*W*ilde
in *America*

DAVID M. FRIEDMAN

Wilde
in America

Oscar Wilde and

the Invention of

Modern Celebrity

W. W. NORTON & COMPANY / New York • London

FOR MARION ETTLINGER

Contents

Wilde
in America

Take Your Show on the Road

On January 3, 1882, a federal customs agent, standing near the Hudson River dock where a British ocean liner had just moored, told an arriving passenger from that ship to present his luggage for inspection.

"Have you anything to declare?" the agent asked, trying not to gawk at the traveler's lavender pants, his puffy white shirt, his green wool coat trimmed at the collar and cuffs in seal fur, and what appeared to be a small turban atop a head of brown hair that fell to the man's shoulders.

"Nothing," Oscar Wilde answered.

Then a pause.

"Nothing but my genius."

THAT THIS STORY is still told, more than a hundred years later, is evidence of Wilde's enduring reputation as the most sardonic wit in the history of the English language. What makes the famous quip all the more comical is how little there was to justify it. For the man reputed to have said those words—and there's debate whether he actually did—was (in either case) not the legendary Irish dramatist, novelist, poet, and essayist we recognize today. Not yet, anyway. Wilde was twenty-seven when he arrived in New York. It would be years before he would write *The Importance of Being Earnest, An Ideal Husband, The Picture of Dorian Gray, De Profundis, The Ballad of Reading Gaol, Intentions,* or any of the works for which we now honor and remember him. Yet in the ten months that followed his passage through customs, Wilde—without writing anything much longer than a letter—did demonstrate a special genius, a genius that made his literary career possible, maybe even inevitable. And Wilde didn't merely fashion his image as a world-class wit after walking onto American soil in 1882. He created an enduring part of the world we live in today.

That part isn't a geographical entity. It is a constellation of values, attitudes, and poses. It is a mindset where everyone thinks they could be famous and, even more to the point, *should* be. It is a belief system in which *celebrity*, a word that once referred exclusively to persons of achievement—artists, athletes, politicians, and so on, even criminals, who left their mark on history through their deeds—has expanded its meaning to include persons famous merely for being famous, a status won by manipulating the media. It is a worldview where fame isn't the end product of a career but the beginning of one. It is the part of modern life we call celebrity culture.

Oscar Wilde called it into existence after leaving the New York waterfront. He did so in a nearly yearlong speaking tour across America, a tour de force of showmanship—and, more often than not, show*boat*manship—that touched down in thirty states, covered approximately fifteen thousand miles, generated more than five hundred newspaper and magazine articles, earned him more money than he had ever earned in his life, and, when it was over, made him the second-most-famous Briton in America, behind only Queen Victoria. (Not bad for a writer who hadn't really written anything.) This "product launch," as we would call it today, was all the more remarkable because Wilde had no training in business and only a little more in public speaking. In an era populated by several of the greatest product marketers in America's history—a list that includes H. J. Heinz, Milton Hershey, and Levi Strauss—Oscar Wilde, whose only product was a self-adoring dandy named Oscar Wilde, may have been the best of them all.

Other Europeans—Dickens and Tocqueville, to name but two—had toured our country before Wilde. But they came to learn about America; Wilde came so America could learn about *him*. Meeting his audiences in an impossible-to-ignore ensemble—satin breeches, black silk stockings, silver-buckled pumps, and a snug velvet coat with lace trim—Wilde sold himself to the American public as a "Professor of Aesthetics," a title for which he had no authentic certification, in roughly 140 lectures (most of them on interior decorating) that brought him face to face with farmers, poets, socialites, preachers, factory workers, prospectors, prostitutes, southern belles, Harvard intellectuals, and, if a newspaper account is accurate, a detachment of Texas Rangers who bestowed upon him the rank of colonel.

Traveling by rail, ferry, and horse-drawn carriage, Wilde spoke before crowds ranging from twenty-five to twenty-five hundred, often embellishing his home-design advice with excerpts from his favorite poems. Maybe it's not surprising some American reporters mocked him as an "ass-thete" and, when other insults failed, as "she." But those rude hacks underestimated their target. Beneath Wilde's delicate persona—the rouge-wearing dandy languidly flinging his hand to his brow as he sang the praises of sconces and embroidered pillows—was a man on a serious mission: to make himself a star, no matter how little he had done (so far) to deserve it.

A stranger in a strange land, Wilde crisscrossed the country from the Atlantic to the Pacific, and from Canada to the Gulf of Mexico, at times joined by a valet, business manager, and, according to letters written to friends in London, two secretaries. He sold autographed photos of himself in theater lobbies, at women's clubs, and on at least one occasion at an amusement park. He was the featured guest at nearly two hundred parties, where he often heard an orchestra play "Oscar Dear!" ("Oscar dear, Oscar dear, How utterly, fluttterly utter you are; Oscar dear, Oscar dear, I think you are awfully wild!"), "The Oscar Wilde Forget Me Not Waltz," and similar ditties composed in his honor. And like most stars, he made a point of socializing with other stars, breakfasting with Henry Wadsworth Longfellow in Boston, drinking homemade wine with Walt Whitman in Camden, New Jersey, and dining with Louisa May Alcott, Henry Ward Beecher, Oliver Wendell Holmes, Henry James, and (one wonders how many people could say this in 1882) both Ulysses S. Grant and Jefferson Davis—though not, in this final instance, it should be noted, at the same time.

No matter whom he drank toasts with, Wilde was clearheaded about his goal, devising a groundbreaking formula for manufacturing fame—one that is still used by many aspiring celebrities today, whether they know it or not. Decades before Norman Mailer, Wilde knew the value of "advertisements for myself." Decades before Andy Warhol, he saw the beauty in commerce and the importance of image in marketing. Decades before Kim Kardashian, he grasped that fame could be fabricated in the media. Decades before *Gawker* or *Us Weekly*, Oscar Wilde created the value system we now call celebrity culture. This is how he did it.

CHAPTER ONE

Build Your Brand

*A*t his parties he was both conductor and soloist; Oscar Wilde saw no conflict in that. He began hosting soirees not long after arriving at Oxford's Magdalen College from Dublin in 1874, holding them on Sunday nights in his rooms overlooking the River Cherwell. His guests, all of them male students (Magdalen wouldn't admit females until 1979), would find their way to a punch bowl of whiskey and gin, alongside a humidor of imported tobacco, next to a rack of long-stemmed clay pipes. The scent of lilies, standing white and exuberant in blue china vases, would drape the air. There was a piano to be played, and it usually was, with spirited vocals from those in attendance, their zeal, if not their skill, enhanced by the grog. Gorgeous etchings of nudes, each one more alluring than the next, populated the walls. But most of all, there was Oscar.

He would dart about the rooms, flipping his hair off his face as he introduced new friends to old with flattery almost as dizzying as the punch. Display was encouraged at his parties, and, if there was hesitation from his guests, Wilde took the lead. To those studying classics (as he was), he would quote long passages from Euripides—in Greek, of course. For literature students, he'd recite Swinburne or Keats, his favorite poets, other than himself. (He would invariably get around to quoting him, too.) Those reading philosophy were challenged with absurdly stated propositions, nearly always of a paradoxical bent. If his voice began to tire, he would mimic the physical quirks of Oxford's most famous dons. And if circumstances demanded, he'd place his six-foot-three-inch frame between guests whose friendly disagreement was about to turn unfriendly, especially if that tension threatened the integrity of his blue china. Few who attended one of Wilde's parties ever forgot the experience, or the host who had invited him. Which was the whole point.

He admitted as much late one Sunday night to two of his closest friends at Oxford, William (Bouncer) Ward and David (Dunskie) Hunter Blair, who had remained at Wilde's after the other guests left. The three students were talking about the future, a pressing personal matter for Ward and Hunter Blair, upperclassmen who were approaching graduation. In truth, the future for both men, because of family obligations, looked settled: Ward would join his father's law firm in Bristol, England; Hunter Blair, a member of the Lowlands aristocracy, would inherit his father's baronetcy in Scotland.

"Oscar, you have twice as much brains in that ridiculous head of yours as both of us put together," Ward said. "What are you going to do with them? What is your real ambition in life?" It took only a moment for Wilde to respond. Becoming a creaky Oxford don was out of the question, he said. He would probably try his luck as a writer. But there was one thing he was sure of:

"Somehow or other I'll be famous, and if not famous, I'll be notorious."

TO READ THOSE words today, knowing how Wilde made good on them—first as the wittiest talker of his age (and maybe of any age); then as the author of peerless stage comedies and serious criticism (not to forget a novel that is still read 125 years after its publication); and finally as the first gay martyr of a sexual revolution that hadn't yet begun (an anomaly that led to his conviction for "gross indecency," a sentence of two years at hard labor, and his death at age forty-six)—it's hard not to shudder at their eerie portentousness. One senses that shudder from the source of the quotation, Hunter Blair, who wrote in his memoir *In Victorian Days* of Wilde's answer: "Surely a prophecy, this, of evil omen."

Hunter Blair's words remind us that any student of history must bear in mind that events in the past were once in the future, which is to say, unknown (and unknowable) to those who would participate in them. Despite Hunter Blair's anxiety, there was nothing preternatural about Wilde's remark. Oscar didn't know his destiny; he only knew what he hoped it would look like. Even so, the words Wilde spoke that night do seem weirdly prophetic on a point that is crucial to understanding his rise and fall—and their lasting impact on our culture. His answer didn't merely show how serious he was about becoming a public figure; it suggests that he grasped, in a precociously modern sense, that the line between fame and notoriety could be blurry. Maybe even non-existent.

His words also hint that he understood the significance of that fuzziness. In the Victorian world Wilde was born in, fame accrued from one's deeds, notoriety from one's persona. The former was bestowed by others as a response to real-world accomplishments. The latter was usually accomplished by oneself, using an identity—or pose—created in one's imagination. Wilde's answer suggests he had intuited something new about the ways one might seek the intoxicating immortality of renown: he suspected notoriety could give birth to fame, or replace it with a flashy new category incorporating the best and worst of notoriety *and* fame. This is the status we now call celebrity. The first step to achieving it, Wilde suspected, was to become known for being well known.

It's likely this idea first occurred to him in the city of his birth,

Dublin, where his parents were very well known. Oscar's father, Dr. William Wilde, had built a stellar career as an eye and ear surgeon, establishing the first hospital in Ireland to focus on diseases of those organs; and, as a member of the Irish Census Commission, he had overseen the first statistical analysis of the public health consequences of the Irish Famine. He was also the author of several well-regarded surgical textbooks, the founding editor of the *Dublin Journal of Medical Science*, and, in his spare time, a prolific compiler of Irish folklore, legends, and superstitions, which he also published. (He spoke Irish fluently.)

Far less impressive was Dr. Wilde's commitment to sobriety. When he was a child, he had been given ale to "cure" a fever. His recovery convinced him alcohol had health-giving properties, a belief he put into daily practice as an adult with a heavy regimen of imbibing. Perhaps it's not surprising, then, that some questioned his skills as a surgeon, no matter how glowing his reputation. According to George Bernard Shaw, who grew up in Dublin, Dr. Wilde operated on Shaw's father to correct a wandering eye that made him look cross-eyed. The surgeon "overdid the correction so much," Shaw later wrote, that his father's eye wandered in the opposite direction for the rest of his life. Even more alarming, Dr. Wilde was said to be a sexual predator or, at the very least, a man unlikely to check his carnal appetites. While unmarried, he fathered three children, for whom he accepted responsibility, and rumor had it there were others out there, unacknowledged. (This despite the fact that he was a short, scrawny man with a disregard for personal hygiene so noticeable it led some Dubliners to joke: "Why are Dr. Wilde's nails so black? Because he scratched himself.")

Even so, Dr. Wilde was one of the most sought-after bachelors in Ireland until November 12, 1851, when, at thirty-six, he married Jane Francesca Agnes Elgee, a Dubliner thirty years of age (though she claimed to be twenty-five) and a woman who in some circles was even more famous than he. Elgee had won that fame contributing fiery, anti-British verse to *The Nation*, the chief organ of the Irish independence movement. Elgee wrote her poetry under the pen name Speranza, but she wasn't one to hide her identity for long. When the editor of *The Nation* was tried in a British court for sedition for publishing a poem of hers containing the line "O! For a hundred thousand muskets glimmering rightly in the light of Heaven!"—muskets held by Irish revolutionaries—Elgee rose from the courtroom gallery and said: "I, and I alone, am the culprit, if culprit there be." After that splendid act of courage, Speranza/Elgee was often recognized on Dublin's streets, where she was usually greeted with cheers.

Dr. Wilde shared his wife's nationalist views, albeit less theatrically. The fact that both were Protestants, a religious affiliation typically associated in Ireland with pro-British, pro-Unionist views, made them an unusual but politically well-matched couple. They were hardly a matched set, however. Jane, who was six feet tall, towered over her husband; she also appeared to outweigh him. In spite of those differences, the Wildes' first child, William Robert Kingsbury Wills Wilde, was born in Dublin on September 26, 1852, in the first home the Wildes occupied as a couple, 21 Westland Row. So was their second, Oscar Fingal O'Flahertie Wills Wilde, on October 16, 1854. Their third, Isola Francesca Emily Wilde, was born on April 2, 1857, at 1 Merrion Square, a much larger house and more fashionable address, where the Wildes had moved shortly after Oscar's birth. This home was staffed by six servants, including a French housekeeper and a German governess whose duties included teaching the Wilde children their native tongues. Mrs. Wilde was proud of her family, even of her somewhat notorious husband, especially after he was knighted, in January 1864, for his work on the Irish census.

Dr. and Mrs. Wilde were now Sir William and Lady Jane Wilde, so an invitation to dine at their home, sent to members of the city's intellectual elite, was a mark of having arrived in Irish society. The Wildes allowed their young sons to sit at the table at those dinner parties—where the liquor and conversation flowed freely—as long as

Oscar and Willie kept silent. Years later, when Oscar was the most popular dinner guest in London, he said it was because he had been forced to hold his tongue as a child that he was so successful in wagging it as an adult. He was joking, of course, but there's no denying that the house on Merrion Square was an important school for Oscar. This education didn't begin in earnest, however, until he won a scholarship to attend Trinity College, Dublin, after graduating from the Portora Royal School in Enniskillen, in what is now Northern Ireland. (His brother, who had also attended Portora, was already at Trinity.)

Now that both the surviving Wilde children were home—Isola had died in 1867 of a lingering fever—Lady Wilde began hosting a weekly party at Merrion Square, where, as she put it, she "agglomerated together all the thinking minds of Dublin" and introduced them (or *re*introduced them) to her sons. These "thinking minds" were invited by a card that read: "At Home, Saturday, 4 p.m. to 7 p.m. *Conversazione*." Lady Wilde's use of Italian was no surprise to her friends. She had long claimed (without evidence) that her maiden name, Elgee, was a corruption of the Italian name Alighieri. (What she was really claiming, then, was that she was descended from Dante.) Despite that preposterous assertion, her invitations were well received, so it was not uncommon for Oscar to find his home occupied every Saturday by more than a hundred people. The guest list for these parties reflected Lady Jane's interest in the arts rather than her husband's in the sciences. In truth, Dr. Wilde was not a regular participant in the *conversazioni*. After a patient of his, Mary Travers, accused him of making unwanted sexual advances on her in his medical office, he spent less time in Dublin and more on Lough Fee, in the west of Ireland, where he had built a summer home.*

Those who did attend the parties were a bohemian bunch, a mix

---

* After Travers published her account of the episode in a Dublin newspaper, Lady Wilde accused her of fabricating the story. This led Travers to sue Lady Wilde for libel. A court ruled in Travers's favor, but awarded her only a farthing (a quarter of a penny).

of poets, actors, political radicals, musicians, journalists, professors, and students. These guests entered rooms lined with Greco-Roman busts intended to recreate the atmosphere of a Platonic symposium—if they could see them: the windows at Merrion Square were curtained, and the only source of light was a series of candles and gas lamps shielded by pink shades. In this artsy ambience poetry was read aloud and music was performed, while other guests argued about politics. There were platters of snacks, bottles of French wine, and bowls of punch refilled by servants forced to push their way through the boisterous throng.

No matter how crowded or dark it got, it was hard to miss Lady Wilde. The Irish writer Henriette Corkran once watched her make an entrance in a long crimson gown that hung over several layers of crinolines. As Lady Wilde walked among her guests, "there was a swaying, swelling movement, like that of a vessel at sea, with the sails filled with wind," Corkran wrote. "Her long, massive face was plastered with white powder; over her blue-black glossy hair was a gilt crown of laurels. She wore white kid gloves, held a scent bottle and a fan. On her broad chest was fastened a series of large brooches, evidently family portraits. . . . This gave her the appearance of a perambulating family mausoleum."

The *Irish Times* liked what it saw. "No. 1 Merrion Square is where one meets all the Dublin celebrities in literature, art and the drama," one article noted. "The affable and courteous hostess is Lady Wilde; the charm in the society to be met in her salons is that it is wholly devoid of snobbism." The last words in that sentence probably referred to the fact that Catholics were as welcome as Protestants, which was rarely true in the milieu the Wildes moved in. Even so, she *was* a snob. Once, when a friend asked permission to bring a "respectable" woman to her next party, Lady Wilde couldn't contain her horror: "You must never employ that description in this house. Only tradespeople," she trilled, "are respectable!" When not making absurd pronouncements or parading among her guests, Speranza was an avid conversationalist, especially about poetry and politics. She had well-defined ideas about how to become a talker worth listening to. "Epigrams are always better than argument in conversation," she said. And "paradox is the very essence of social wit."

Was anyone listening (or watching) more closely than her second son? It hardly seems possible. We have no photographs of Lady Wilde's parties to examine, but it is easy to imagine Oscar standing in a corner of his living room, sipping punch and holding a cigarette, affecting a worldliness way beyond his years, as he observed his unforgettably costumed (and cosmeticated) mother as she took a star turn in her own home, charming and cajoling the most accomplished, the most admired, and, in some cases, the most gossiped-about people in Dublin. We know he was so awed by her success as a party host that he tried to take some credit for it himself. "I want to introduce you to my mother," he told a friend from Trinity College, whom he was inviting to Merrion Square. "She and I have founded a Society for the Suppression of Virtue."

That was quite an exaggeration by Oscar, who knew perfectly well that the defining personality at his mother's parties was hers. Not that Lady Wilde would have minded his fib. Self-promotion, she understood, had its own code, one with little connection to truth-telling—and this was a truth she had made sure to pass on to her son. Indeed, it would be difficult to overstate the influence of Lady Wilde on the teenager who would become the famous and notorious Oscar Wilde. It was from Lady Wilde that Oscar learned that identity is a kind of fiction, and that being oneself is a form of playacting. It was from her that Oscar learned that appearances have their own reality. It was from her that Oscar learned that the most important act of creativity is the creation of one's image. And it was from her, the woman who rose to her feet in a packed courtroom to unmask herself as the "seditious" poet Speranza, that Oscar learned it was not enough to stand up; one had to stand out.

That Oscar would choose conversation as his means of standing out was, to be sure, the result of observing his mother. But he had a second teacher in this as well, a regular guest at Lady Wilde's salons, a person he knew intimately. This was his classics tutor at Trinity College, Rev. John Pentland Mahaffy, a man that many in Dublin called the greatest raconteur in Ireland. (Mahaffy certainly thought so.) And like Lady Wilde, he had rules for excelling at conversation that he passed on to anyone who would listen.

Oscar listened. Some said it was impossible not to. "Until you heard Mahaffy," one Dubliner said, "you hadn't realized how language could be used to hypnotize." The true master of conversation, taught Mahaffy (who would later author a book on the subject), is the one who leavens seriousness with humor: "For if a person is to require others to listen to him, it must be by presenting human life under a fresh and piquant aspect—in fact, as a little comedy." This law, Mahaffy declared, was especially useful in arguments. Once, while debating an Irish feminist, he was challenged by this question: "Sir, you are a man. I am a woman. What is the essential difference between us?" It took only a second for Mahaffy to answer: "Madam, I cannot conceive."

Along with puns, Mahaffy (like Speranza) championed the epigram. "Poets are born, not paid," he liked to say. And "It is the spectator and not life that art mirrors." Oscar would later appropriate many of these for himself. Equally influential on the future party wit and author was Mahaffy's insistence that "a liar is a better ingredient in company than a scrupulously truthful man," and that details are the enemy of good talk. The goal of any good conversationalist, Mahaffy said, "is not to instruct but to divert, and to ask him, 'Is that really true?' shows that the objector is a blockhead." Once, while speaking to the provost of Trinity College, Mahaffy bragged, "I was only once caned in my life, and that was for telling the truth," to which the provost replied, "It certainly cured you, Mahaffy." Years later Wilde would write that "the telling of beautiful untrue things is the proper aim of Art," and he would have Lord Henry Wotton, the aristocrat who tantalizes Dorian Gray with his talk in Wilde's novel, tell his protégé: "One should absorb the colour of life, but one should never remember its details. Details are always vulgar." Some have guessed Mahaffy was a model for Wotton. What's certain is that he was a model for Oscar Wilde.

Perhaps the tutor's greatest impact came in early 1874, when, as Wilde was in his third year at Trinity (where he had just won a prize for Greek translation), Mahaffy urged his nineteen-year-old pupil to continue his studies in England. Mahaffy's motivation is hard to pin down. Perhaps he was an alpha male banishing a young rival from his turf. We know he thought Trinity's classics program the equal of any in Europe, but, like many Irish Protestants, he was awed by the older English universities. Lady Wilde liked the idea; Willie Wilde was already in England, studying law in London. Dr. Wilde gave his approval, so now it was up to Oscar. In March 1874 he learned that Oxford's Magdalen College was awarding two Demyships—scholarships worth £95 per year—in classics to the top scorers in an examination given on June 23. Wilde took the test and finished first. "You're not quite clever enough for us here, Oscar," Mahaffy told his pupil. "Better run off to Oxford."

So he did, matriculating on October 17, 1874. Wilde had absorbed a great deal from his eccentric tutor, as he had from his even more eccentric mother. He saw how diligently both had worked to fashion their public identities, using spectacle and wit to leave their marks on the world. At Oxford, the medieval birthplace of English academia, Oscar Wilde would begin to leave his own mark.

THE MOST IMPORTANT thing Wilde learned in Dublin was a truth about himself: he wanted to be famous. Such an urge requires a substantial ego, and, in Wilde's case, that was virtually a genetic inheritance. Both his parents were driven by high self-regard to achieve fame—Lady Wilde as a published poet and essayist on Irish independence, Sir William as a published scientist and folklorist. The "published" part was important. Neither was content to have his or her work unacknowledged by the community. But his parents' success, Wilde came to see as a teenager, had been achieved in a provincial capital. That would not be enough for him. Wilde's own ego, though still forming, was already of such substance that he was determined to surpass his parents.

So he arrived as Oxford with a goal—one he soon realized would not be so easy to achieve. He was hardly a typical first-year student, and not merely because he had already spent three years at college in Dublin. What really separated him was class. His father's knighthood may have counted for much in Ireland, as did Wilde's degree from Portora. But at Oxford nearly everyone came from Eton, Harrow, or Winchester, the most prestigious schools in Britain, and half of his classmates seemed to belong to families with titles dating back to the Magna Carta. (The youngest son of Queen Victoria, Prince Leopold, was there.) Embarrassed by his own middle-class origins, Wilde decided some shedding was in order. He shaved off the sideburns that marked him as a provincial. He lost his Irish accent. He shipped many of his clothes back to Dublin, replacing them with the tweed jackets and blue neckties favored at Magdalen. He purchased formalwear. It took little time for him to go native. "If I were alone on a desert island and had my things," he told a new friend. "I would dress for dinner every night." Wilde was desperate to fit in, but he also wanted to stand out. He was confident the skills he had learned in Dublin would make that second goal possible, for if Mahaffy had convinced him of anything, it was the power of good talk. "Many men," his Trinity tutor often said, "owe the whole of a great success in life to this and nothing else." All he needed to harness that force at Oxford, Wilde was certain, was the right conversation topic. He found what he was looking for at classes taught by John Ruskin, the university's Slade Professor of Fine Art.

Wilde was awestruck by Ruskin's talks on the power and meaning of beauty, lectures that seemed more like public ecstasies than podium presentations. The professor's commitment to his subject was the stuff of legend at Oxford. He was once seen staggering across Magdalen Bridge, seemingly drunk; in reality, so the story went, he was walking with his eyes closed because he had seen a sunset of such loveliness that he hoped, by keeping his eyes shut, to retain the image in his mind until he got home to write about it. Myth or not, Wilde was soon attending Ruskin's art lectures—sometimes instead of his assigned Greek or Latin classes—to hear Ruskin describe beauty as evidence of God's presence on Earth (and not just in nature). Indeed, much of the aesthetic movement inspired by Ruskin had earthly goals. In opposition to the Industrial Revolution, it championed handmade goods and decorative ornamentation in the making of furniture, ceramics, metal-work, stained glass, textiles, wallpapers, books, and so on. One must "get rid at once of any idea of Decorative art being a degraded or a separate kind of art," Ruskin wrote in *The Two Paths.* Wilde found in Ruskin not just his new mentor and friend (they took long walks together through Oxfordshire) but his new conversation topic—*and* his new identity: he would become the self-anointed leader of Oxford's student aesthetes, preaching to his classmates the Divine Gospel of Beauty and the superiority of decorative handmade goods to ugly manufactured ones. And while doing so, he would make him*self* the most talked-about student talker on campus.

His usual venue was the dining hall. He would gush at length about the loveliness of Pre-Raphaelite painting—work championed by Ruskin—and the overriding importance of color in art. ("Of all God's gifts to the sight of man, colour is the holiest, the most divine, the most solemn," Ruskin taught. Years later Wilde wrote: "Mere colour, unspoiled by meaning, and unallied with definite form, can speak to the soul in a thousand different ways.") He repeated Ruskin's lesson that "the most beautiful things in the world are the most useless: pea-cocks and lilies, for instance." He declared that, were he given godlike powers, he would order all the factories in Britain banished to an island off the mainland and give the city of Manchester back to the shepherds. It wasn't easy for anyone else to get a word in during these soliloquies, but complaints were few. There was something irresistible, one classmate said, about Wilde's "sureness of himself."

Confident talk was just part of it. Wilde had learned from his mother the importance of scenery, costume, and appearance in creating a persona. Soon an unfinished oil painting appeared on an easel in his rooms. He said he was working on it, but no one ever saw him holding a brush. Reproductions of works by (the real painters) Dante Gabriel Rossetti and John Everett Millais found space on his walls. His purchase of blue china vases was similarly inspired by his wish to "exist beautifully." When a quip of his—"I find it harder and harder every day to live up to my blue china"—was repeated around campus, an unexpected consequence thrilled him: he was condemned in a sermon at a nearby church. Wilde's remark was "a form of heathenism," Rev. John W. Burgon told his flock, "which it is our bounden duty to fight against and to crush out." That Rev. Burgon had condemned Darwin from the same pulpit only made Wilde prouder. When the "scandal" was covered in the *Oxford and Cambridge Undergraduate's Journal*, he was euphoric. It was getting harder and harder for him to leave his rooms without being recognized.

That was partly because he no longer looked like everyone else. He began to leave his formalwear in his closet, instead wearing an aesthetic "uniform": baggy trousers and a blousy white shirt under a dark frock coat that hung "like drapery," wrote Horace G. Hutchinson, an Oxford classmate, in his memoir. Wilde let his hair grow; some said he altered his posture to match the languid sensibility prized by aesthetes. He couldn't—or wouldn't—keep his head upright, Hutchinson wrote: "It fell sideways, like a lily bloom too heavy for its stalk." Wilde was seeking a reaction, even outrage, from his fellow students, and he got it. The Oxford elites, he knew, revered swaggering hussars, burly sports heroes, and brave explorers. Not aesthetes with droopy posture.

Hutchinson's comments were probably a coded criticism of Wilde as—to use the modern usage—a homosexual, a word that wouldn't appear in English until 1892 (as an adjective) and not until 1912 as a noun. Hutchinson made his remarks in 1920, long after Wilde's downfall for "gross indecency," so it's likely he assumed that at Oxford Wilde had already been "indecent." In truth, there's no conclusive evidence Wilde lived as a homosexual, secretly or not, at Magdalen. Most experts believe he didn't have his first homosexual experience until 1886 or 1887—in either case, several years after graduating from Oxford—with Robert (Robbie) Ross, later to become his literary executor.*

We know that in 1875 Wilde met a young woman from Dublin named Florence Balcombe. A mutual attraction ensued; gifts were exchanged, and they even talked of marrying one day. (In the end, Balcombe wed a different Irishman, Bram Stoker, later to become immortal as the author of *Dracula*.) But we also know that at Oxford Wilde was in close contact with at least two men who loved men, though neither was enrolled at the university: the artist Frank Miles, a man described by the gay author Rupert Croft-Cooke as "one of those sophisticated queers who tell women what they should wear, have rather exaggerated good manners and camp outrageously, preferably among titled people"; and the titled person Lord Ronald Gower, the pleasure-seeking youngest son of the Duke of Sutherland—and a man often put forth, along with John Mahaffy, as the model for Lord Henry Wotton in *The Picture of Dorian Gray*. That Wilde was aware he had classmates at Oxford who were drawn to same-sex relationships is also clear. This is from a letter he sent to William (Bouncer) Ward, in August 1876: "Last night I strolled into the theatre . . . and to my surprise saw Todd and young Ward the quire boy in a private box. . . . I believe Todd only mentally spoons the boy, but . . . he looked awfully nervous and uncomfortable" when he knew Wilde had seen him.

---

* Ross boasted that "I was the first boy Oscar had." If accurate, Ross would have been seventeen or eighteen at the time. (He also claimed he seduced Wilde.) Three books that argue that Wilde was a homosexual at Oxford are *Sexual Heretics*, by Brian Reade (1970), *The Unrecorded Life of Oscar Wilde*, by Rupert Croft-Cooke (1972), and *The Secret Life of Oscar Wilde*, by Neil McKenna (2003).

If Hutchinson's snickering about Wilde's posture was meant to hint that Wilde had something to be nervous about at Oxford, it's impossible to know with certainty if he was correct. But Hutchinson was correct when he credited Wilde with inventing a new type of poseur there. "The ordinary poseur tries to conceal his pose. But Wilde," he wrote, "knew himself to be a poseur and made no effort to conceal it. He posed as a poseur."

Here Hutchinson was spot on. Wilde's persona at Oxford *was* a pose—in fact, a series of poses: sometimes bait and switch (the serious scholar who pretended to be too enamored of lilies and sunflowers to open a book), sometimes shape-shifting (the Irishman who played the Englishman), and sometimes pure make-believe (Wilde the "painter"). He could strike those poses without embarrassment because, long before academics invented the field of performance studies, he grasped that the line between "staged" and "lived" behavior was faint. The actor playing Hamlet and the student playing the aesthete, Wilde was convinced, were doing the same thing: inhabiting a character and performing for an audience—often for fun, but always for a reason.

Wilde's playacting at Oxford was done intentionally and in public, with goals that were clear to him, if not to everyone else: to become well known as the aesthete's aesthete, then to translate that renown into a career. This was the reverse of the vocational path usually taken by young men of promise in Victorian England. Fame would *launch* Wilde's career, not cap it. On a spring night in 1877, he pushed that process forward with the most eye-catching performance of his life so far.

THE OCCASION WAS the opening of the new Grosvenor Gallery, in London. Its proprietor, Sir Coutts Lindsay, had committed his gallery to exhibiting new work, especially by Pre-Raphaelite painters such as Edward Burne-Jones and John Everett Millais, that was at times overlooked by the Royal Academy. The invitation to a private viewing on

May 1, 1877, could not have come at a better time for Wilde. Despite an excellent academic record—he had won a "first" the previous semester in Honour Moderations, a part of Oxford's rigorous classics curriculum—he had been suspended for missing the first three weeks of the current term, tardiness caused by a trip he took through Greece with John Mahaffy. "I was sent down from Oxford," Wilde wrote later, "for being the first undergraduate to visit Olympia." It was no joke at the time, however. Suspension meant he lost his room privileges on campus. So, temporarily homeless, Wilde went to London, where he stayed with Frank Miles, whose career as a portraitist of society beauties was just taking off. Oxford's loss, Wilde vowed, would be London's gain. He wouldn't just show up at the Grosvenor. He would make sure the entire city heard about it.

That wouldn't be easy. Baronet Lindsay, whose wife was a Rothschild, had spent £150,000 (the equivalent of £14 million today) to make his gallery the talk of the town. A Palladian doorway, salvaged from a crumbling church in Italy, was installed at the entrance, and James McNeill Whistler was hired to paint a frieze on the coved ceiling of the main exhibition hall, which visitors reached by ascending a fifteen-foot marble stairway. Gilded Ionic pilasters, purchased from a defunct opera house in Paris, appeared at intervals along the gallery walls, which were lined with red silk. The floor was covered with Oriental rugs, and the corners of each exhibition room were inhabited by plush Italian chairs and potted plants on consoles, making the Grosvenor appear less a gallery than the interior of a Venetian palace. The effect, both inside and out, was spectacular.

This setting only encouraged Wilde to make a spectacle of him*self.* Aware this was his London debut, he made his guiding principle the truism that one never gets a second chance to make a first impression.[*] So in an exquisite space occupied by the Prince of Wales, the states-

---

[*] This aphorism is often credited to Wilde, but there's no evidence that he deserves the honor.

man William Gladstone, the scholar John Ruskin, and other notables, Oscar Wilde—a twenty-two-year-old undergraduate (and a suspended one, at that)—outshone them all. He did so with an unforgettable act of peacockery, strutting about the Grosvenor in an evening jacket specially tailored, shaped, decorated, and tinted so that, when viewed from the rear, it transformed its wearer into a walking, talking musical instrument: a cello. In a room lined with works of art, Wilde stole the show by wearing one.

He introduced himself to nearly everyone in sight (except, as prohibited by protocol, His Royal Highness), then commented on the paintings, using his exuberance to hold the attention he'd grabbed with his jacket. The whole point of going to the Grosvenor, Wilde understood, was to be seen. He was thrilled by the splash he had made—even more so when *Punch*, the popular English humor magazine committed to lampooning the follies of the fashionable, took notice of him. *Punch* used verse to express its "admiration" for the Oxford student's performance at the Grosvenor:

> *The haunt of the very aesthetic,*
> *Here comes the supremely intense,*
> *The long-haired and hyper-poetic,*
> *Whose sound is mistaken for sense.*
> *And many a maid will mutter,*
> *When Oscar looms large in her sight,*
> *"He's quite too consummately utter,*
> *As well as too utterly quite."*

Wilde got an assignment to review the Grosvenor opening for *Dublin University Magazine*, a journal that had published some poems of his and several essays on Irish folklore written by his father. That Oscar envisioned this commission as an act of self-advertisement is made clear from a letter he sent to Keningale Cook, the magazine's editor, after turning in his first draft. Apparently Cook had questioned his decision to write the piece in the first person. "I always say I and not 'we,'" wrote Wilde. "We belongs to the days of anonymous articles, not to signed articles like mine." Cook wasn't Wilde's only important correspondent after the opening. He mailed a letter to William Gladstone in which he included a poem he had written titled "On the Massacre of the Christians in Bulgaria," a real-life event Gladstone had forcefully condemned in Parliament. Unlike the tone he took with Cook, Wilde's tone with Gladstone was sycophantic and disingenuous. But it had the same goal: promoting Oscar Wilde.

"I am little more than a boy and have no literary interest in London," the twenty-three-year-old wrote, "but perhaps if you saw any good stuff in the lines I send you, some editor (of the *Nineteenth Century* perhaps or the *Spectator*) might publish them: and I feel sure that you can appreciate the very great longing that one has when young to have words of one's own published for men to read." Read today, the words "no literary interest in London," and Wilde's calling himself "little more than a boy," are risible. Gladstone told Wilde to send his poem to the *Spectator* himself, where it was rejected. Wilde's search for glory was far from over, however. When his review of the Grosvenor show was published, Wilde, his suspension now complete, sent a copy to Walter Pater, Oxford's second-most-famous professor of art history. Wilde had never taken a course from Pater. But he had read his book, *Studies in the History of the Renaissance*, which he later described to William Butler Yeats as "my golden book; I never travel anywhere without it." There were parts of *Studies*, Wilde's friends at Magdalen knew, that he had committed to memory. "Not the fruit of experience, but experience itself is the end," Pater wrote, and Wilde often repeated aloud:

A counted number of pulses only is given to us of a variegated, dramatic life. How may we see in them all that is to be seen in them by the finest senses? How can we pass most swiftly from point to point, and be present always at the focus where the greatest number of vital forces unite in their purest energy? To burn always with this hard, gemlike flame, to maintain this ecstasy, is success in life.

Pater was hardly living that fiery life himself. To borrow the author Hesketh Pearson's line, he was "one of those timid, old-maidish scholarly recluses who, fearing even the uncertainties of marriage, preach the gospel of living dangerously." Even so, Pater overcame his shyness to invite Wilde to tea, a meeting that took place in October 1877. "Why do you always write poetry?" Pater asked his guest. "Why do you not write prose? Prose is much more difficult." The two men, so unlike, became close, often lunching together in Wilde's rooms. That an undergraduate could form a bond with not one (Ruskin) but two (Ruskin and Pater) of Oxford's most famous dons did not go unnoticed. Wilde's status among students as the aesthete's aesthete was now indisputable.

This stature reached even greater heights the following year, when Wilde submitted an entry for the Newdigate Prize, the award given annually to the poem written by an Oxford undergraduate judged to be the "best composition in English verse" on a subject chosen by the university's professor of poetry. The subject selected in 1878, as luck would have it, was Ravenna, a city in Italy Wilde had visited the previous year with John Mahaffy when they were on their way to Greece. On June 10 Wilde was notified that he had won the prize, the first Magdalen man to do so in fifty years, and an accomplishment that put him in extremely distinguished company. Past honorees included Matthew Arnold, John Ruskin, John Addington Symonds, and—this name particularly tickled Wilde—John W. Burgon, the Oxford cleric who had famously decried Oscar's "blue china" lament. Wilde's delight at the honor was exceeded only by that of his mother, then dealing in Dublin with complications arising from the settling of her husband's estate. (Sir William had died in 1876.) "Oh, Gloria, Gloria! Thank you a million times for the telegram," she began:

It is the first pleasant throb of joy I have had this year. How I long to read the poem. We, after all, we have *Genius*—that is something attorneys can't take away. Oh, I do hope you will now have some joy in your heart. You have got *honour* and *recognition*—and this at only 22 is a grand thing.

(Wilde was actually twenty-three.)

Not everyone was thrilled. W. S. Gilbert, the librettist who had just made a splash in London with his operetta *H.M.S Pinafore*, had been watching the aesthetic movement, and Wilde, with consternation for some time. It's possible he had seen Wilde in his cello coat at the Grosvenor gallery; if not, he surely heard about it. When told that Wilde had won the Newdigate, Gilbert harrumphed: "I understand that some young man wins this prize every year." Aided by his partner Arthur Sullivan, he would have more to say about aesthetes in the future. In the meantime, Wilde had more good news: in July he earned a second first, this one in "Greats," another part of the classics curriculum. "The dons are 'astonied' (sic) beyond words—the Bad Boy doing so well in the end!" he wrote to Bouncer Ward. By the time Wilde graduated from Oxford in November 1878, he was one of the most honored members of his class. But not all the news was happy. It was around this time that Wilde learned Florence Balcombe had accepted Bram Stoker's marriage proposal. He reacted peevishly, asking her to return some jewelry he had given her. "Worthless though the trinket be, to me it serves as a memory of two sweet years—the sweetest of all the years of my youth," he wrote. There were also financial matters to be dealt with. Properties had to be sold in Ireland, including the house on Merrion Square, if Oscar, his mother, and his brother, who had rejected a career in law for one in journalism, were to have sufficient incomes.

Despite such issues, Wilde's time at Oxford had clearly been a great triumph. He won fame, firsts, friends (as well as a few enemies), and one of the most glittering prizes the university had to offer. But the work he had started there, Wilde knew, wasn't finished. He'd had a successful out-of-town tryout. It was time to move his show to a larger stage.

IN JANUARY 1879, Wilde and Frank Miles moved into a three-story house in London, the largest city in the world (population: nearly five million), where the first electric streetlights had just gone up. The building on Salisbury Street had a river view, so Wilde christened it "Thames House," but the name promised a grandeur the structure didn't deliver. It was really just three apartments, linked by a creaky staircase. Miles lived and worked in a studio at the top, where the light was best; Wilde lived on the floor beneath him; the ground floor was leased to a student neither man knew. In a letter to a friend at Oxford, Wilde described his new home as "untidy" but "romantic."

The most romantic thing about it was the shrine he had built to Lillie Langtry, the society beauty who owed her fame to her status as the mistress of the Prince of Wales. Upon entering Wilde's home, one's attention was irresistibly drawn to the end of his living room, where Edward Poynter's oil portrait of Langtry sat on an easel, next to two blue vases, each filled with lilies and peacock feathers. Langtry reclined in a sensuous pose in the portrait, wearing a low-cut golden bodice and clutching a yellow rose—a symbol of adultery in Victorian times—to her bosom. The painting had debuted in 1878 at the Royal Academy, making Mrs. Langtry (she was married to an Irish yachts-man) even more notorious than she already was. That only deepened Wilde's fascination with her, so much so that he used part of his inheritance from his father's estate to buy the portrait.

He had met Langtry at a previous studio used by Miles. "I want to introduce you to the most beautiful woman in the world," Miles said that day. According to Lord Ronald Gower, Miles and Wilde soon hatched a plan. "I with my pencil," Miles said, "and Oscar with his pen will make her the Joconde and the Laura of this century."

(Joconde was Da Vinci's *La Giaconda*, better known as *Mona Lisa*; Laura was the poet Petrarch's inspiration.) We don't know if Langtry was immediately conscious of the "conspiracy," but we do know her first impressions of Wilde. "His face was large, and so colourless that a few pale freckles of good size were oddly conspicuous," she wrote in *The Days I Knew.*

> He had a well-shaped mouth, with somewhat coarse lips and greenish—hued teeth. The plainness of his face, however, was redeemed by the splendour of his great, eager eyes. . . . [His] nails, I regretfully record, did not receive the attention they deserved. . . . To me he was always grotesque in appearance. . . . That he possessed a remarkably fascinating and compelling personality . . . is beyond question, and there was about him an enthusiasm singularly captivating. He had one of the most alluring voices I have ever listened to, round and soft, and full of variety and expression.

Wilde was oblivious to the less flattering of Langtry's opinions because he had something else on his mind. Langtry's connection to the prince meant she was invited to the best parties in London—and that was where Wilde wanted to be. He didn't have the bloodline normally required to enter society, but he knew there were other ways to get in. For Langtry, it had been her beauty; for Wilde, it would take a special performance. He believed any poet worthy of the name needed a public passion; if it was unrequited, that only made it *more* poetic. Lillie Langtry would be his passion.

So he showered her with public adoration that was impossible to ignore, not just by Langtry but by all of London society. What Wilde understood, as no one before him ever had, was that worship could be a career move. He "always made a point of bringing me flowers," Langtry wrote in her memoir, "but he [couldn't] afford great posies, so . . . he would buy me a single gorgeous amaryllis . . . and stroll down Piccadilly, carefully carrying the solitary flower." It was said that Mr. Langtry returned home late one night after a long night of socializing (without his wife) to find Wilde asleep outside the entrance to the Langtrys' apartment, snoring as he clutched a solitary blossom to his heaving chest. This story was repeated all over London, though some doubted its veracity. No matter: Wilde knew a higher truth was at work. As he would write in *The Picture of Dorian Gray*, "There is only one thing in the world worse than being talked about, and that is *not* being talked about."

He invited Mrs. Langtry to parties in his home on Salisbury Street. He gave her advice on fashion and told her what novels to read. He took her to museums and art galleries. He urged her to become an actress and found her an acting coach. He even became her personal classics tutor. When Sir Charles Newton, the man who unearthed the Mausoleum at Halicarnassus—one of the Seven Wonders of the Ancient World—gave a lecture at King's College, London, Wilde brought Langtry there in a carriage, from which they alighted, waving like royalty to their fellow lecture-goers. After Langtry studied the *Iliad*, Wilde wrote a poem about her titled "The New Helen."

> *O Helen! Helen! Helen! Yet a while*
>> Yet for a little while, O tarry here,
> *Till the dawn cometh and the shadows flee!*
>> For in the gladsome sunlight of thy smile
> *Of heaven or hell I have no thought or fear,*
>> *Seeing that I know no other God but thee.*

Wilde the adoring poet began to display in London the same aesthetic languor that had so irritated some of his classmates at Oxford: he would hail a cab to cross a street and ask for physical assistance to cross a room. His visits to the theater became dramas: he would arrive half an hour before curtain, then make a series of highly visible appearances around the auditorium, greeting the rich and titled. "There goes that bloody fool Oscar Wilde," one playgoer grumbled. When told of the remark, Wilde actually seemed proud. "It's extraordinary how soon one gets known in London," he said. He was right. The *Biograph and Review*, a kind of Who's Who of Victorian England, ran a profile of him in its 1880 annual edition, just a year after he had arrived in the capital. It began:

> Oscar Wilde, though he may be considered to have his career still before him, has already attained prominence as one of the elect in a certain modern school of which he is held to be not the least of the apostles. He is a believer in the religion of beauty, a marked figure among the newest group of Aesthetics, a dweller in the high places of feeling.

Time, a British weekly with no link to the current journal, published a cartoon in 1880 titled "The Bard of Beauty" in which Wilde, smirking in a top hat, caused lilies to grow wherever his feet touched the ground. It was in *Punch*, however, that the use of cartoons to mock Wilde reached its apogee, especially in a series of drawings that often appeared under the heading "Nincompoopiana." Most were drawn by George du Maurier, who had studied painting in Paris alongside James Whistler but now used pen and ink to make fun of a certain aesthete's flowing locks and his fondness for flowers. At first this dandy was identified in the drawings as Maudle or Jellaby Postlethwaite—the first an allusion to Wilde's alma matter, Magdalen College (pronounced Maudlin), the second a reference to Wilde's habit of calling himself the "Apostle of Aestheticism." It wasn't long, however, before—lest anyone miss the joke—the character was called Oscuro Wildgoose. Wilde certainly hadn't missed it. One night at an art opening, Whistler noticed that both Du Maurier and Wilde were in attendance. After bringing them together, Whistler asked, "Which of you two created the other, eh?" Du Maurier wasn't thrilled, but Wilde was delighted. He understood—ninety years before Roland Barthes made the point in an essay on Albert

Einstein—that appearing in a cartoon is "the sign [one] has become a legend."

The legend created by Du Maurier's cartoons enabled Wilde to achieve the first goal he had set for himself in London. He was mingling almost nightly at parties with the most celebrated figures of the day, a list that included not just Whistler and Mrs. Langtry but the novelist and former prime minister Benjamin Disraeli (now Lord Beaconsfield), Disraeli's longtime rival (and current prime minister) William Gladstone, and the future PMs H. H. Asquith, Arthur Balfour, and Lord Rosebery. Wilde enjoyed socializing with politicians, but he saved his special attention for the actresses Ellen Terry and Sarah Bernhardt. He became close friends with both stars; his relationship with Bernhardt, however, took on a special weight: she became one of his role models. As Henry James had written of her, after Bernhardt's London debut in 1879, "she is a celebrity because, apparently, she desires it with an intensity that has rarely been equaled, and because for this end all means are alike to her." These words were not intended by James as praise, but Wilde took them as career advice.

When Bernhardt returned to England in 1880, after touring America, he showed his fealty to his new mentor by casting an armful of flowers at her feet as she stepped off the ship and onto terra firma. The press coverage of this act of adoration was huge and, best of all from Wilde's standpoint, as much about him as it was about her. Not that Bernhardt held a grudge. She was a regular guest at parties thrown by Wilde at Thames House, on one occasion leaving her autograph on the paneling in his living room. (Bernhardt's English was spotty, so she and Wilde conversed in French.) Wilde was euphoric about that autograph, his friendship with "the Divine Sarah," his rapid rise in society, and, most of all, about the attention he was getting from the press. But he knew the next phase of his project would be even more critical to his future success: from now on, *he*—not Miss Bernhardt or Mrs. Langtry—would have to be the work of art on display.

Sometimes with props. One night he appeared at the artist Louise Jopling's studio wearing a live snake around his neck. Even without an exotic scarf, Wilde used fashion to present himself as a work of art. His typical uniform was a bespoke black frock coat with a daisy or carnation in his lapel buttonhole, enlivened by a brightly flowered waistcoat over a solid-colored silk shirt, usually cream, with a white cravat held in place by an antique intaglio amethyst pin, all of it over light-colored trousers and polished black boots. He would hold a walking stick in one hand, leaving the other free to carry pale lavender gloves, items whose primary function was to punctuate, with a well-timed flick, his remarks, which were legion and, before long, legendary.

Despite his excellent fashion sense, Wilde knew he could never be a living work of visual art in the same manner as Mrs. Langtry or Miss Bernhardt, who, after all, were professional beauties. So he would be what he *could* be: a living work of conversational art. He could talk beautifully about beauty, and he soon realized this skill was much prized by the blue-blooded women who were the true gatekeepers of London society. So what if much of what he said was lifted from Ruskin's lectures at Oxford or from Pater's writings? His listeners didn't know that, and, even more to the point, Ruskin and Pater were not available to serve as their guides to the art world, and Wilde was. He was so often observed taking his society "students" to exhibitions in London that the artist William Powell Frith immortalized his status in a painting he called *A Private Viewing at the Royal Academy*. The painting has roughly fifty people depicted in it, but one man stands out: Oscar Wilde, in a frock coat and top hat, holding a book in his hand, gesturing toward the art on display, about which he is speaking to a fashionably dressed group that includes Lillie Langtry and the actors Henry Irving and Ellen Terry. (Farther away, too far away to be listening, stand the poet Robert Browning, the biologist Thomas Huxley, and the novelist Anthony Trollope.) Wilde was so visible in London as the Aesthete About Town, and so successful at the attention-getting vocation he had given himself, that the essayist Max Beer-bohm would write: "Beauty had existed long before 1880, [but it] was Mr. Oscar Wilde who managed her *début*."

Art wasn't Wilde's only conversation subject, especially not at the parties he was so eager to attend. To ensure he kept getting those invitations, he perfected a verbal trick: replacing a word in a sentence with its unexpected opposite. This sleight of tongue enabled him to take subjects that others deemed serious and treat them irreverently, or take matters that others thought trivial and treat them with great solemnity—producing amusement either way. This made Wilde not just a well-dressed occupant of a seat at a dinner table. It made him a veritable bon mot machine:

"I can resist everything except temptation."

"If one tells the truth, one is sure, sooner or later, to be found out."

"Don't be led astray down the path of virtue."

"Only shallow people do not judge by appearances."

"I can sympathize with everything except suffering."

"True friends stab you in the front."

He seemed to have an endless supply, many of which he would later repeat in his comedies and other writings. But that was far off in the future. It is important that we fully credit the poise it took in 1880 for Wilde, a barely published writer in his early twenties, to command the spotlight before dinner-party audiences that were almost always older and more accomplished than he. Years later, in *A Woman of No Importance*, he would write, "A man who can dominate a London dinner table can dominate the world." He was speaking from experience.

What Wilde's listeners at those tables didn't know was that his remarks weren't always as spontaneous as they seemed. The novelist Coulson Kernahan described in his memoir how Wilde, when the two of them were alone, once asked Kernahan for his views on religion. After Kernahan answered at length, Wilde said, "You are so evidently, so unmistakably sincere and most of all so truthful, that I can't believe a single word you say." Noticing the smug look on Wilde's face, Kernahan asked, "Where are you dining tonight, Wilde?" When Wilde gave the name of a well-known English aristocrat, Kernahan said, "Ah. And who is the guest you have marked down upon whom, when everybody is listening, to work off that carefully prepared impromptu wheeze which you have just fired off on me?" Wilde's smile revealed that Kernahan had hit the bull's-eye.

Though he was always ready to perform at dinner parties, Wilde never forced the issue. He would usually start by talking quietly to the person seated next to him, making sure, however, that he was heard by at least one other dinner guest. If his "impromptu wheeze" was on target, the table would fall silent soon enough, and the attention of all would belong to him. He was able to hold it because he had excellent timing, because his humor was almost never mean-spirited, and because he loved performing. For most people it was irresistible—but not all. W. S. Gilbert was exasperated when he observed Wilde at a party. "I wish I could talk like you," he said. "I'd keep my mouth shut and claim it as a virtue!" He was made even crankier by Wilde's response: "Ah, that would be selfish! I could deny myself the pleasure of talking, but not others the pleasure of listening." The Polish actress Helena Modjeska, in London to make her West End debut as Camille, was also perplexed by Wilde's social success: "What has he done, this young man, that one meets him everywhere? Oh, yes, he talks well, but what has he done? He has written nothing, he does not sing or paint or act—he does nothing but talk. I do not understand."

But the Prince of Wales did, or at least wanted to. "I do not know Mr. Wilde," he said, though he surely knew *of* him, "and not to know Mr. Wilde is not to be known." This oversight was corrected in the spring of 1881 at the house on Tite Street where Wilde and Miles had moved the previous summer. (Wilde christened it "Keats House," because the previous occupants had been named Skeates.) The occasion was a party cum séance. The account in the society column of the

Ladies' Treasury magazine was hardly written with flair. Even so, Wilde was delighted. What better way to show you've arrived in society than for the world to learn you've held hands around a table in a dark room with a royal, several blue-blooded grandees, and their friends, trying to commune with the dead:

> Mr. W. Irving Bishop, the "thought reader," recently gave a private *séance* at Keats house, Chelsea. The company consisted of His Royal Highness the Prince of Wales, Lady Mandeville, Lady Archibald, the Marquisa Santurce, Mrs. Langtry, Lord Donoughmore, Mr. Irving, Mr. Booth, Mr. Whistler, Mr. Frank Miles, Mr. Oscar Wilde, and others.

(Mr. Booth was the American actor Edwin Booth, the brother of John Wilkes Booth.) George Gissing, in his novel *New Grub Street,* published in 1891, noted that men no longer "succeed in literature [so] that they may get into society," but "get into society [so] that they may succeed in literature." This path to success had been pioneered by Oscar Wilde more than a decade earlier.

But to Wilde's detractors, the séance at Keats House—and *all* of Wilde's social climbing—were proof that his true talent was for making an obsequious fool of himself. They were wrong. Wilde had done something far more serious and difficult: he had made a *commodity* of himself. The key step in that process had been transforming his personality, formed in Dublin and polished at Oxford, into a multifaceted brand in London: Wilde the Party Wit, Wilde the Style Guru, Wilde the Art Connoisseur, Wilde the Celebrated Friend of the Celebrated, even Wilde the Subject of Gossip and Sarcastic Cartoons. Some of these personae brought him more pleasure than others, but all of them increased his profile. As he had promised his friends at Oxford, Wilde had become famous. Now he was ready to get serious about being a famous writer.

• • •

THAT WILDE WAS confident of his imminent literary success, and of his current notoriety, is shown by the letter he sent to the London publisher David Bogue. "I am anxious to publish a volume of poems immediately.... Possibly my name requires no introduction." It appears he was right: by the summer of 1881 Wilde was a published author, though self-published was more accurate. The contract made him responsible for all printing costs, which were considerable. He insisted his book be bound in vellum and printed on handmade paper. Whatever the expense, he was ready to pay. A friend of Wilde's would say that Wilde told him: "If you wish for reputation and fame in the world, and success during your lifetime, you [must] seize every opportunity of advertising yourself. Remember the Latin saying, 'Fame springs from one's own house.'" If his literary fame had to spring from a vanity publishing house, that was fine with Wilde.

He sent his book to the poets Matthew Arnold, Robert Browning, and Algernon Swinburne; to Prime Minister William Gladstone; and, of course, to Lillie Langtry. ("To Helen," he wrote in hers, "Formerly of Troy, now of London.") All replied positively or at least politely. But several critics did not. "*Poems by Oscar Wilde* is the title of the book, which comes to us arrayed in white vellum and gold," began the unsigned review in *Punch*. "There is a certain amount of originality in the binding, but that is more than can be said of the inside of the volume. Mr. Wilde may be aesthetic, but he is not original. This is a volume of echoes—it is Swinburne and water." A cartoon in *Punch* drawn by Edward Linley Sambourne depicted Wilde as a human sunflower. The caption read:

> *Aesthete of Aesthetes!*
>   *What's in a name?*
> *The poet is WILDE,*
>   *But his poetry's tame.*

There was more pain to come, and, worse still, from an unexpected source. The Oxford Union, the university's debating society, had asked Wilde, a former member, to send a copy of *Poems* for its library. He happily did so, only to be told later that its formal acceptance required a majority vote from its members. To the great embarrassment of the Newdigate Prize winner, the vote went against him. "It is not that these poems are thin—and they *are* thin," said the leader of the anti-Wilde students, Oliver Elton, later to become a professor of literature at Harvard. "It is not that they are immoral—and they *are* immoral.

> It is that they are for the most part not by their putative father at all, but by a number of better-known and more deservedly reputed authors. They are in fact by William Shakespeare, by Philip Sidney, by John Donne, by Lord Byron, by William Morris, by Algernon Swinburne, and by sixty more. . . . The Union Library already contains better and fuller editions of all these poets: the volume which we are offered is theirs, not Mr. Wilde's: and I move that it not be accepted.

In truth, the charge that Wilde's poetry was immoral had already exacted a price. After Frank Miles's father, a Church of England cleric (and his son's chief financial patron), read one of Wilde's poems that referred to sexual acts between a man and a statue, and another that spoke of kissing the mouth of sin, he ordered his son, who was the leaseholder at Tite Street, to expel Wilde from their shared home. "My son must not be contaminated!" Canon Miles wrote.

After Wilde moved in temporarily with his mother, now living in London (where she was again hosting parties), he decided that if Oscar Wilde the Poet found his path to literary glory blocked, perhaps Oscar Wilde the Dramatist would not. Between nights out, he had written his first play. Set in Russia, the plot of *Vera; or, The Nihilists* was based on a real event: the shooting of the St. Petersburg police chief, in 1878, by a young female revolutionary who had been born into the Russian gentry. Along with radical politics, the play offered romance. Vera is torn between her passion for the masses, which has led her to plot the assassination of the czar, and her passion for her lover, the czar's son. It was a serious play for a party wit, but the subject Wilde was most serious about hadn't changed. He admitted as much in a letter to Edward F. Smyth Pigott, the examiner of plays for the lord chamberlain. "I am working at dramatic art because it's the democratic art, and I want fame," he wrote. In the fall of 1881 it was announced that *Vera* would open in London in December, with the title role played by Mrs. Bernard Beere, a name forgotten today but then belonging to an actress of some note. Wilde was thrilled.

But not for long. That year saw two assassinations—of Czar Alexander II in Russia, and of President James A. Garfield in the United States—that affected the political climate in Britain. The subject matter of *Vera*, which had been reported in the press, was now deemed an insult to the queen. Finally it was announced that *Vera* would not debut after all. The British humor magazine *Moonbeam* delighted in reporting the news:

> Mr. Oscar Wilde has been induced to withdraw his drama, *Vera; or, The Nihilists,* which was to have been produced at one of our London theatres. We wonder who it was that succeeded in persuading this gentleman to refrain from thus once more courting publicity? As a Scotsman might say, "it must ha' been *vera* deefficult!"

Wilde was crushed; he also began to worry about his finances. His income from his father's estate was dwindling, and it cost money to be a well-dressed party guest. Even so, his confidence in his career plan remained high. Long before psychologists began to teach visualization as a means of achieving one's goals, Wilde's vision of his future was both steadfast and clear: he would translate his personal fame into money and a career as a writer. What he couldn't foresee was the man who would step forward to help him.

W. S. Gilbert was working on a libretto for a show he hoped would match the success of his second hit, *The Pirates of Penzance*, which opened in 1880. His first idea was to expand upon a comic ballad he had written years earlier about two pastors who compete to "outmeek" each other. Then he got a better idea. Instead of rival curates, his operetta would have rival aesthetes—the equally narcissistic Bunthorne and Grosvenor—who would vie for the hand of a maiden named Patience. The lead male roles envisioned by Gilbert were composites lampooning several well-known aesthetes, including Dante Gabriel Rossetti, Algernon Swinburne, James Whistler, and Oscar Wilde. But the public would take a more focused view of what was going on in *Patience; or Bunthorne's Bride*. And it quickly became obvious, after its premiere in April 1881, Londoners' recognition of the model for Bunthorne was as clear as Wilde's ambition was transparent. It was hard to argue with that conclusion, after hearing these words, sung by Bunthorne in act one:

> *Though the Philistines may jostle,*
> *You will rank as an apostle,*
> *In the high aesthetic band.*
> *If you walk down Piccadilly*
> *With a poppy or a lily*
> *In your medieval hand.*

Wilde had heard he might be the object of some satire from Gilbert, so he sent a letter to the actor George Grossmith, then rehearsing to play Bunthorne: "I should like to go to the first night of your new opera and would be obliged if you would ask the Box Office to reserve a three guinea box for me. . . . I am looking forward to being greatly amused." And he was, even before the curtain went up. The critic for *The Era* wrote that there was "a fierce clamour of screams, yells and hisses which descended from the Gallery signaling the arrival of Mr. Oscar Wilde himself" on opening night. "For there, with the sacred flower, stood the exponent of uncut hair, Ajax-like, defying the Gods." Later, when Bunthorne sang of himself as the flower-carrying "apostle in the high aesthetic band," stared into Wilde's box, this audience would which only made Wilde happier.

A witness to both commotions was Richard D'Oyly Carte, Gilbert & Sullivan's producer. If *Patience* was a hit, and the eight curtain calls on opening night led him to think it would be, he might finance an American production, as he had for *The Pirates of Penzance* and *H.M.S. Pinafore.* But Carte was nervous: he noticed that several of Gilbert's jokes about aestheticism had passed over the heads of the audience in London. How then, he wondered, would an audience in America— where the British aesthete was not a native species—get any of those jokes? Buoyed by the demand for tickets in London, however, he approved a New York production, to open in September 1881. Still anxious about the show's "legs," Carte wrote to Helen Lenoir, his former assistant in London who was then managing his New York office. Lenoir (who would later become Carte's second wife) passed on an idea she had heard from a friend in Manhattan: why not send over a real British aesthete (maybe Oscar Wilde?) and have him present a series of lectures in America ("On Beauty," perhaps?), delivered in the same aesthetic costume (breeches, buckled shoes, a velvet coat, and so on) worn by Bunthorne in *Patience?* And to make the link (and joke) even clearer to their American cousins, perhaps he could be convinced to walk down Broadway with a poppy or a lily in his medieval hand.

This was asking a lot, even of a self-promoter as eager as Wilde. Lenoir's plan was a Russian doll of antivanity: it required Wilde, no stranger to high self-regard, to make a fool of himself in public by playing "himself" as a real-life Bunthorne, a role fashioned by Gilbert to make Wilde and *all* aesthetes appear fools. In a clever stroke, Carte used Wilde's vanity to get the response he wanted. Instead of contacting Wilde himself, he had Lenoir's colleague in New York, Col. W. F. Morse, the office's business manager and press agent, cable Wilde from the Carte bureau at 1267 Broadway. This gave Wilde not only the false impression that he was as well known in America as he was in England, but the equally false idea that there were lecture agents in America eager to book him. "Responsible agent asks me to enquire if you will consider offer he makes for fifty readings. . . . This is confidential. Answer," wrote Morse. There's no evidence Morse knew of any American agents clamoring for Wilde to lecture in their cities when this was sent, and certainly not in fifty of them. But Wilde didn't know that. And for him the timing was perfect. The telegram arrived at the very moment rumors were beginning to spread in London that *Vera* would never open. So . . ."Yes, if offer good," Wilde replied on October 1, 1881. And it was: half the gate receipts for the lecture tour, with all expenses covered.

Wilde had never given a lecture before, and what he knew of America, besides what he had gleaned from the poetry of Walt Whitman and Edgar Allan Poe, could be written on the palm of one of his lavender gloves. But that wouldn't stop him. After making his agreement with the Carte organization, he asked Hermann Vezin, an American actor then working in London, for elocution lessons. "I want a natural style, with a touch of affectation," Wilde said. "Haven't you already got that, Oscar?" Vezin asked. As for the subject of his lectures, Wilde had no fears. Weren't there dozens of well-born ladies in London who could testify how beautifully he spoke about beauty? And didn't he know many of the artists who had created that beauty? Men such as Rossetti, Burne-Jones, Whistler, and Swinburne? To make sure he met people of similar aesthetic rank in America, Wilde asked Burne-Jones to send a letter of introduction on his behalf to Charles Eliot Norton, a professor of art history at Harvard. "The gentleman who brings this little note to you is my friend Mr. Oscar Wilde," Burne-Jones's letter began:

[He] has much brightened this last of my declining years and I did promise him that if . . . a journey to America should ever come to pass that I would give him some little message to carry from me to thee. So behold it: and any kindness shewn to him is shewn to me.

THE TOUR OF America wouldn't just be a great adventure, Wilde was certain. It would be a great drama, one in which he would be both author and star—and if all went well, it would earn him a significant sum of money. His optimism was momentarily dashed, however, when word of his tour leaked to the press. The *Sporting Times* in London (a journal that covered society, not sports) had a laugh at the idea of Carte's dispatching Wilde as a "sandwich man"—someone to walk around with a billboard on his shoulders—for *Patience* and then claimed, falsely, that Carte had changed his mind when he realized he could get men in America with "longer hair" to do the job "for half the price." The *New York Herald* wrote an editorial on Wilde's possible arrival that took the form of a warning to all Americans: "In ancient mythology there is no more curious figure than that of the youth who pined for love of his own image and who was subsequently transformed to a flower. In modern life Narcissus is apt to be a nuisance. We fear that he is coming to our shores."

Once again Carte manipulated Wilde's vanity to put matters right. "Wilde is slightly sensitive," Carte wrote Lenoir. "I suggested to him that it would be a good boon for him if he were to go one evening to see *Patience*" again, in London. Carte told Wilde "he would probably be recognized" at the theater if he did so. "This idea," Carte wrote, "he quite took to." Wilde saw *Patience* for the second time; he was recognized (which both flattered and exhilarated him); the trip to America was still on. "I told [Wilde]," Carte wrote Lenoir, "he must not mind my using a little bunkum to push him in America."

Clearly, Carte was using Wilde. But Wilde, who knew a fair bit about bunkum, was using *Carte*. The aesthete had worked hard to advance his career in London with, he had to admit, mixed results, despite his inarguable success as a party wit. But he wasn't discouraged. Perhaps all he needed was a change of venue—and wasn't kind Mr. Carte offering that very thing? Years earlier, in a letter to his friend William (Bouncer) Ward, Wilde had confessed that his "two great gods" in life were "Money and Ambition." They still were. On Christmas Eve, 1881, he walked onto the SS *Arizona*, headed for America, to grab the former and further the latter.

CHAPTER TWO

Work the Room

*I*f Wilde was eager to get to New York quickly, he was on the right ship. When launched from Liverpool in May 1879, the SS *Arizona*, burning 125 tons of coal per day in thirty-nine furnaces, made the fastest maiden voyage across the Atlantic in nautical history and, a year later, set a new world record for the Liverpool–New York run: seven days, ten hours, and forty-seven minutes. Making that record even more impressive was that, a few months earlier, *Arizona* had crashed full speed into an iceberg the ship's lookouts had mistaken for a low-hanging cloud. "My God, men, where were your eyes?" said Capt. Thomas Jones, after returning to the bridge from his cabin. Jones couldn't have been happy with what he saw: *Arizona* had a hole in its bow resembling a railroad tunnel; it was listing heavily to the starboard; and it was taking on water at a rapid rate. But the good news was that the ship's interior walls had held, so the leak wasn't spreading. After limping back to Canada, *Arizona* made temporary repairs, then steamed to Scotland, where its bow was rebuilt. Having survived the iceberg, *Arizona*'s reputation for speed was now matched by a reputation for strength: it was considered unsinkable.

That was probably how, in December 1881, passenger 114 on *Arizona*, identified on the manifest as "Oscar Wilde, Gentleman," was feeling about himself. The literary setbacks he had experienced in London were ancient history as he luxuriated in his first-class stateroom, furnished with an upholstered reading chair, an inlaid chest of drawers and matching vanity, a (shared) toilet with a mahogany seat, and a twelve-inch porthole through which, when the mood struck him, he could gaze upon the sea, hoping not to see an iceberg. If Wilde required any personal service, a pneumatic bell, when rung, brought a prompt response from a nearby steward.

When he wished to mingle with other passengers—some of them, anyway—he could walk from his cabin to the Grand Saloon, which covered the entire width of *Arizona*, the walls of its entranceway decorated with frescoes depicting the English countryside. As Wilde would soon learn, the word *saloon* had a gamier connotation in America. On a ship such as *Arizona*, however, the saloon was the elegant space where passengers with first-class tickets took their meals and other pleasures, often in formal dress, while holders of steerage and second-class tickets had to make do with facilities resembling at best a cafeteria and at worst something one might experience in an orphanage.

At one end of the saloon was a library, where Wilde planned to write his lecture for America, and, above it, a room with a large bank of plate-glass windows at its front that offered a wide and protected view of the sea. Wilde passed pleasant moments in both areas, but the section of the saloon where he spent most of his time was its well-stocked bar, where socializing took place before and after the evening meal, as a pianist in evening clothes played in the background. Wilde had developed a taste for champagne as the darling of London's dinner-party set and, along with it, an equally strong predilection for showing off. The bar was an excellent setting for both.

He was delighted that his accommodations were top drawer. The deal he had struck with the Carte organization was vague; it stipulated that his traveling expenses would be covered, but it made no mention of *how* he would be traveling. Now he knew. It's possible that Richard D'Oyly Carte, one of the savviest impresarios of his era, was implementing a well-thought-out plan: he had sent many British performers, most of them stars of unquestioned stature, to tour the United States in the past. But now he was sending Oscar Wilde, a man who had yet to become a star—except in his own mind—to be a star in a country where most people had never heard of him. Perhaps if Carte made sure the *Arizona* treated Wilde like a star, he would play the part more convincingly when he arrived.

Carte had instructed Wilde to write his lecture while on the ship, but Wilde failed to get it done. The lure of the Grand Saloon bar, it seems, was too much to resist. But while Wilde was playing, the Carte office in New York was working—and had been for weeks. Even before Wilde walked onto *Arizona*, Col. W. F. Morse, the Carte operative who had sent the cable offering Wilde a lecture tour, mailed a solicitation letter to booking agents between Washington and Boston. Like many salesmen, Morse embellished the truth in his pitch, but what's curious about his letter is how he seemed to disassociate the Carte organization from the man it was ostensibly promoting. "I have lately had a correspondence with Mr. Oscar Wilde, the new English Poet, with reference to a tour in the U.S.," Morse began, apparently unaware that this client was Irish.

> My attention was first drawn to him for the reason, that while we were preparing for the opera "Patience" in New York, his name was often quoted as the originator of the aesthetic idea, and the author of a volume of poems lately published, which had made a profound sensation in English society. It was suggested to me, that if Mr. Wilde were brought to this country with the view of illustrating in a public way his idea of the aesthetic, that not only would society be glad to hear the man and receive him socially, but also, that the general public would be interested in hearing

from him a true and correct explanation of this latest form of fashionable madness.

Poems hadn't made a profound sensation in English society. Nor was there a consensus that Wilde was the originator of the aesthetic idea. But he would undeniably have been miffed to hear his worldview referred to as "madness," fashionable or not. Despite that final comment—or maybe because of it—Morse got bookings from most of the agents he contacted. Now he began to court the press, preparing an eight-page pamphlet on Wilde that was enclosed in an envelope made of thick marbled paper, with each addressee's name (and that of the Carte organization) printed in maroon ink, with the occasional word underlined in turquoise. Morse then mailed the pamphlet to every newspaper in the cities where Wilde was to appear.

This document, written in prose almost as bedizened as the covering in which it had been mailed, exalted Wilde as a man well equipped by a singularly enthusiastic temperament, and specially trained by a tutelage under the world-renowned scholar John Ruskin, to be the high priest in the new religion of beauty. Wilde had accepted that calling, the pamphlet declared, "with a soul steeped in the splendor of a religion which is preached through color and glow." Wilde had been called to preach this faith in America, the American press was told— and this was surely the biggest whopper in the text—"owing to repeated and urgent invitations from his friends and admirers in this country."

Yet at the same time this "official" message was circulating, Morse, striking a "just between you and me" pose, was whispering to his numerous friends in the New York press that Wilde was the inspiration for the absurd character Bunthorne in *Patience,* and he confessed that the whole purpose of that new Gilbert & Sullivan operetta was to satirize "the professors of ultra-refinement who preach the gospel of morbid languor and sickly sensuousness, which is half real and half affected by its High Priests for the purpose of gaining social notoriety." (These very words had been used in a pamphlet prepared by the Carte organization in Britain to promote touring companies of *Patience* in that nation's provinces.) Moreover, the poseurs satirized in *Patience* had reaped their ill-deserved fame, Morse said, by exhibiting an eccentricity of taste for, and an unhealthy admiration of, exhaustion, corruption, and decay. The conclusion seems inescapable: while Wilde was amusing himself in *Arizona*'s Grand Saloon, the Carte organization was selling his lecture tour to the American press as a freak show.

It was sound business strategy. The most popular commercial attraction in the United States, until it was destroyed by fire in the late 1860s, was P. T. Barnum's American Museum. There, in a five-story building on Broadway in Lower Manhattan, exhibits of anatomical oddities and historical curios—some alive and authentic (Tom Thumb and the Siamese twins Chang and Eng) and others not so much (The Trunk of the Tree Under Which Jesus's Disciples Sat)—combined to sell thirty million tickets, a number matching the population of the entire United States. One reason for that astonishing success, Morse understood, was the willing role played in promoting Barnum's humbuggery by the American press, which seemed to love nothing more than writing about the silly and the strange, no matter how seriously the subjects of their journalism took themselves.

WILDE'S SHIP ARRIVED off the coast of Staten Island, at the entrance to New York Harbor, on the evening of January 2, 1882. *Arizona* couldn't clear quarantine and dock in Manhattan until the next morning, so it dropped anchor. But the local press, apparently sent into a lather by Morse's promotional campaign, refused to wait. Several newsmen hired a small boat to take them to the ship, where, after climbing on board, they found Wilde and encircled him, an event that both alarmed and flattered the "High Priest of Beauty," who had no idea they were coming. Morse's pamphlet had told the reporters Wilde had come to America to advance the cause of aestheticism. The newsmen demanded a definition of that strange foreign philosophy.

Wilde was used to being surrounded, but not like this. The groups that gathered around him in London, usually at parties or art exhibitions, were composed of stage actresses such as Sarah Bernhardt and Ellen Terry, society beauties such as Lillie Langtry and Lady Archibald (both of whom had participated in the séance where Wilde was introduced to the Prince of Wales), or fellow aesthetes such as Frank Miles and Lord Ronald Gower. Certainly not aggressive newspaper hacks. So it took a moment for Wilde to regain his composure before he answered. "Aestheticism is a search after the signs of the beautiful. It is the science through which men look after the correlation which exists in the arts," the *New York World* quoted him as saying the next day. (Employing the usage of Victorian Britain, Wilde said "after" where we today would say "for.")

The *World* would be just about the only paper in New York to report that answer. The other newsmen on the ship—those looking for a freak, not a philosopher—instead wrote in "scientific" detail about Wilde's physiognomy, fashion choices, and phonetics. Barnum's American Museum had once exhibited a four-and-a-half-foot-tall black man with a large nose, bulging eyes, and a tiny pointed head with a solitary tuft of hair at the point—ostensibly the "Missing Link" between man and monkey—under a lurid banner that asked: "WHAT IS IT?" Now the New York press was asking and answering the same question about Wilde.

"He was found near the Captain's room," a reporter for the *New York Times* wrote. "He opened his large mouth as though about to laugh, and displayed white teeth of good size, but he made no noise.

He is over six feet tall in height and has broad shoulders. He is not heavily built, but looks like a not particularly athletic man. His face is oval in shape, with a rather massive chin, and a nose of more than ordinary size. His complexion would be difficult to describe except perhaps . . . as pretty. He wears his brown hair so long that it rests in a curling fashion far down upon his shoulders. His face was smooth, no sign of a beard yet having shown itself. He wore a low-necked white shirt, with a turn-down collar of extraordinary size, and a large light-blue scarf. His hands were in the pockets of his fur-lined ulster, and a turban was perched on his head. He wore pantaloons of light color, and patent-leather shoes. . . . His laugh was a succession of broad "haw, haw, haws."

A reporter from another paper added:

His manner of talking is somewhat affected, his great peculiarity being a rhythmic chant in which every fourth syllable is accentuated. Thus, when asked what was his mission in America he replied in a sing-song tone: "I came from *Eng*-land because I *thought* Ameri-*ca* was the best *place* to see."

A fellow passenger, asked if he had heard Wilde make any comments about their voyage, said that Wilde told him: "I am not exactly pleased with the Atlantic. It is not so majestic as I expected. The roaring ocean does not roar." The context for such words, if Wilde really said them, was that years earlier, while sailing to Italy with John Mahaffy, he had witnessed a squall in the Mediterranean he described as "the grandest sight I ever saw." Wilde's comment about the unexpectedly pacific Atlantic—genuine or not—was printed all over America and cabled to England, where the London weekly *Truth* published a letter that said: "I am disappointed in Mr. Wilde." Signed: "THE ATLANTIC OCEAN."

More reporters came to the Manhattan waterfront the next morning to meet the "real Bunthorne," including one from the *New York Sun* who claimed he heard passengers on *Arizona* singing these lines from *Patience* as Wilde left the ship:

A pallid and thin young man,
A haggard and lank young man,
A greenery-yallery, Grosvenor Gallery,
Foot-in-the-grave young man!

After Wilde emerged from customs, a journalist from *The New York Post* challenged the lank aesthete to justify his obsession with beauty. "I am here to diffuse beauty, and I have no objection to saying that," Wilde answered. "Man is hungry for beauty. The ridicule which aesthetes have been subjected to is only the envy of blind, unhappy souls who cannot find beauty, . . . [which] in fact is all around us." The reporter, either dim or determined to be rude (or both), looked across the river to a grain elevator in New Jersey. "Might beauty be in both the lily and [in that silo] in Hoboken?"

"Something of the kind," Wilde said, before he was pulled away by Colonel Morse, who took him, by carriage, away from the noisy waterfront to a quiet breakfast at Delmonico's, the restaurant on Fifth Avenue and Twenty-sixth Street said to be New York's finest. (It was definitely the first in the city to have tablecloths and printed menus.) Later the same carriage took the two men to a hotel not far from the Carte agency's office, at 1237 Broadway, where Wilde checked into a two-room suite. (A few days later Wilde moved into a private residence in Manhattan, on East Twenty-eighth Street.) Before returning to his office, Morse told Wilde that he would have a valet at his service in New York, as well as a carriage and driver. He also reminded him of his obligation to finish writing his lecture, which was to be delivered less than a week later, on January 9, at Chickering Hall.

Built for Chickering & Sons, a firm that manufactured pianos, that venue was a four-story brick building, trimmed in marble, at the corner of Fifth Avenue and Eighteenth Street that had a piano showroom on the ground floor, topped by a graceful auditorium, with balcony, that could seat 1,250. Though it was designed for recitals, Chickering Hall was a popular location for lectures, and in 1877 it was the site used by Alexander Graham Bell to demonstrate his new invention, the telephone, to New Yorkers. (Bell made the world's first long-distance call there, from Manhattan to New Brunswick, New Jersey.)

Wilde was slow to take up his task. The man who had once walked through rural Oxfordshire with the legendary John Ruskin now walked, alone and unrecognized, through the streets of Manhattan. Later he would describe his first impressions: "Everybody seems in a hurry to catch a train." "There are no pageants, and no gorgeous ceremonies. I saw only two processions: one was the Fire Brigade preceded by the Police, the other was the Police preceded by the Fire Brigade." And: "In America life is one long expectoration."

Wilde was even more distracted by Manhattan's social life, and for that the blame goes to Colonel Morse. He had sent announcements of Wilde's arrival to the Very Important People of New York and let it be known, through his social connections, that Wilde would make an excellent party guest. Soon Wilde's valet was carrying piles of invitations on a silver tray to Wilde, for review. Wilde was thrilled to be so in demand and wrote a bubbly letter to Mrs. George Lewis, the wife of his English solicitor, in which he compared his own popularity in New York to that of the most sought-after party guest in London. "I now understand why the Royal Boy"—the Prince of Wales—"is in good humour always. It is delightful to be a *petit roi.*"

Wilde received those invitations because, to the wealthy women who sent them, he was not the freak the press had taken him for. He was the Ambassador of Aestheticism, a European of taste and refinement who could help American women achieve the goal they had set for themselves: making their newly prosperous nation a more civilized place to live (which in most cases meant mimicking Europe). The husbands of these women lived for money and reaped their rewards. The wives would live for art and beauty and reap theirs. And now, here in New York, was Mr. Oscar Wilde, one of the English aesthetic movement's leading lights (or so they had been told), an art critic, dramatist, and prize-winning poet who had not only studied with the connoisseur John Ruskin, but personally knew the designer William Morris, whose teachings on beauty, craftsmanship, and interior decorating were then making such a large impact inside American homes.

Wilde's first hosts in New York, Mr. and Mrs. Augustus A. Hayes, Jr., opened their townhouse on East Twenty-fifth Street for a party in Wilde's honor on January 5. Though it was held between three and six p.m., on a Thursday, the turnout was impressive. Among those attending were the mayor of New York, William R. Grace; Justice John R. Brady of the New York Supreme Court (who had administered the oath of office to President Chester A. Arthur); the pastors of Grace and Trinity Churches, Rev. Dr. Potter and Rev. Mr. Douglass; and several dozen visibly excited, culture-worshiping New York society women, many of them dressed in "aesthetic" gowns—long, loose-fitting, unstructured garments, usually solid-colored, that hung from the shoulder rather than from the waist.

"A line of private conveyances with liveried coachmen filled the street and invited guests were constantly arriving or departing," reported the *New York Times*. Wilde made his entrance in a black velvet Prince Albert coat and billowing white shirt with a large collar, accessorized by a robin's-egg-blue scarf tied loosely around his neck. Once inside, he was placed in an alcove between the two large parlors that occupied most of the second floor of the Hayeses' townhouse. The dim lighting there no doubt seemed familiar to him. As had been Lady Wilde's custom at the family home in Dublin, Mrs. Hayes had shuttered her house with dark curtains, using only candles and gas lamps covered with rose-colored shades for illumination. Even so, the lighting was sufficient for a reporter from the *New York World* to make this assessment of the guest of honor: "His face is that of a colossal maiden untroubled by heated vision but over which at times beams a certain joyousness, wholly Greek, at the sight of the largeness or beauty of nature. In its lines it is essentially feminine, but these are on so large a scale that their soft curves indicate none of the weakness which might hastily attach to the adjective. Otherwise his sturdy physique is as English as if trained in athletics instead of aesthetics." A large ceremonial parasol, handmade in Japan, was suspended from the ceiling above where Wilde had stationed his "sturdy physique." This theatrical setting, intensified by the mood lighting, gave Wilde the appearance of "a heathen idol," the reporter from the *World* wrote.

Guests were introduced there to the idol, who answered questions about his lecture plans, the elements of good poetry, the charms of Pre-Raphaelite painting, and, of course, the aesthetic movement. He loved playing the *petit roi*, meeting his "subjects." As he would write to his friend Mrs. Lewis: "I stand at the top of the reception rooms when I go out, and for two hours they defile past for introduction. I bow graciously and sometimes honour them with a royal observation." "Royal" observations such as this, declaimed to a group of adoring females who had surrounded him: "America reminds me of one of Edgar Allan Poe's exquisite poems." Why? "Because it is full of belles." And this, said to a woman who asked for advice on arranging decorative screens in her Manhattan apartment: "Why arrange them at all? Why not just let them *occur*?"

It was a memorable debut, but Wilde would give an even more important performance later that day. After the party ended at the Hayeses', Wilde accompanied his hosts and nine other New Yorkers to the Standard Theatre on West Thirty-third Street, where *Patience* was playing. They were joined on this crosstown trip by a reporter from the *New York Tribune*, so Wilde knew his words and actions were on the record. He wasn't especially eager to see *Patience*—he had already seen it twice in London. But he *was* eager to do something special once he got there.

His group had reserved two adjoining boxes, and their entrance was noticed by their fellow theatergoers. This became obvious when, as had previously transpired in London, virtually the entire New York audience turned as one to stare into Wilde's box at the moment when the actor playing Bunthorne (J. H. Ryley)—wearing breeches, black stockings, patent-leather pumps, a black velvet coat, and an unusually large-collared shirt—began to sing:

Am I alone,
*   and unobserved? I am!*
Then let me own
*   I'm an aesthetic sham!*
This air severe
*   is but a mere veneer!*
This cynic smile
*   is but a wile of guile!*
This costume chaste
*   is but good taste misplaced!*

Let me confess! . . .

I am not fond of uttering platitudes
*   in stained-glass attitudes.*
In short, my mediaevalism's affectation,
*   born of a morbid love of admiration!*

Wilde knew the moment was coming, so he was prepared. This is how the *Tribune* reporter described what happened: "[As] the whole audience turned and looked at Mr. Wilde, he leaned toward one of the ladies [in his box] and said with a smile while looking at Bunthorne, 'This is the compliment that mediocrity pays to those who are not mediocre.'"

As a dinner-party wit in England, Wilde had witnessed the power of his personality, but he had used that power mainly for social advancement. By saying those words in front of the *Tribune* reporter, Wilde was declaring that he would now use that power for *professional* advancement: while in America, the most commercial nation on Earth, he would do business like an American and sell his product for financial gain. The key to making that enterprise successful, he understood, was realizing that his product wasn't Bunthorne. It was himself. In committing to this business plan, he anticipated a paradigm shift in the law and commerce (and, though no one knew it yet, politics). Not long after his arrival in the States, a legal dispute arose between the Southern Pacific Railroad and Santa Clara County, California, over a tax bill. This conflict led to the Supreme Court ruling establishing the "doctrine of corporate personhood," a doctrine confirmed more than a century later in *Citizens United* and memorably restated in 2012 by the presidential candidate Mitt Romney as "corporations are people, my friend." What Wilde grasped in 1882—decades before any other celebrity—was that the reverse was equally true.

So he worked the room, wherever it was. On the night of January 8 he put his product on display at three parties held by three grandes dames of New York society. (Colonel Morse helped Wilde decide which invitations to accept during his stay in New York.) First he dined at the Gramercy Park home of Mrs. John Bigelow and her husband, the former American ambassador to France, who had asked a small circle of friends to meet "the young aesthete," as their invitation described the twenty-seven-year-old guest of honor. (Wilde had told the New York press he was twenty-six.) After that meal, Wilde's carriage driver took him to a reception at the Fifth Avenue apartment of Mrs. Paran Stevens, one of the wealthiest widows in the city and an opinion leader among the social elite; and, after that, to the East Thirty-eighth Street home of Mrs. D. G. Croly, better known to New Yorkers as the pioneering female newspaper columnist Jennie June. In truth, Croly had organized her gala so that her guests could meet Louisa May Alcott, whose success with *Little Women* and other novels had made her the best-selling female writer in the United States. But Wilde, whose *Poems* had barely sold a few hundred copies, wasn't intimidated. As the *New York Tribune* reported, he arrived at eleven p.m., and, as he had seen his friend Sarah Bernhardt do so often to other guests at parties in London, he "immediately drew off part of the crowd which had formed around Miss Alcott," making him*self* the center of attention. All in a night's work, he wrote to the English actor Norman Forbes-Robertson:

I am torn to bits by Society. Immense receptions, wonderful dinners, crowds wait for my carriage. I wave a gloved hand and an ivory cane and they cheer. Girls very lovely, men simple and intellectual. Rooms are hung with white lilies for me everywhere. I have "Boy" (champagne) at intervals, also two secretaries, one to write my autograph and answer the hundreds of letters that come begging for it. Another, whose hair is brown, to send locks of his own hair to the young ladies who write asking for mine; he is rapidly becoming bald.

The bit about the balding secretary was blarney. But Wilde understood he had two audiences to impress now: one in New York, where he was on display; the other in London, where people were reading about him almost daily in the British press. Besides, as his mentor John Mahaffy had taught him in Dublin, the ultimate sin in storytelling isn't lying. It's being dull.

So it's no surprise Wilde was exaggerating when he said all New York was cheering him on. The poet and essayist Edmund Clarence Stedman, a lion of the city's literary scene, wrote in his diary on January 5: "This Philistine town is making a fool of itself over Oscar Wilde. Pah!" After seeing his name wrongly included in the press on a list of attendees at Mrs. Croly's party, Stedman wrote a letter to a friend in Boston:

The genuine writers [and] poets of this city have kept out of [Wilde's] way and are not over-pleased with the present revelation of the state of culture on Murray Hill. I do not blame a clever hum-bug, like Wilde, for taking advantage of their snobbery, and idiocy, and making all the money he can. He is a shrewd man of the world. . . . Before leaving London, [he] procured—through the influence of his titled patronesses—*hundreds* of letters of introduction, addressed to all leading writers and fashionables in our chief cities. He has sent me two. . . . I have declined to acknowledge them. . . . As I have devoted months to pointing out the talents of other English poets—genuine workers who would scorn such advertising—no one suspects me of jealousy. It is simply self-respect, and contempt for our rich people here who see no difference between Longfellow and Emerson and Bryant—and Wilde!

Another lion(ess) of the New York literary establishment who avoided Wilde, though not precisely for the same reason, was the poet Emma Lazarus, who in 1883 would write "The New Colossus," the poem excerpted on the base of the Statue of Liberty ("Give me your tired, your poor, Your huddled masses yearning to breathe free. . . .") "I have not seen Oscar Wilde & have little or no curiosity to see him," she wrote to a friend in January 1882:

[But] I do not agree [with those who say] that "he is beneath contempt"—intellectually—he has written together with a lot of trash & verbiage, some charming & some manly verse—"Ave Imperiatrix" is I think a fine poem, & could only have been written by a man of genuine imagination & talent. But for the very reason that he is *not* a fool, & knows what he is about, I think he is the more to be despised & shunned by all sensible people, for making such a consummate ass of himself. The bare-faced courting of a vulgar notoriety, in a man with well-founded pretensions to good birth, good breeding, & an intelligence conspicuously above the average is, I really do think, something "beneath contempt."

Somehow Wilde found the time between making friends (and enemies) to write his lecture, in longhand, which was given to a secretary in the Carte office, who used a new machine called the Type Writer—it had become commercially available in 1867—to render his document into easily legible text. In a note to Mrs. Lewis in London,

Wilde expressed anxiety about his speaking debut: "If I am not a success . . . I shall be very wretched." Actually, by one important measure his lecture was already a success: according to the delighted Colonel Morse, every ticket had been sold.

CARRIAGES BEGAN DISCHARGING passengers at Chickering Hall shortly after seven p.m., on January 9, as scalpers on the sidewalk did a brisk business selling tickets for two dollars, twice their face value. Wilde would tell his friends in London that each ticket holder walked by an elegant display case—fully six feet tall, he bragged—with a poster inside announcing in muscular boldface: TONIGHT Mr. OSCAR WILDE on The ENGLISH RENAISSANCE OF ART.

That was a serious topic, and it's likely some arrivals were wondering how seriously to take it—and maybe even wondering how seriously its *presenter* would be taking it. After all, British magazines, many of which were available in New York, had been drawing Wilde as a fool for years, and now every daily in Manhattan was charting his flattery of society matrons, an exercise that hardly seemed worthy of a serious lecturer on a serious intellectual topic. Adding to the confusion was the fact that the Carte organization was telling everyone that Wilde, who had graduated with first-class honors from Oxford, was nonetheless the real-life Bunthorne, the grandiose boob whose dandyish dishonesty and nattering narcissism formed the humorous core of *Patience*, the latest box-office smash from the masters of the operetta, Gilbert & Sullivan.

Wilde's topic had emerged from the letter Morse sent to booking agents weeks earlier in which he claimed Wilde had prepared two lectures for America, "The Poetical Methods of Shakespeare" and "The Beautiful as Seen in Everyday Life"; if neither piqued the agents' interest, he said, Wilde was ready to read a lyric poem of his own composition. The agents chose "The Beautiful . . ." After arriving in New York, however, Wilde, who in truth hadn't prepared any lectures,

altered that selection to become an account of the origins and achievements of the English aesthetic movement. Morse wasn't thrilled about
the change, but he took comfort in knowing that the American public
had shown a willingness to buy tickets to all sorts of lecture programs,
from the folksy travel adventures of Mark Twain to the horrific tales
of polygamy voiced by Ann Eliza Young, the runaway nineteenth
wife—or twenty-seventh, depending on who was counting—of the
Mormon patriarch Brigham Young. Morse had made only two
demands of Wilde regarding his talk: that while delivering it he dress
like Bunthorne, which meant in breeches; and that he mention *Patience*
at least once. That Chickering Hall was sold out made Morse feel his
work in presenting his client to America had paid off where it counted
most—at the box office.

Wilde believed he had done that job himself. Now it was time to
work the room—the biggest he had been in so far. If he peeked out
from behind the curtain at Chickering Hall, he would have seen hundreds of women in free-flowing aesthetic gowns (which also meant
corset-free, as the aesthetic code demanded), nearly all of them accompanied by husbands or other male escorts in conservative wool suits. A
group of last-minute ticket buyers, described by the *New York Tribune*
as "aesthetic and pallid young men in banged hair," were "leaning in
mediaeval attitudes" in the standing-room section.

Those "pallid" young men probably didn't know it, but Wilde had
never given a lecture; even so, his years in Oxford and London had
given him a well-defined sense of occasion, so he was ready to perform. There were two chairs on the stage behind the lecture stand, one
to the left, the other to the right. An Oriental rug lay beneath all three
objects. A brown screen was suspended from the ceiling as a backdrop.
At around 8:10 P.M., the stage gaslights flashed on full, and Colonel
Morse and Wilde emerged from the wings and walked toward the
chairs, Morse taking the lead, Wilde taking his time. The occasion, he
knew, demanded that he be observed. Closely.

The audience gasped. Its 1,250 members were staring, many with open mouths, at a six-foot-three-inch man wearing a snug black velvet coat with lavender satin piping and a frill of white lace at the wrists, black satin breeches with silk bows that encased his legs at the knee, black silk stockings that, when caught by the lights, flashed white at the calves, and patent-leather pumps with lustrous silver buckles. His accessories were designed to produce a contrast, and they succeeded: a white silk waistcoat, cut low, with a white handkerchief drooping—not peeking—from one pocket; a gold watch fob hanging from another; and white kid gloves with black ornamental stitching at the seams. He wore a starched white shirtfront with an enormous stud—a diamond flanked by two pearls—near the center of the garment that reflected the nearby gaslights. The shirt had a wide Byronic, turn-down collar that enveloped a white muslin bowtie (hand-tied, of course). Wilde's dark hair hung to his shoulders and framed a clean-shaven, milky face that showed hints of powder and rouge. He carried a black cape over one shoulder and a slim black leather case in in his free hand. When he reached his chair, he sat down. The audience was still applauding.

After some late arrivals were seated, Colonel Morse rose from his chair and walked to the edge of the stage. "I have the great honor," he said, "to introduce to you Oscar Wilde, who will deliver to you his lecture on 'The English Renaissance.'" Then, with a bow, Morse retired to the wings. Wilde opened his leather case, removed his typed manuscript, then stood up and walked a step or two to the lecture stand, where he placed the text before him. He cleared his throat and looked out at the audience, aiming a pleased smile and a subtle wave of his gloved hand at a face—a woman's—that he recognized. Just as Bunthorne might. Chatter and laughter rippled through the Hall.

"Among the many debts which we owe to the supreme aesthetic faculty of Goethe," Wilde began, "is that he was the first to teach us to define beauty in terms the most concrete possible, to realise it, I mean, always in its special manifestations." The audible excitement in the audience morphed into silence—some to better hear what Wilde was saying, others in shock at *what* he was saying. "So in the lecture which I have the honour to deliver before you," Wilde continued,

> I will not try to give you any abstract definition of beauty—any such universal formula for it as was sought for by the philosophy of the eighteenth century—still less to communicate to you that which in its essence is incommunicable, the virtue by which a particular picture or poem affects us with a unique and special joy; but rather to point out to you the general ideas which characterise the great English Renaissance of Art in this century, to discover their source, as far as that is possible, and to estimate their future, as far as that is possible.

This wasn't Bunthorne the "aesthetic sham." This was Oscar Wilde the prizewinning scholar who had studied with Ruskin and dined with Pater, two names that would soon be dropped as Wilde continued, just as Goethe's had in the first sentence, along with those of—and this is just a partial list—Homer, Plato, Theocritus, Chaucer, Dante, Michelangelo, Rubens, Rousseau, Ruskin, Byron, Shelley, Wordsworth, Swinburne, Schiller, Baudelaire, and Gautier (the French poet and critic who had popularized the aesthetic slogan "Art for Art's sake" or, as he had written, "*l'art pour l'art*.")

As his listeners now realized, Wilde's promised survey of the origins of aestheticism would be unrelentingly serious, briefly chronicling the contributions of Greek art, medieval art, and Florentine art, until he came to the men he deemed the shapers of the current renaissance he had come to speak about, figures he would pay homage to at length. These were men such as Keats (for writing "Beauty is truth, truth beauty. That is all Ye know on earth, and all ye need to know"); Rossetti, Burne-Jones, and the other members of the Pre-Raphaelite Brotherhood (for painting from nature and for championing realism over abstraction); and William Morris (for his insistence upon the importance of the decorative arts, and for his commitment to the highest standards of design and craftsmanship in the making of that art). Wilde was demanding of his listeners not just a surface grasp of the history of Western civilization but a rigorous schooling in it, the kind of education not readily available in America in 1882, except perhaps at Harvard. One can only wonder what his listeners made of these words:

> It is to no avail that the Muse of Poetry be called, even by such a clarion note as Whitman's, to migrate from Greece and Ionia and to placard REMOVED and TO LET on the rocks of the snowy Parnassus. Calliope's call is not yet closed, nor are the epics of Asia ended; the Sphinx is not yet silent, nor the fountain of Castaly dry.

Wilde had promised Morse he would give his American listeners a show—and hadn't his jaw-dropping costume fulfilled that requirement? But he had promised himself that the product he would be selling in America would be Oscar Wilde. So he didn't merely work the room at Chickering Hall; he worked to show he was the smartest person in it. This was an unexpected turn for his audience, most of whom had come to see the man considered the wittiest (and foppiest) man in London, a person now the target of considerable mockery in Gilbert & Sullivan's *Patience*, then playing to full houses at the nearby Standard Theatre. But on this night, Wilde had his own goal: to show America that a caricature like Bunthorne—as he'd said at the Standard Theatre—is just the compliment that mediocrity pays to those who are not mediocre.

So on he went, despite the occasional yawn from a listener, to speak of André Chénier's observation that "the storm of revolution blows out the torch of poetry"; of how "art never harms itself by keeping aloof from the social problems of the day"; and of how the immortal Keats had sounded the clarion call of the current renaissance when he said, "I have no reverence for the public, nor for anything in existence but the Eternal Being, the memory of great men, and the principle of Beauty." Eventually Wilde honored his promise to Morse, but in a way that subverted that promise. This is how a reporter for the *New York Herald* heard it:

> I am asking, as you have listened for a hundred nights to my friend Mr. Arthur Sullivan's charming opera *Patience* (laughter), that you will listen to me for one night (renewed laughter); and as you have had satire, you may make the satire a little more piquant by knowing a little more of the truth; and that, in any case, you will not take the brilliant lines of Mr. Gilbert any more as a revelation of the aesthetic movement than you would judge of the splendour of the sun or the majesty of the sea by the dust that dances in the beams of the bubble breaks on the wave. (Applause.)

Could the dividing line have been drawn any clearer? Wilde equals "splendour of the sun"; Bunthorne equals dancing, bubbly "dust." Moments later Wilde added: "You have heard . . . of two flowers connected with the aesthetic movement and said . . . to be [eaten by] aesthetic young men." (This comical claim, met by more laughter from Wilde's audience, was sung by Bunthorne, in act one of *Patience*.)

> Well, let me tell you that the reason we love the lily and the sunflower, in spite of what Mr. Gilbert may tell you, is not for any vegetable fashion at all. It is because these two lovely flowers are the two most perfect models of design, the most naturally adapted for decorative art—the gaudy leonine beauty of the one and the precious loveliness of the other giving to the artist the most entire and perfect joy.

What he wanted, Wilde said, was for his audience to experience that joy themselves.

And so with you: let there be no flower in your meadows that does not wreathe its tendrils around your pillows, no little leaf in your Titan forests that does not lend its form to design, no curving spray of wild rose or briar that does not live forever in carved arch or window or marble, no bird in your air that is not giving the iridescent wonder of its colour, the exquisite curves of its wings in flight, to make more precious the preciousness of simple adornment. For the voices that have their dwelling in sea and mountain are not the chosen music of liberty only. Other messages are there in the wonder of wind-swept heights and the majesty of silent deep—messages that, if you will listen to them, will give you the wonder of all new imagination, the treasure of all new beauty.

Wilde paused, then looked at his audience. "We spend our days looking for the secret of life. Well, the secret of life is in art."

With that revelation, he gathered his papers into his case, stepped beside the lecture stand, bowed, and walked off stage, as his audience applauded—some in admiration, others happy the arcane program had finally ended. When the most persistent of those clappers induced Wilde to return from the wings to take a second bow, a reporter for the *New York Times* noticed that he "blushed like a school-girl."

IF WILDE HAD been asked to review his own performance, he probably would have found it wanting. He had aimed high with his text, but he worried that he hadn't reached the peaks regularly achieved at Oxford by John Ruskin, an orator, as Wilde would later write, "to [whom] the gods gave eloquence such as they have given to none other, so that [his] message might come to us with the fire of passion, and the marvel of music, making the deaf to hear, and the blind to see." Wilde suspected that, despite his florid finish, most of the men and women at Chickering Hall had left the auditorium as deaf and blind as they had arrived. It occurred to him that he might have to replace his current lecture topic with something with a broader appeal.

But he took solace in knowing that the stage at Chickering Hall was not the only one he would be appearing on in America, and not even the only one he'd be performing on that night. Minutes after taking his second bow, Wilde was ushered out of the stage door and into his waiting carriage by the unusually bubbly Colonel Morse, who congratulated his client on his great success, pointing out that only a handful of American lecturers—men such as the clergyman and social reformer Henry Ward Beecher and the atheist and freethinker Robert G. Ingersoll—could be counted on to sell more than $1,000 worth of tickets on a given night in America, as Wilde just had. Joined in the carriage by Mrs. Morse, the two men took a mile-long ride up Fifth Avenue to the home of Mrs. John Mack, one of the leading ladies of New York society, who had organized a party for the Irish poet and aesthete who had just made that highly profitable speaking debut.

Once inside Mrs. Mack's home, one of the grandest on Fifth Avenue, Wilde was escorted by his glowing, aesthetically gowned hostess into her parlor, decorated on this night with huge displays of lilies and sunflowers, as an orchestra played—without irony—"God Save the Queen." This was a stage Wilde was confident of conquering. "Scores upon scores of beautiful and elegantly dressed ladies crowded each other in their effort to grasp his hand," noted a reporter for the *New York Herald*. Wilde, the only man in the parlor wearing breeches, was easy to find, and he "showed remarkable self-possession, meeting them all with a courteous welcome. Any ordinary young man," the *Herald* was certain, "would have been nervous." But not Wilde, who spent hours delighting his admirers—and himself—by listening to their compliments and responding with humorous "impromptu wheezes." In a letter to a friend in England, Wilde joked about having to endure the spotlight so: "Loving virtuous obscurity as much as I do, you can judge how much I dislike this lionizing."

As Wilde was working the room at Mrs. Mack's, journalists were writing their reviews. The *New York World* praised his "long melodious sentences, seldom involved, always clear, that unfolded his meaning as graceful curves reveal a beautiful figure," and the *New York Herald*, which days earlier had confessed it "viewed Mr. Wilde's [aesthetic] teachings with alarm," now, after listening to them in person, commended their "quality of thought." The *New York Times* filled most of its allotted space with a detailed description of Wilde's audience and the speaker's extravagant costume, but made no judgment of the lecturer or his lecture, other than to describe his voice as "sepulchral." The *Daily Graphic*, in a piece headlined "THE FOOLER AND THE FOOLS," made no effort to hide its contempt. "The craze over Oscar Wilde will not be of long duration," it said.

> It received a fatal blow last night, when all the sensible men and women in the audience which had gathered to hear and see him began quickly to feel ashamed of themselves and to wish that they had stayed at home. They began to see that they had been duped into aiding a young Irishman to make a pot of money, simply because he had possessed the shrewdness to . . . impersonate in the flesh what a *Punch* artist had depicted with pen and ink. . . . [Wilde's talk] was delivered in a prosy and dull monotone. . . . There was nothing in it striking, original or new.

Wilde had the positive reviews mailed to his mother and several friends in London, a list that included James Whistler and Lillie Langtry. Then he returned to work, which meant putting himself on display at more parties. His host on January 11 was Samuel Cutler Ward, known to his innumerable friends in New York and Washington as "Uncle Sam." Ward was the nation's preeminent lobbyist, an occupation that in 1882 was only about half as disreputable as, but far more corrupt than, it is now. Ward had received a letter of introduction about Wilde from Wilde's friend in London, Lord Houghton, a member of Parliament and patron of the arts (and erotica) who was an early champion of Swinburne. After receiving Houghton's letter, Ward, who often contributed poems to the press, sent some of his own verse to Wilde. "In two days I got a better critique of them than ever appeared in the newspapers," he wrote in a letter to his niece. Then, after the two men were introduced at a luncheon at the Merchants Club in Lower Manhattan, Wilde "quoted several of [Ward's] Lyric lines" back to him, lines that, according to Ward, Wilde said "he very much envied." The two professional flatterers became fast friends.

On January 11 the flattery was all aimed at Wilde. As was reported in the *New York Times,* "Oscar Wilde was entertained at dinner last evening by Sam Ward . . . at Mr. Ward's apartments at 84 Clinton Place" (now West Eighth Street, between Fifth and Sixth Avenues). The meal was catered by Pinard, a French chef so famous in New York society in 1882 that he was identified by only one name. Two calla lilies tied with a red ribbon were placed in front of Wilde's plate; each guest was given a lily of the valley to place in his buttonhole. To further the flowery theme, Ward had his friend the composer Stephen Mallett sing "The Valley Lily" to the guest of honor, a song Mallett had recently cowritten with Ward, who provided the words. In reality, the song had been written not for Wilde but for a society beauty named Miss Jessie Keene, which explains these opening lyrics:

> *Take, O gardener, to the maiden*
> *In whose praise the harp I string.*
> *Take at morn a basket laden*
> *With the loveliest blooms of Spring.*

By night's end, after a bounteous feast and innumerable toasts, Ward had promised to send letters on Wilde's behalf to the poet Henry Wadsworth Longfellow in Boston, and to the former president Ulysses S. Grant, now living in Manhattan. "He is no slouch," Ward wrote of Wilde to his niece.

The next evening Wilde attended a party at the Gramercy Park home of gen. George McClellan, the former head of the Union Army in the Civil War, the losing presidential candidate of the Democratic Party in 1864, and now a titan of the New York social scene. Two days after that, Ambassador John Bigelow took Wilde to dinner at the Century Association, a preserve of New York's wealthy and well-connected located just east of Union Square, where Wilde was reminded that there were some in New York who still viewed him as a freak. The club member James Herbert Morse, then the headmaster of an elite New York private school, wrote in his diary: "At the Century last night John Bigelow brought as his guest Oscar Wilde, the 'Aesthetic Messiah.' Much curiosity was shown by members who were familiar with the Bunthorne features—by the medical men among us there was much quiet comment on his peculiar appearance. One would hardly expect any but silly girls to take to the face or the other effeminate features of the man, or to languish under his sweetish smile." Another member, showing an even greater scorn for Wilde (as well as a talent for puns), was overheard to say: "Where is she? Have you seen her? Well, why not say 'she'? I understand she's a Charlotte-Ann."

But Wilde kept smiling in the nights to come as he was feted (for the second time) by Mrs. Paran Stevens, and, for the first time, by Mr. and Mrs. Samuel L. M. Barlow. Barlow was a power broker in Democratic Party politics and a well-heeled attorney who was said to have once been paid $25,000—the equivalent of more than half a million dollars today—for a half-hour's legal work. Whether that was true or not, Barlow had earned enough from his law practice to build a double-wide brownstone on the corner of Madison Avenue and Forty-third Street, a home that *Cosmopolitan* magazine—then a far different magazine from the *Cosmo* of today—described to its readers as "filled with pictures, engravings, bric-a-brac, bronzes, books and all the fine things that men of culture, taste and wealth enjoy." It was in this luxurious setting, one that surely reminded Wilde of the aristocratic homes he had dined in so often in London, that the "Aesthetic Messiah" held court, capturing the cream of New York society in his thrall. He had come. He had preached the Gospel of Beauty. He had risen.

"Nothing like it since Dickens," Wilde boasted of his success in a letter to Norman Forbes-Robertson, alluding to the trips Dickens had made to New York, and other parts of America, in 1842 and 1867. Wilde's self-puffery was comically overstated, even by his standards. When Dickens arrived in New York in 1842, he and his wife were feted at a ball on Valentine's Day where three thousand guests heard an orchestra strike up Handel's "Here the Conquering Hero Comes"; Mr. and Mrs. Dickens entered a room where a giant oil portrait of the author was suspended from the balcony and a series of tableaux vivants depicted scenes from several of his most famous works, among them *Oliver Twist*, *The Pickwick Papers*, and *Nicholas Nickleby*. When not dancing, the three thousand revelers feasted on fifty hams, fifty beef tongues, ten thousand pickled oysters, twenty-eight thousand stewed oysters, four thousand candy kisses, and countless magnums of champagne that had been prepared and assembled by a staff of 140 men and women.

That was a splash Wilde hadn't come close to matching—but there was something about his success in New York that Dickens hadn't matched. When Dickens arrived in the United States, he was already a household name throughout the English-speaking world, a man whose novels were widely read in America (though all too often, to his great dismay, in pirated editions that paid him no royalties). Wilde, on the other hand, arrived as a writer who had published almost nothing and was famous merely for being famous, and even that accomplishment, achieved in England, was news to most Americans.

But it was no longer news to New Yorkers. Though he had been in the city less than two weeks, Wilde, after a relentless series of performances on public and private stages, had made himself into an (almost) irresistible attraction. The press in New York couldn't get enough of him. According to clippings compiled a century ago by the New York–

based independent scholar Richard Butler Glaenzer, the *New York Daily Graphic*, a popular evening tabloid in this period, published twenty-two different items on Wilde in January 1882, fourteen of them accounts of his comings and goings (some factual, most satirical), one of them a harsh review of his maiden lecture at Chickering Hall, and the rest of them cartoons (four) or poems (three).

Sarcastic poetry was the medium of choice for the *Graphic's* rival, the *New York Sun*, which published nine poems about Wilde while he was staying in New York, one of which, "The Aesthetic Boom: The New Narcissus," opened with these lines:

> *A conscious youth, who poses to the crowd*
> *In dress fantastical and aspect strange,*
> *Afflicted with a sentimental mange,*
> *So scarce he moves and scarcely speaks aloud*
> *I swear I love him not!*

At the same time doggerel such as this was being published and read all over New York, Wilde was feted in the most fashionable homes in the city and, best of all, had become someone whom New Yorkers paid money to see on the lecture stage. The Irish dandy had come to America with a plan to become a star. It was working.

In the midst of this social, vocational, and financial whirlwind, Richard D'Oyly Carte arrived from London on the SS *Servia*. Carte and Wilde, joined by Colonel Morse, had a meal at Delmonico's at which Morse gave his boss a firsthand account (and accounting) of Wilde's success at Chickering Hall, a debut that had increased the demand not only for Wilde's services at other American lecture venues but for tickets for *Patience.* Carte listened with palpable pleasure. Not long afterward a reporter found the British impresario and asked for his opinion of the "Bunthorne in the flesh."

"[He's] a clever young man," Carte said. "I think I shall send him around the country."

CHAPTER THREE

Strike a Pose

*I*t had taken Wilde only days to make an impression in America. Before he left New York, he went to a building on Union Square to make that impression permanent. His destination was the studio of Napoleon Sarony, the most acclaimed portrait photographer in the United States, a status he had solidified in the 1870s, when he began to specialize in highly stylized portraits of actors, musicians, authors, and other figures from the world of entertainment. Born in Canada to a French mother and a Prussian father, Sarony was one of the first photographers in America to exploit the market for celebrity portraits, reproducing them in large quantities, then placing them with retailers, who sold them to the public. The *New York Times*, in an article headlined "FACES OF NOTED PEOPLE *The Popular Craze for Photographs of Celebrities*," published shortly after Wilde's arrival in America, found six shops in Manhattan specializing in such items, businesses with combined sales, the paper reported, in the hundreds of thousands of dollars per year.

A typical celebrity portrait was mounted on cardboard and measured four by six and a half inches, though some were smaller. One

New York dealer claimed to have fifty thousand in stock, at prices ranging from a few pennies to five bucks. Among his biggest sellers were photos of the American actress Lillian Russell, whom Wilde had just seen in the title role in *Patience* at the Standard Theatre in New York; the international opera star Adelina Patti, a Carte agency client then making her second lucrative tour of America (and who, years later, Wilde's most famous fictional creation, Dorian Gray, would "hear" at London's Royal Opera House); and Wilde's glamorous new friend and self-promoter extraordinaire, the French actress Sarah Bernhardt. Many, if not most, of the photo dealer's most popular items had originated in Sarony's studio on Union Square.

Sarony's reputation was so exalted that Bernhardt said her chief reason for coming to the States in 1880, for her first American tour, was to have her photo taken by him. The press, after learning Sarony paid her a $1,500 sitting fee—the equivalent of about $35,000 today—snickered that her remark was less about art than about personal financial gain. But the arrangement wasn't merely mercenary. Bernhardt was eager to work with Sarony because she knew the power of photography to shape a career. Portraits of her taken in Paris in the 1860s by Nadar (born Gaspard-Félix Tournachon) had been instrumental in transforming a young bit player into a star of the French theater. One admirer of those photos, the novelist Henry James, wrote of her: "She has in a supreme degree what the French call the *génie de la réclame*—the advertising genius." Posing for Sarony to shape her image in America was one more example of Bernhardt's *génie*.

Wilde was eager to display his own *génie* in America, so he followed his friend's lead, though in his case there was no sitting fee. He waived that payment not merely because he was in no position to demand one, but because he knew Bernhardt's first collaboration with Sarony—there would be more in the years to come—had produced some of the most memorable (and career-enhancing) portraits of her (or anyone else) ever made. In one photo from the 1880 session, Sarony posed Bernhardt supine on a sofa, her slim frame encased in a lacy gown, a long braid of hair resting on her breast, her right arm hanging limply to the floor, her eyes closed, and her delicate mouth slightly open. In another, he placed her next to a table topped by a Greek urn, sitting in an elegant high-backed chair, her head caressed by a gauzy hood, the rest of her wrapped in a belted robe Aphrodite might have worn on Mount Olympus, as Bernhardt stared wide-eyed into the distance, looking tragic and erotic—simultaneously.

These portraits created such a charged environment for Bernhardt in America that her opening-night audience on November 8, 1880, at Booth's Theatre in New York—after watching a three-hour play in French in which she didn't even appear until the second act—gave her twenty-nine curtain calls, while showering the stage with a cannonade of long-stemmed roses. An hour later Bernhardt was nearly trampled at the stage door by frenzied fans of both sexes hoping to touch her or to yank an ostrich feather out of her hat, as older gentlemen in evening wear presented their shirt cuffs for her signature, only to be outmaneuvered by a young girl with an autograph book who, realizing her pen was out of ink, sank her teeth into her own wrist, then dipped her pen point into her pooling blood.

Wilde understood such displays. He had thrown bouquets of flowers at Bernhardt's feet when her ship docked in England, after her American tour. Now, two years later, he approached his own appointment with Sarony with anticipation. He knew he required Sarony's professional assistance far more than Bernhardt did. She was an internationally famous actress when she arrived in America; he was a Brit in breeches whom most Americans had never heard of. Bernhardt's goal was to have Sarony help her spread her notoriety in the States; Wilde's was to have Sarony help him *create* his. In exchange for Sarony's professional services, Wilde signed a contract stipulating that he would sit for no other formal portraits, or for any other photographer, while he was in America.

In truth, Wilde had already had a taste of the notoriety a photographic portrait could generate. Before he left London, the Carte organization sent him to Elliott & Fry, a well-established studio on Baker Street, to have a photograph made to publicize his American tour in the British press. In the resulting portrait, occasionally published under the pompous (or was it mocking?) title "The Apostle of the Aesthetes," Wilde stood in a long wool overcoat trimmed in fur, a velvet jacket visible beneath it, while holding a cane and a top hat in his right hand. Apparently this was too much for another dapper aesthete about town to bear. "Oscar,—How dare you! What means this unseemly carnival?" James Whistler wrote, in a letter published in the London weekly the *World*. "Restore these things to Nathan, and never let me find you masquerading in the combined costumes of a degraded Kossuth and Mr. Mantalini!" (Nathan was a costumer in London's theater district; Lajos Kossuth was a Hungarian revolutionary who had lived in exile in England in the 1850s; Mr. Mantalini was a gigolo with an extravagant fashion sense in Charles Dickens's novel *Nicholas Nickleby*.)

WHEN, AFTER A short carriage ride, Wilde arrived at 37 Union Square, he looked up at a five-story building—all of which was occupied by Sarony—to see that the exterior of the fourth floor was almost entirely obscured by a reproduction of Sarony's signature in letters ten feet tall, the same autograph found at the bottom of each of his portraits. Wilde's valet carried a hatbox, a dressing case (we would say toiletry kit), and a suitcase (Wilde preferred "portmanteau") filled with changes of clothing, as Wilde made his way into the photographer's reception area on the ground floor. Most photographers of this period, hoping to make their sitters comfortable, modeled these areas after a typical Victorian drawing room, with upholstered chairs, paintings of pastoral scenes, potted plants, and so on, sometimes even a piano and a fireplace. Not Sarony. His reception area was designed to inspire awe. In *New York's Great Industries*, a book published not long after Wilde spent the day with Sarony, the journalist Richard Edwards described his own sense of wonder as he walked into that eighty-foot-deep room, where he found himself gawking at "a genuine Egyptian mummy in a fine state of preservation," assorted "Buddhist idols," a "Chinese bell weighing many hundreds of pounds," an "Australian Aboriginal war-cleaver made of iron-wood and teak," a collection of "Toltec and Aztec pottery—perhaps the finest extant in the world," full suits of medieval armor from Europe and Japan, a lacquered Russian sleigh-coach, and, suspended from the ceiling, a stuffed crocodile.

The theatricality of the room recalled Lady Jane Wilde's *conversazione* parties in Dublin. When Sarony entered the space, Wilde encountered the same flair for showmanship in the photographer. It was Sarony's custom to meet new clients with a red fez on his head (with prominent tassel), while wearing a tight-fitting military-style jacket with cloth-colored buttons and abundant piping over baggy trousers tucked into black cavalry boots, the thick heels of which elevated him above his natural height, which was barely more than five feet. Wilde, who was more than a foot taller, probably couldn't help noticing from that vantage point that Sarony's eyes nearly disappeared under dense eyebrows. His mouth was similarly hard to locate, thanks to a bushy goatee with a waxed, upturned mustache that hadn't encountered scissors in some time.

Sarony ushered Wilde into a freight elevator that took him, his luggage, and Sarony to the photographer's studio, on a higher floor. This was an expansive and airy room, but not so airy that Wilde could ignore the odor, which one journalist, after visiting Sarony's, described as "the smell of a chemical warehouse on fire." Most of this piquant aroma emanated from Sarony's nearby darkroom, the rest from the emulsion on the dozens of glass-plate negatives that one of his assistants had prepared for the day's session. The room had tall windows with adjustable blinds. (Artificial lighting wasn't used as a matter of course by photographers until after the First World War.) Large reflector screens were also at the ready. There were tapestries and exotic wallpapers for backdrops (most of them on stands with wheels), chairs of all shapes and sizes, sofas, consoles, vases, sculptures, throw rugs, and assorted bric-a-brac to be used as compositional "extras." Sarony had pioneered the use of such accessories in photographic portrait-making in America, and, by doing so, one of his contemporaries (and professional rivals) wrote, he "took our beloved science out of a rut and placed it on the pedestal of art."

Near the center of Sarony's studio stood a bulky large-format camera on a heavy wooden stand supported by three legs. Pleated bellows connected the lens at the front of the camera with the focusing section and glass-plate holder at the rear. A recent technological advance— the gelatin dry-plate process—had reduced exposure times in portrait photography from one minute (or more) to about three seconds. Even so, that was a long time to keep still. This explained the presence of a strange device, not far from Sarony's camera, that was made of metal and bore an eerie resemblance to a human skeleton, but with small rubber knobs placed at the end of its "ribs." This was Sarony's posing machine, which, after being positioned discreetly behind the sitter, enabled him, using the device's restraints for the torso, arms, and head, to immobilize his sitter in the poses he desired, for the time it took him to make an exposure. The machine had been invented by Sarony's brother Oliver (born Olivier), who ran a successful portrait studio of his own in a resort town in the north of England. Napoleon Sarony marketed and distributed his brother's machine in the United States and Canada. *Galaxy*, an American literary magazine, published a profile of Sarony in which the writer of the piece referred to the device as an "iron instrument of torture." Considering how many sitters happily returned again and again to 37 Union Square to have their portraits taken, this appears to have been an exaggeration.

"A picturesque subject indeed!" said Sarony, while admiring Wilde's fur-lined wool coat, the white cane he carried in his yellow-gloved hands, and his long flowing hair. The first photographs they would make together would feature nearly all of them. By this time several of Sarony's assistants—at the peak of his fame he had thirty—would have entered the shooting space. Most of them were responsible for tending to the photographer's props, but one would take a position next to Sarony's camera. This was because Sarony did not make his exposures himself, at least not in the "hands-on" sense; his preferred method was to compose his photographs from several feet away, working like a theater director at a rehearsal, cajoling and flattering his subjects into different expressions and positions. When photographing the British middleweight boxer Jem Mace, a champion both in the bare-knuckles era and in the modern (gloved) era that followed it, Sarony surprised the pugilist, on this occasion dressed in top hat and tails, by commencing to shadow box, throwing out jabs, crosses, and uppercuts while moving back and forth in front of Mace, until the prizefighter gave Sarony the expression he wanted. Then and only then would Sarony signal his camera operator, who would remove the lens cap from the camera to capture the image his employer desired and, after consulting his watch, replace it seconds later. (Mechanical shutters for cameras weren't perfected until the 1890s.)

On the day Wilde and Sarony spent together, they produced twenty-seven photographs. In the most famous of these images, Wilde is wearing the clothing he had worn to deliver his lecture at Chickering Hall: the satin breeches, the black silk stockings, the patent-leather shoes, the velvet jacket, and so on that had provoked an audible gasp from his audience and so much comment in the press. Though there's no documentary evidence, it is logical to assume that Wilde was encouraged to pose in his "Bunthorne" costume at Sarony's by the Carte organization. In photo eighteen, one of the most frequently reproduced from the session, Wilde sits at the end of a sofa that is covered with elaborately patterned cloth, resting his head on his left hand, holding a book of poetry in his right; a large signet ring is visible on his third finger. His legs, exposed by his breeches and encased in black stockings, are manly and attractive; his face is youthful yet transmits a worldly self-knowledge; his wavy hair is parted in the middle, framing his face and curling around his ears; his eyes meet

the viewer without evasion. Though his clothes evoke a famously risible character from an operetta by Gilbert & Sullivan, Wilde himself
does not: his mien in photo eighteen is both sober and sedate. Despite
the theatrical outfit, he projects intelligence, poetic sensibility, and the
self-possessed attitude of a young artist coming into his own. In
another photograph taken in the same clothing on this sofa, Wilde
leans back, lost in a reverie, a state apparently inspired by the book of
poetry in his hand. Nearly a century later, another young aesthete,
Truman Capote, would strike a similar pose to promote his own bur-
geoning literary career.

In portrait twenty-two Wilde sits in a chair, having once again
donned his wool overcoat. The garment's massive fur collar, which
nearly envelops his head, gives him a somewhat bearish aspect. Wilde
has replaced his satin breeches with dark wool trousers. In his right
hand he holds his cane and, as he often did at parties, a pair of leather
gloves. His left hand supports his face, which stares into Sarony's camera with a challenging directness. The index finger of this hand points
at Wilde's temple, as if to say, *There's a serious mind at work here. Under-
estimate it at your peril.*

Several other photographs from the session show Wilde standing.
In one of them, his cape—the same one he carried onto the stage at
Chickering Hall—is draped on his shoulder. His right arm, partially
obscured by the cape and bent at the shoulder, rests on his waist. In his
left hand he holds a cane and a wide-brimmed black hat. His hair
hangs freely to his shoulders; his gaze, positioned at an angle to Sarony's lens, is self-assured. He looks like an explorer. In another vertical
shot Wilde has wrapped his cape around his body and placed his hat
upon his head. His chin is elevated, suggesting supreme confidence. In
the late nineteenth century, a period of explosive growth for portrait
photography, the power of photography to freeze a moment—to stop
time—was appreciated by its consumers, the cultural historian Jane
M. Gaines has written, as a symbolic victory of mortal life over the
certainty of death. This "truth" was certainly embraced (and embod-

ied) by Wilde in this photo: he is triumphant; he is seductive; he is *vampiric*. He is convinced of his impending immortality—if not as a person, as a personality; if not as a man, as a legend.

THAT WE ARE still looking at these portraits today suggests that the photographs made that winter day at Union Square indeed made Wilde immortal. What's certain is that their impact in 1882 was as far-reaching as it was immediate. Wilde's sold-out appearance at Chickering Hall, and the resulting press coverage, made the photos big sellers at stores that sold such items for much of the next twelve months, prompting Wilde to tell the *Manchester* (England) *Examiner and Times* that the demand "far exceeds any possible supply." That was hyperbole, but we know that the Sarony portraits were reproduced on posters, brochures, and other promotional materials that received wide distribution in America—so much so that a reporter for the *Dayton Daily Democrat*, sent to interview Wilde before his speaking engagement in that city, wrote of his subject: "His face is well known to our readers through the thousands of pictures that have been scattered over the country since his arrival upon American soil."

Wilde wanted that face to be even better known. He wrote to Richard D'Oyly Carte in London, asking that "some large lithographs of me" be sent "to small cities" in America "where the local men spend so little on advertising. The photograph of me with my head looking over my shoulder would be the best—just the head and fur collar. Will you see to this?" (This was probably photo twenty-three from the Sarony session.) Such visual materials not only helped boost ticket sales for Wilde's lectures as he traveled across America, but soon made him, the media historian Robert Jay writes, one of the most recognized figures in the United States in 1882—certainly the most recognized foreign visitor. Wilde's visual bond with his American audience was further enhanced when the portraits became source material for newspaper and magazine illustrators across the continent, including

America's preeminent cartoonist, Thomas Nast, who drew several likenesses of Wilde for *Harper's Weekly*, all of them based on the images made at Sarony's. And, as Wilde surely would have wanted us to know, he did his own part in marketing his portraits and spreading his renown, on several occasions selling autographed photos of himself in the lobbies of the theaters where he spoke.

The sociologist Chris Rojek, writing 120 years later, coined the term "staged celebrity" to describe "the calculated technologies and strategies of performance and self-projection designed to achieve a status of monumentality." Wilde's calculated effort to project himself as a star to the American public via reproducible images in 1882 shows his precocious understanding of mass communications. To grasp the full measure of his contribution to that cultural force, one must understand his actual role in the photographs produced at Sarony's studio. Wilde wasn't a passive sitter in those portraits. He was their true creator.

For Wilde, it was a matter of control—or more accurately, regaining control—of something extremely important to him: his image. As a great talker, he never undervalued the importance of being heard. But he knew it was equally important to be seen. As a student at Oxford, he had fashioned his image almost exclusively through visual statements: eccentric "aesthetic" clothing, unusual hair length, an intentionally "languid" posture, and near-constant posturing, all of it conceived to show his classmates that he was someone called to greatness. For a while he had to be content with merely looking the part, but when he won the Newdigate Prize for poetry, Wilde's belief in his own readily visible genius was confirmed where to him it mattered most: in public.

He had planned to project the same visual persona in London but learned that his success in that endeavor was no longer under his exclusive control. His image, a product of his own design at Oxford, was now being designed—literally—by others: caricaturists such as George Du Maurier and Edward Linley Sambourne, who made their livings making fun of Wilde, drawing him as physically unattractive (his large head and prominent teeth were frequent subjects of caricature) in their illustrations for the humor magazine *Punch*. To be sure, these drawings helped make their target a household name—and, equally important to Wilde, a houseguest—in many of the fashionable homes of London. Wilde adored going to those parties, where he got to dress up and issue the "impromptu wheezes" that made others laugh, so when he was asked his opinion of those satirical drawings, he said he found them as amusing as everyone else did. That response was sincere, up to a point: Wilde was delighted to be deemed a person worthy of attention in the London press, but he wasn't completely comfortable with the kind of attention he was getting.

One reason for that ambivalence was the work of the biologist Francis Galton, now infamous as the father of eugenics, but then one of the most respected scientists in Britain. A cousin of Charles Darwin, Galton had begun to argue in the 1870s that there was a biological link between genius and physical attractiveness: if you didn't have the latter, you weren't likely to have the former. Galton "documented" this assertion with photographs published in scientific journals just as Wilde was establishing himself as a party wit in London. These photos were close-up portraits of English and Irish criminals, impoverished Jews from London's East End, and other "undesirables" in which Galton made multiple exposures of one facial image upon another. The resulting composites, Galton said, proved his thesis: the undesirables were not merely biologically unfit and intellectually second-rate; the indisputable aesthetic "truth" arising from the photographs was that they were physically unattractive.

Wilde suspected this belief in the body-mind, beauty-genius connection had crossed the Atlantic and taken root in America. What else could explain the obsessive attention paid by American journalists to his appearance? That many of the descriptions published here were unflattering was a blow to his vanity, but even more worrying to him was what those comments suggested to his potential audience in America about his intellectual powers. Wilde, you see, agreed with

Galton on the body-mind connection. Though Wilde was said to have declared his genius to an American customs inspector upon his arrival, the articles about him in the New York press told him that Americans were determined to make up their own minds, not just by hearing him but by seeing him.

That's why the afternoon he spent with Sarony was one of the most important days of his nearly yearlong stay in America. That photo shoot was Wilde's attempt to take charge of the "genius assessment" process: to use photography to regain control of his public image, control that he had partially lost in England to Messrs. Du Maurier and Sambourne and that, now that he was in America, he was in danger of losing to a bunch of newspaper hacks who were only too happy to write nasty things about his looks. In the photos he would make at Sarony's, Oscar Wilde would decide what image Oscar Wilde would present to America.

While there's no denying that Sarony had a stellar reputation as a maker of photographic images, it's far more likely that Wilde posed *for* him rather than was posed *by* him. Some biographers of Wilde assert that he went to Sarony's at the insistence of his American handler, Colonel Morse, and had little or no knowledge of who Sarony was, or what he could do for him. But this is hard to credit considering Wilde's close friendship with Sarah Bernhardt, the subject of several of Sarony's most famous photographs. And while it is plausible that Bernhardt, an actress who had worked with many theater directors over the years, would have responded positively to Sarony's direction of her at her shoot, it is hard to understand why Wilde would have required, or even wanted, such direction for himself. He had already spent years "directing" himself at Oxford and in London, where he lived his life in public as a never-ending performance. He arrived at Sarony's not merely with a suitcase full of clothing, but with an extensive history of posing—and all of those poses were of his own invention. To be Oscar Wilde was to be the star, writer, and director of a one-man show. He already knew the image he wanted to project in America. A century earlier the Scots poet Robert Burns had written: "O wad some Power the giftie gie us, To see oursels as ithers see us!" In 1882 Wilde took Burns's musing about one's image in the world to heart, and then some: he would make the world see him as he saw himself.

The part Wilde acted at Sarony's studio was the role he had chosen to play in America, despite his dearth of real-world accomplishments: the confident, well-dressed, well-bred, well-read, physically attractive poet, intellectual, and art connoisseur who had sailed across the Atlantic to lecture on aesthetics and, while doing so, become a celebrity. This "fake it till you make it" strategy, researchers at the business schools of Harvard and Columbia would report more than century later, actually works. Wilde wasn't just posing at Sarony's; he was "power posing," a concept developed by those researchers who wrote in the journal *Psychological Science* that "by holding one's body in expansive, 'high-power' poses" the poser enhances his own status (and his testosterone levels), and, even more important, the receptivity of those viewing him to those 'power claims.'" It's also relevant to remember in this context that Wilde was a man of the theater: a playwright (albeit unproduced) and a close confidant of several of the leading actors of the Victorian stage. He understood drama and how to create it before an audience, whether in an auditorium or in a photography studio. He enjoyed striking poses for Sarony, just as much he enjoyed performing at dinner parties. Wilde's self-scripted performance at Sarony's would be captured on specially treated glass plates in Sarony's camera, then developed, printed, and reproduced for mass consumption across America. The resulting photographs would go on tour, "performing" Wilde's chosen persona on theatrical posters and promotional brochures every bit as much as Wilde would be performing it in the flesh at lecture halls, opera houses, and women's clubs.

Three decades after Wilde's death, the philosopher Walter Benjamin published the influential essay "The Work of Art in the Age of Mechanical Reproduction," in which he praised photography for its "democratizing" ability to reach a mass audience beyond the privileged elite to whom the appreciation of art had been limited in the past. But Benjamin worried that such easy reproducibility had a negative consequence: it destroyed the "aura" of original works of art. What Wilde understood in 1882—years before anyone else—was that mass-produced images create a new kind of aura: the aura of celebrity. Equally important, he showed as he traveled across the hemisphere's first democracy that such easily accessible images "democratize" the very definition of celebrity: virtually *anyone* can become a star.

Wilde arrived at Sarony's New York studio prepared to make his photos more than portraits, which is to say, more than just images presenting an interesting face. He would make them *pictures.* The difference, he had learned from John Ruskin at Oxford, was that pictures tell a story. (Wilde's belief in that distinction explains why he later chose the title *The Picture of Dorian Gray* for his only novel, rather than *The Portrait of Dorian Gray.*) In January 1882 Wilde was telling the story he wanted to tell America about himself: A very special person had landed among them. Not just a man of genius. A living work of art.

To tell that story, he chose the objects he brought to Sarony's with care. The most important was the book of poetry he holds in so many of the photos shot there. This was *Poems,* the collection of his verse that scoffers in England always made sure to describe (accurately) as self-published. Far more significant, however, was that *Poems* was self-designed to show Wilde's superior artistic taste. The white vellum and gold leaf on the cover signified there was beauty—and genius—inside. By holding *Poems* in his hand, Wilde was sending the same message about himself.

Though he didn't know it yet, this message was about to be heard in England. Not long after Wilde arrived in America, the British critic Walter Hamilton, after considering Wilde's poetry and art criticism in a book Hamilton called *The Aesthetic Movement in England*, called Wilde an "undoubted genius." This was the first such declaration about Wilde—by anyone other than Wilde—ever made in print. (In truth, the only "undoubted genius" Wilde had demonstrated at this point in time was his genius for publicity and for getting party invitations; apparently that was enough for Hamilton.) It was Wilde's plan that the pictures he made at Sarony's studio would help prompt many more such pronouncements about him as he crossed America.

AS WE'LL SEE, Americans were not unanimous in granting him stature as a genius. But Wilde succeeded far beyond his hopes in a similar, yet different context: he was so proficient at using reproducible images to sell himself as a product in America that images of him were used to sell *other* products in America. The medium that his photographic image dominated in 1882 was the trade card, a place where, to borrow a phrase from today, Wilde's face "went viral."

Trade cards were illustrated advertisements for products or events that were printed on cardboard in sizes approximating those of the celebrity portraits shot by Sarony. Trade cards were originally conceived of as disposable, but that changed in 1876, the year of the hugely popular Centennial Exhibition in Philadelphia, which attracted nearly nine million visitors, roughly one-fifth of America's population. At the Philadelphia fair, a commercial setting where trade cards were ubiquitous, American visitors were so amazed to see new technological marvels such as the telephone, the telegraph, and the mechanical calculator that many accepted—and held on to—trade cards for those products, as well as those for new consumer items such as Heinz ketchup and Hires' root beer. When these visitors returned home, many of them mounted those cards in albums that they showed to friends and relatives as mementos of their trip to Philadelphia, launching a new national mania for card collecting and scrapbooks. As a result, for the next decade or so—until the fad faded in the 1890s—trade cards were made and marketed as something Americans would want to save.

According to Kit Barry, the founder of the Ephemera Archive for American Studies, there was one man whose face appeared on those "savable" cards more often than any other celebrity in 1882—in fact, even more than any homegrown American. This was Oscar Wilde. Quite a few of those trade cards, it's not surprising, were made to promote Gilbert & Sullivan's *Patience*. What is surprising is that the most of them were not. In those cards, Wilde's visage—clearly lifted from the pictures he made at Sarony's—was used by American manufacturers to promote products ranging from cigars to kitchen stoves. Certainly the most unexpected use of the aesthete's face from photo twenty-two at Sarony's—the one in which Wilde is sitting in a chair, his head nearly enveloped by his fur-lined coat—was on a trade card promoting "Mme Marie Fontaine's Bosom Beautifier For Beautifying & Enlarging The Bust." The card showed a lovely young maiden, blond-haired and rosy-cheeked, watering some sunflowers, which hover above an inserted photo of the smiling Mr. Wilde, whose lips are tinted ruby red. On the card's reverse side was this message from the product's manufacturer. (All italics were in the original.)

> This preparation will be appreciated by all ladies who are deficient or lacking in that necessary development of the bust, so essential to a handsome figure. It will *in every instance*, where the instructions are faithfully followed, *enlarge and beautify the bosom*, in both old and young ladies. Where the bosoms have become soft and flaccid, from whatever cause, its use will restore them, rendering them *firm and hard*.

Just as Oscar Wilde liked them, one has to assume.

Apparently the mere presence of Wilde's face on the card—no words from him endorsing the product appeared anywhere on it—was by itself so successful at increasing sales of the "Bosom Beautifier" that the manufacturer used the same card, with new text, to promote "Mme Fontaine's Freckle Cure." According to Barry, the appearance of Wilde on these and so many other trade cards in 1882—Barry has found nearly a hundred of them—shows that Wilde was "the first modern marketed celebrity in our culture."

Wilde was marketed as a celebrity so often by people other than himself that it led to a Supreme Court case now considered a landmark in the history of American copyright law. What happened was this: in late 1882 the Burrow-Giles Lithographic Company in New York printed 85,000 slightly altered copies of photograph eighteen from Wilde's session with Sarony, the picture in which Wilde is sitting in breeches at the end of a sofa, holding his book of poetry in his hand. (The huge volume of that order is yet more evidence of Wilde's success at establishing his physical image in America.) Burrow-Giles was contracted to make those lithographs by the Ehrich Brothers department store, on Eighth Avenue and Twenty-fourth Street, as part of an advertising campaign by that emporium to sell men's hats in flyers and newspaper advertisements distributed throughout the metropolitan area. Apparently a hat, which Wilde is not wearing in the original photo, was, according to the Ehrich Brothers, the one fashion accessory the well-known dandy had overlooked when putting together his charming ensemble.

Though Wilde probably would have been tickled by the campaign had it been brought to his attention, Sarony was not amused at all. Because he had neither authorized nor been paid for the use of this particular photograph, Sarony—claiming ownership and, even more to the point, *authorship*—of the image, sued Burrow-Giles for copyright infringement. While it's true that Sarony had neither approved nor been paid for the images of Wilde that had already been used on trade cards such as those promoting Mme Fontaine's Bosom Beautifier and Freckle Cure, Sarony decided to sue Burrow-Giles because of the size of the print run for Ehrich Brothers, and because the resulting advertisements were appearing all over New York, where he lived and worked. After the case was argued in the Circuit Court of New York, Southern District, in April 1883, the judge ruled in Sarony's favor.

Burrow-Giles challenged that ruling, claiming in a countersuit that Sarony hadn't authored or created anything original in the photo of Wilde now being used to sell hats. Instead, Sarony had merely used a mechanical device—his camera—to make a visual record of something, or someone, already in existence: Oscar Wilde. If there was an original work of art (or artist) in the photograph in dispute, the attorney for Burrow-Giles argued, it was Wilde and Wilde alone. (This was certainly an argument Wilde would have seconded.) The appeal reached the Supreme Court in December 1883, a year after Wilde returned to England. As the *New York Times* reported, in a piece headlined "DID SARONY INVENT OSCAR WILDE?", the argument made in court by Sarony's attorney was that Sarony indeed had "invented" the "picture in controversy," by "posing Oscar Wilde before the camera, selecting his costume as well as the draperies and other accessories, and arranging the said Oscar Wilde in a graceful position." This "made Sarony [the] author or inventor" of the picture and, by extension, its subject. Counsel for Burrow-Giles replied that if Sarony really was claiming to have invented Oscar Wilde, he had mistaken his remedy: he should have taken out a patent. To claim a copyright, the printing firm's attorney argued, the person claiming protection must be the author of the article on which the copyright is granted, and the work in question must be original. "Mr. Sarony was not the creator [or author] of Oscar Wilde," the *Times* wrote, summarizing the attorney's position, "and the photograph was not original," so it was not worthy of copyright.

In March 1884 the Supreme Court upheld the decision of the lower court, and Sarony was granted copyright protection against the image of Wilde reprinted 85,000 times by Burrow-Giles, was awarded $12,000 in damages—nearly $300,000 today. Oscar Wilde thought of himself as a living work of art, but the Supreme Court ruled he was a work of fiction, authored by Napoleon Sarony.

THERE'S NO EVIDENCE that Wilde was following the court's deliberations in *Burrow-Giles v. Sarony* as they were happening, which isn't too surprising, considering he was back in England when the case was argued. But we know that Wilde did eventually learn of the court's ruling because, several years later, he took some small revenge on the man who claimed to have invented him.

He did so in one of his first published stories, "The Canterville Ghost," which appeared in two installments in the English magazine the *Court and Society Review*, beginning in February 1887. As the title suggests, it was a ghost story. But it was no ordinary horror tale: rather than scaring his readers, Wilde was amusing them. As the story opens, a high-ranking American diplomat is about to purchase Canterville Chase, a stately home in the English countryside that he will occupy with his wife and four children, despite a warning from its seller, Lord Canterville, that the house is haunted by the ghost of one the lord's ancestors: Sir Simon de Canterville, who murdered his wife in the same mansion in the year 1575. (In fact, the current Lord Canterville had moved out of the house because of the ghost's near-nightly appearances.)

But the wealthy American is neither concerned nor worried. "I will take the furniture and the ghost at valuation" and everything else that comes with the house, he tells Lord Canterville. The American isn't scared because, as he puts it, "I come from a modern country, where we have everything that money can buy" and "I reckon that if there were such a thing as a ghost in Europe, we'd have it at home in a very short time in one of our public museums, or on the road as a show."

The rest of Wilde's story recounts a series of encounters between Sir Simon's ghost and members of the diplomat's family—encounters told (and sympathetically, at that) from the point of view of the ghost. Sir Simon's ghost is appalled by the lack of respect the new owners of Canterville Chase are showing him. When he makes his first appearance before them, groaning loudly while covered in rattling chains—a getup intended to scare the family—the diplomat merely offers him a bottle of Tammany Rising Sun Lubricator. This American-made product, the diplomat tells him, will surely eliminate any and all excessive sounds emanating from his jangling iron restraints. The ghost is similarly offended when the Americans use another of their American-made products, Pinkerton's Champion Stain Remover and Paragon Detergent, to wash clean the bloodstain on the floor of the library—the spot where Sir Simon murdered his wife three centuries earlier.

But perhaps the greatest offense to Sir Simon's ghostly dignity is how the Americans have redecorated the house he haunts. Before the Americans' arrival, the grand entrance hall of Canterville Chase was dominated by the presence of beautiful oil paintings of several generations of Cantervilles. But now they are gone, replaced by large—and to the ghost's eyes, laughably vulgar—photographs of the American diplomat and his wife. These highly stylized photographs, the ghost (and Oscar Wilde) can't help noticing, are the products of yet another marketing-savvy American manufacturer:

A man named Saroni.

CHAPTER FOUR

Celebrity Is Contagious

*W*hatever pique Wilde felt later about Sarony's claim of having "invented" him, we know he didn't feel any resentment toward Sarony in 1882. To the contrary, Wilde was so pleased with the photographs made at Sarony's studio that he had several dozen pictures printed for his personal use. These photos weren't the pocket-size cards Sarony retailed in shops across the United States, however. The portraits in Wilde's possession were nearly three times larger, measuring approximately eleven by fourteen inches, and were intended for framing. We know this because one of the first Americans to receive (and frame) one of these large portraits—a sixty-two-year-old man, partially paralyzed by stroke, living in southern New Jersey with his brother and sister-in-law—made mention of it in a letter he wrote to a friend on January 31: "Oscar Wilde sent me his picture yesterday, a photo a foot & a half long, nearly full length, very good." A week earlier this same man wrote in another letter: "Have you read about Oscar Wilde? He has been to see me & spent an afternoon—He is a fine large handsome youngster," Walt Whitman then said of his guest, before giving that visitor his ultimate compliment: "[He] had the *good sense* to take a great fancy to *me!*"

The two-hour meeting between the dandified, self-anointed "Professor of Aesthetics" and the shaggy, self-described "old rough" who had revolutionized American poetry with his masterpiece *Leaves of Grass*, took place on January 18, 1882, in the home of Mr. and Mrs. George Whitman, at 431 Stevens Street, in Camden, New Jersey, a city not then as blighted as it is today but nevertheless a city of meager economic stature. This encounter has been examined in many books and scholarly journals in the intervening years, usually through the lens of what is now called queer history, or as an interesting, if not particularly consequential, moment in the history of Western literature. Neither of those approaches takes the full measure of the meeting's true significance. For Oscar Wilde didn't travel from Philadelphia to Camden to talk to Walt Whitman about gender roles or poetry, though he was always ready to pontificate about the latter. What really drew him to the house on Stevens Street was the opportunity to discuss fame. He wanted to listen to the singer of "Song of Myself": an older man with inexhaustible energy—despite his infirmity—for self-promotion; an international icon who had exploited the fuzzy line between acclaim and notoriety in his own life; a media-savvy poet who understood the crucial role of image in the making of a literary career *and* the central role of photography in the making of that image. It would be hard to imagine a more apt pairing of student and teacher.

THE STORY OF how the two men met begins on January 16, the day Wilde left New York by taking a ferry across the Hudson River from West Thirty-fourth Street to the Exchange Place slip in Jersey City, New Jersey, a short walk from the Pennsylvania Railroad station where he would board a train for Philadelphia, the second stop on his lecture tour. According to an eyewitness, a reporter for the *Philadel-*

phia Press who met Wilde at the dock in New York and accompanied him to his destination, Wilde began this journey in a less-than-animated mood. "I am very tired," he said, after his valet struggled—without any help from him—to ensure that not one piece in Wilde's towering pile of luggage was left behind on terra firma. "I was up late last night dining" at the home of a prominent New York society hostess, "and afterward [went] to a reception" at the palatial home of one of New York's leading political power brokers. Even worse than being tired, from Wilde's point of view, was that he was famished. He had missed breakfast while rushing to make his ferry.

Two events soon lifted his mood. The first was the audible buzz that greeted his arrival in Jersey City. "Look, there he is. See him? That's Oscar Wilde," said several travelers waiting there to board the ferry for the return trip to New York. This happened, the *Philadelphia Press* reporter wrote, when Wilde stepped off the ferry, his tall frame wrapped in his fur-lined green coat, his shoulder-length hair tossed this way and that by the wind, and his face flashing a smile at being recognized. The second pressing issue was resolved when he purchased and wolfed down a sandwich. When his train was announced, Wilde, now reinvigorated, walked to the smoking compartment of the Pullman car *Jupiter* on the Philadelphia Express, where he took a seat across from the reporter and next to the man who had arranged for him to be there: Colonel Morse of the Carte agency.

Not yet in the mood to be interviewed, Wilde removed two books from his briefcase, *Fors Clavigera* and *The Poetry of Architecture*, both written by John Ruskin, and read—or pretended to read—portions of each. He broke his silence moments later when the train moved through the swampy New Jersey meadowlands. "How dreadful these marshes are," he said to the reporter. "What a pity! And how unnecessary. They might plant them with something; so many beautiful things will grow in a marsh. Why, they might have great fields of calla lilies growing there." Before long, the fledgling lecturer and the seasoned journalist were conversing on all sorts of aesthetic topics, beginning with the need for the elevation of taste in men's clothing. ("Velvet is such a beautiful material," Wilde said. "Why do not men wear it? Gray or brown or black velvet is always beautiful.") Then it was on to the wondrous illustrations in William Blake's books of verse, the skill of Dickens and Thackeray in conveying the tempestuous sweep of London life in their novels, the use of sunflower motifs in wallpapers and on embroidered pillows, and the part played by climate and geography in the making of beautiful furniture. On and on it went until the reporter asked, "What poet do you most admire in American literature, Mr. Wilde?" It took only a second for the Newdigate Prize winner to answer: "I think Walt Whitman and [Ralph Waldo] Emerson have given the world more than anyone else. I do so hope to meet Mr. Whitman." Wilde was apparently aware that the poet lived just across the Delaware River from Philadelphia. "Perhaps he is not so widely read in England, but England never appreciates a poet until he is dead."

Wilde's use of the word "dead" was revealing. In truth, the American poet he most admired—Edgar Allan Poe—*was* dead. It's likely he named Whitman and Emerson because they were alive, though in Emerson's case just barely, and because he hoped to meet them both. Wilde had learned an important lesson about self-marketing when he was establishing himself as a party wit in London, hobnobbing nightly with actors, writers, artists, and society beauties: celebrity is contagious.

His seemingly spontaneous response to the reporter was probably not as spontaneous as it seemed. Wilde planned to absorb the star power of as many American luminaries as he could while touring the States, just as he had in Britain from the famous Londoners he had charmed while sitting next to them at dinner parties—proximity that had helped to make *him* a star (or at least a well-known man about town). So as his train motored south through New Jersey, he resumed his florid discourse on Whitman.

"I admire him intensely," he told his interviewer, before slipping into name-dropping mode: "Dante Rossetti, [Algernon] Swinburne, William Morris and I often discuss him." In reality, Swinburne and Wilde were mere acquaintances and had not "often" discussed anything. But that didn't stop Wilde from adding, as if he were repeating something from their "frequent" discussions: "There is something so Greek and sane about [Whitman's] poetry; it is so universal, so comprehensive."

By the time these words were published in the *Philadelphia Press*, Wilde was in his suite at the Aldine Hotel, at 1920 Chestnut Street, where his well-documented presence made him a much-sought-after party guest—so much so that Wilde's valet was stationed outside his hotel room, telling bearers of new invitations: "Massa Wilde is too busy to recept today." Two well-connected Philadelphians—George Childs, the publisher of the *Philadelphia Public Ledger,* and J. M. Stoddart, the editor and publisher of the literary journal *Stoddart's Review*—had taken charge of Wilde's social calendar. On January 16, the night of his arrival, he was feted by yet another publisher, Robert Stuart Davis of Philadelphia's *Evening Call*, at his mansion near Rittenhouse Square. Davis had mailed out more than three hundred invitations, including one to President Chester A. Arthur, whose social secretary sent his regrets. Among those who did attend his party were the former governor of Pennsylvania John F. Hartranft, a retired major general in the Union Army and winner of the Medal of Honor for his service in the Civil War; the former three-term mayor of Philadelphia William S. Stokley; the vice provost of the University of Pennsylvania Charles P. Krauth; and the poet, short story writer, and critic Louisa Chandler Moulton, who had traveled down from Boston. After a magnificent meal at Davis's, during which, as one newspaper account put it, the guest of honor eagerly "surrendered his devotion to the aesthetic to the cravings of the inner man," Wilde retired to his host's library, where he "shared the delight and wonder of all the guests at a curiously woven mandarin's silk bed quilt, saved from the sack of Pekin . . . and gazed yearningly on a piano cover, which was a Persian rug of cloth of gold, having embroidered upon it the conventionalized tree of life."

On January 17, the night of Wilde's talk at Horticultural Hall, in

Philadelphia's Fairmount Park, Stoddart would be hosting a postlecture reception for Wilde at his home on North Nineteenth Street. The next evening he would be feted at Childs's residence on Walnut Street. Both men, aware of Wilde's interest in Whitman, had invited the poet to their parties, but the bard had begged off, writing: "I am an invalid . . . suffering an extra bad spell & forbidden from going out nights this weather—Please give my hearty salutation & American welcome to Mr. Wilde." After reading Wilde's comments about him in the *Philadelphia Press*, however, Whitman—as Wilde had surely hoped— decided to offer that American welcome personally, writing this in a letter sent to Wilde's hotel:

"Walt Whitman will be in from 2 till 3½ this afternoon [January 18] & will be most happy to see Mr. Wilde & Mr. Stoddart."

This letter couldn't have come at a better time for Wilde. His lecture the previous night, though well attended, had not been well received. There was some giggling when he walked on stage in his breeches and patent-leather pumps, some yawning after he began to speak, and an unmistakable swell of applause when he stopped lecturing for a moment to raise a glass of water to his lips. Maybe it's not surprising that, when interviewed by a reporter later that night at Stoddart's home, Wilde confessed that "my hearers [at the lecture] were so cold I several times thought of stopping and saying, 'You don't like this, and there is no use of my going on.'" Had Wilde done so, it would have pleased the critic from the *Philadelphia Times* who, in a piece headlined "The Shoddy and Aesthetic Climaxes," called Wilde "a weak, vain, pretentious crank," a view seconded by another local reviewer who guessed that "Oscar Wilde always dresses in mourning out of respect for the memory of his wits."

Whitman's invitation did much to raise the lecturer's spirits. After breakfast the next morning, Wilde and Stoddart ferried across the Delaware River to Camden. When they arrived in New Jersey, Stoddart hired a carriage to cover the short distance between the dock and Whitman's home. Wilde, dressed in brown velvet, but in trousers rather than breeches, had obviously planned his opening remarks before the door to that home was opened by Whitman. "I come as a poet to call upon a poet," he said, to which Whitman replied, "Go ahead." So he did: "I have come to you as one with whom I have been acquainted almost from the cradle."

This was true—mostly. Lady Wilde had purchased a copy of *Poems*, by Whitman, in or shortly after 1867, when Oscar would have been entering his teens. The first book by Whitman to be published in Great Britain, *Poems* was a selection from *Leaves of Grass* edited by William Michael Rossetti, who was Whitman's earliest champion in that country and the brother of the poet and pre-Raphaelite painter Dante Gabriel Rossetti, whom Wilde had claimed, somewhat exaggeratedly, as a close friend to the reporter from the *Philadelphia Press*. Lady Wilde, her son now told Whitman, shared William Rossetti's passion for the American bard of free verse and had often read his poetry aloud to Oscar and his brother, though surely not, as Oscar claimed, when they were infants. Later Oscar and his friends at Oxford brought Whitman's poetry with them on walks through the nearby countryside, where they declaimed his verse to each other— and, Wilde said, to the natural beauty all around them. Whitman, who adored being adored as few others ever have, was delighted to hear this. After taking it all in, he went to the cupboard and removed a bottle of his sister-in-law Louisa's homemade elderberry wine. The two men began to empty it.

They were unlikely drinking companions. Wilde had a double first from one of the most prestigious universities in the world; Whitman left school at age eleven. Wilde said it was getting "harder and harder . . . to live up to [his] blue china"; Whitman scorned the "old teacups treasur'd by our grand-aunts." Wilde was a clotheshorse; Whitman cared nothing for fashion. Wilde was a polished talker and epigrammist; Whitman spoke in short, occasionally ungrammatical bursts. Wilde was a snob and an elitist; Whitman (in his own words) "talk[ed] readily with niggers." Physically, they were an odd couple as well: Wilde was clean-shaven, Whitman bearded; and Wilde looked younger than his twenty-seven years, while Whitman looked older than his sixty-two because of a series of strokes—he called them "whacks"—that had weakened his left arm and leg and left him partially paralyzed. (He could still walk and climb stairs, but slowly.)

Despite such differences, the two men enjoyed each other's company. "I will call you Oscar," Whitman said. "I like that so much," Wilde replied. He was delighted to be in such close proximity to the man who, as Wilde had hoped to do for himself, had launched his career with a self-published book of poems. Unlike Wilde, however, Whitman had received extravagant praise for his self-published book from a man at the pinnacle of intellectual life in the country where it was published: Ralph Waldo Emerson, the "Sage of Concord, Massachusetts," who wrote to Whitman in July 1855, after receiving a copy (from Whitman) of the first edition of *Leaves*:

> I am not blind to the worth of the wonderful gift of "LEAVES OF GRASS." I find it the most extraordinary piece of wit and wisdom that America has yet contributed. . . . I find incomparable things said incomparably well, as they must be. I find the courage of treatment which so delights us, and which large perception only can inspire. I greet you at the beginning of a great career.

Whitman, a self-taught genius at self-promotion, printed the full text of Emerson's letter as an appendix to the 1856 edition of *Leaves* and, in a bit of self-aggrandizement never before seen in American letters, had the words "I greet you at the beginning of a great career. R.W. Emerson" embossed on the book's spine.

So Wilde, who craved to read words like that about himself, accepted the invitation from his host to accompany him to his den on the third floor, where, as Whitman said, they could be on "thee and thou terms." (It appears that Stoddart excused himself at this time,

exiting the house on Stevens Street and returning a few hours later.)
Wilde would tell his friends in London he was shocked by the squalor
of the upstairs room where Whitman wrote his poetry. Dust and clut-
ter were everywhere, and the only place for Wilde to sit, a low stool
near Whitman's desk, was covered by a messy pile of newspapers
Whitman had saved because he was mentioned in them. After
Wilde—who mailed his own positive press clippings back to friends
and family in London—moved that pile and took his seat, the two
men continued talking.

Most of what we know of their conversation comes from an interview Whitman gave to the *Philadelphia Press*. According to the quotes
printed in that account, the main subject was poetry. Whitman claimed
to admire the verse of Britain's poet laureate, Alfred, Lord Tennyson,
yet described it as "almost always perfumed . . . to an extreme of sweet-
ness." Then he asked his guest: "Are not you young fellows going to
shove the established idols aside, Tennyson and the rest?"

"Tennyson's rank is too well fixed," Wilde said, "and we love him
too much. But he has not allowed himself to be a part of the living
world. . . . We, on the other hand, move in the very heart of today."
The "we" Wilde was referring to was the British aesthetic movement,
about which Whitman had some reservations; he expressed them after
Wilde said, "I can't listen to anyone unless he attracts me by a charming style, or by beauty of theme." "Why, Oscar," Whitman said, "it
always seems to me that the fellow who makes a dead set at beauty by
itself is in a bad way. My idea is that beauty is a result, not an abstraction." Rather than arguing, Wilde said, "Yes, I remember you have
said, 'All beauty comes from beautiful blood and a beautiful brain,'
and . . . I think so, too." Though Whitman had made his position
clear, he didn't wish to stop the aesthetic movement. "You are young
and ardent," he said, "and the field is wide, and if you want my advice,
[I say] go ahead."

Not long after the *Philadelphia Press* article was published, a "clas-
sical dialogue" between the poets "Paumanokides" and "Narcissus"

appeared, without a byline, under the title "NARCISSUS IN CAMDEN," in *Century*, the literary magazine that, a few years later, would introduce the American public to a character named Huckleberry Finn. The opening section of the dialogue read:

PAUMANOKIDES:

Who may this be?
This young man clad unusually, with loose locks,
Languorous, glidingly toward me advancing,
Toward the ceiling of my chamber his orbic and expressive
eye-balls uprolling. . . .
Sit down, young man!
I do not know you, but I love you with burning intensity. . . .

NARCISSUS:

O clarion, from whose brazen throat
Strange sounds across the seas are blown,
Where England, girt as with a moat,
A strong sea-lion sits alone!
A pilgrim from that white-cliffed shore,
What joy, large flower of Western land,
To seek thy democratic door,
With eager hand to clasp thy hand!*

This was excellent poetic parody, but its mockery left a major target unscathed. For Whitman's advice to Wilde to "go ahead" on his aesthetic quest, coupled with his remark about "shov[ing] the established idols aside," suggests that the subtext of his "thee and thou" conversation on poetry with Wilde wasn't literary form; it was how to build a career in public, with all the preening and posing that self-

---

* The author was later revealed to be Helen Gray Cone, eventually to become chair of the English department at Hunter College, in New York.

glorifying achievement requires. A piece of evidence supporting this view is the fact that one of the first things Whitman did when he reached his den was to give Wilde a recent photographic portrait of himself.

This was significant, even beyond the blatant self-reverence, because Whitman had pioneered the idea that a literary man in search of fame should fashion himself as a literary artifact. The first edition of *Leaves of Grass*, published in 1855, did not include Whitman's name on the title page. Instead, he used as his frontispiece an engraving made from a photo taken of him in 1854, when he was thirty-five, by his friend Gabriel Harrison. This engraving is now considered, the scholars Ed Folsom and Charles M. Price write in the Whitman Internet Archive, "the most influential portrait in the history of American poetry," and "the most famous frontispiece in [all of] literary history."

It was not common in the late nineteenth century for a book of verse to come with a portrait of its author—*Poems*, the book Wilde published in 1881, didn't have one—and the few that did made sure to present the poet as a gentleman: in a dark suit with a dark tie knotted at a closed collar, hatless and seated, often in profile, and always shown from the chest up. Whitman's portrait broke all those "rules." He stands tall in workman's garb; he wears no coat or tie; his collar is open; his left hand is in one pocket of his slacks; his right rests on his hip; a large-brimmed hat sits at a cocky angle atop his head; and his eyes meet the reader with a stare simultaneously casual and challenging, a look almost as ambiguous as Mona Lisa's smile. But one thing about the portrait is clear: it was the first "author photo" in history to present the author with a button fly. As Whitman himself would write in one of his many self-authored reviews of *Leaves*: "Its author is Walt Whitman and his book is a reproduction of the author. His name is not on the frontispiece, but his portrait, half-length, is. The contents of the book form a daguerreotype of his inner being, and the title page bears a representation of its physical tabernacle."

This depiction of Whitman's "tabernacle" (along with the updated depictions in later editions of *Leaves*)—and the "look at me" attitude all of those portraits projected—were as important as Emerson's praise in making Whitman a literary man worthy of consideration. These portraits *demanded* that attention be paid to Whitman, just as Wilde expected his portraits by Sarony would for him, even if Wilde's tabernacle, at his insistence, was presented with a decidedly more aesthetic attitude. This is not to suggest that all the attention paid to Whitman's engraved portrait in the first edition of *Leaves* was positive. Whitman wrote that it "was very much hatcheted by the fellows at the time [of its publication]—war was waged on it." Even so, he used the same portrait on several later editions of *Leaves*, including the selections published in Britain that Wilde read. To paraphrase the velvet-clad visitor to Whitman's home in January 1882, the only thing worse than being hatcheted is *not* being hatcheted.

We don't know which portrait Whitman gave to Wilde that day in Camden, but it's a good bet it was the one he was preparing to use on the book he published several months later, *Specimen Days and Collect*, an assemblage of travel diaries, nature writing, and Civil War reminiscences. (Whitman had spent the war years in Washington, working as a government clerk and volunteering as a hospital visitor and nurse's aide.) This portrait wasn't an engraving; it was a photograph taken at the Philadelphia studio of W. Curtis Taylor in 1877, showing Whitman in profile, his beard forming an unruly white nest around his face. He is sitting in a wicker chair wearing a large hat, an open-necked shirt, and a buttoned cardigan. His left hand is partially hidden inside a pocket; his right—which Whitman is staring at—is lifted in front of his face. He is staring at it because a butterfly is perched on his index finger.

This portrait, which Whitman described as "2/3rd length with hat outdoor rustic," was said to be his favorite out of the more than one hundred he posed for in his lifetime—more than any other nineteenth-century author save Mark Twain. Photographers "have used me for a show-horse again and again and again," Whitman once complained. But another animal metaphor explains why he was so eager to accept that "exploitation." "The public is a thick-skinned beast," he once said, "and you have to keep whacking away at its hide to let it know you're there."

The butterfly portrait was a highly effective example of that "whacking away"—one that caused some controversy, which only made Whitman fonder of it. His friend William Roscoe Thayer, a Harvard-trained historian who moved to Philadelphia shortly after Wilde visited Camden, was dubious of the photo's authenticity, a suspicion he expressed to Whitman's face. "I've always had the knack of attracting birds and butterflies and other wild critters," Whitman told him. Thayer kept silent at the time but later mused, "How it happened that a butterfly should have been waiting in the studio on the chance that Walt might drop in to be photographed . . . I have never been able to explain." It was explained half a century later when a scholar at the Library of Congress discovered the actual "butterfly"—it was made of cardboard—and proved that, rather than being attracted to Whitman, it had been tied to his finger with a piece of string.

Even if the butterfly portrait was not the photo Whitman gave to Wilde—it could have been the equally dramatic portrait made by Sarony in 1878, in which the poet seems to be sitting on the rim of a volcano—Whitman was teaching his guest a lesson: fame as a literary man is only partly about literature; it is also, maybe even mostly, about committing oneself to a public performance, an act—whether done on stage (Whitman gave lectures on the death of Abraham Lincoln that convinced many of his listeners, falsely, that he had witnessed it), or performed before a portraitist with a camera—with all the theatrics implied in the word *act*.

For Whitman, this role-playing wasn't phony. Every pose he struck on stage and on film, no matter how outlandish, was to his mind both natural and authentic, if not in the sense that his friend William Roscoe Thayer could understand, but in a way that Wilde *did*. This type of authenticity—the fashioning of an image one would be faithful to in public—Wilde had experienced while performing as an aesthete at Oxford and in London. Even so, it was meaningful to have its truth verified by a man who had proved its efficacy. Wilde had always believed there was nothing inglorious about seeking glory. By handing Wilde one of his many portraits, the supremely image-conscious Whitman—a writer who had launched his career without a byline but with a picture of himself—was confirming Wilde's instinct.

"God bless you, Oscar," Whitman said at the door, when Wilde, rejoined by Stoddart, took his leave. On the carriage ride to the ferry, Stoddart, a well-known epicure, joked that it must have been hard for Wilde to swallow the homemade elderberry wine his host had offered. For one of the few times in his life, Wilde rejected an invitation to snobbery. "If it had been vinegar I should have drunk it all the same," he said, "for I have an admiration for that man which I can hardly express." When interviewed a few days later, he expanded on this theme, saying of Whitman, "He is the grandest man I have ever seen . . . The simplest, most natural . . . character I have ever met."

Decades later, when the magnitude of Whitman's ceaseless (and occasionally deceitful) efforts at self-promotion were fully exposed by scholars, some critics took Wilde to task for that remark. The foppish Irishman, they said, was so hopelessly naïve that he failed to grasp that Whitman's simplicity and naturalness were nothing but a charade, a theatrical performance for public consumption. In reality, it was Wilde's critics who were showing their lack of sophistication. Wilde knew how complicated it was to project simplicity. His critics did not.

WILDE LEFT WHITMAN'S home, and Philadelphia, a bigger celebrity than when he arrived, which was a feat of some consequence. Philadelphia was the second-largest city in America in 1882, behind only New York. But Wilde would soon learn another truth about living in the public eye, one he had not anticipated: celebrity isn't merely contagious; it can make others ill. This lesson was taught to him by two men—the first a once-famous, now-forgotten journalist, the other a novelist whose place in the Western canon is unassailable. Teacher number one was the Scotsman Archibald Forbes, a former soldier in the Royal Dragoons turned battlefield reporter, who was crossing America at the same time as Wilde, speaking on "The Inner Life of a War Correspondent," a talk he presented wearing a chest full of medals that included the Iron Cross and the French Legion of Honor. It is a sign of Forbes's considerable fame in January 1882 that, when he spoke on this topic two months earlier, in a sold-out auditorium in Hartford, Connecticut, he was introduced by Mark Twain.

Already in New York when Wilde arrived, Forbes (like Wilde, a client of the Carte organization) saw the traveling aesthete as a commercial rival, despite their shared management, and was not pleased to see the attention given by the American press to his competitor, a man he viewed as having done nothing to deserve that notice, except as a charlatan in clown's garb. "Oscar Wilde is here," Forbes wrote in a letter to a friend. "He wears knee breeches. . . . He can't lecture worth a cent, but he draws crowds . . . and fools them all." Much of this was true, but the letter also contained this assertion, which was not: Forbes claimed that P. T. Barnum, who had recently bought Jumbo the Elephant from the London zoo for $10,000, had offered Wilde several hundred dollars to lead the famous pachyderm through several American cities, if Wilde wore breeches and carried a sunflower in one hand and a lily in the other. Several months later the *Cincinnati Gazette* would have some Forbesian fun with the same inaccurate claim: "It is reported that Barnum has made an offer to Oscar Wilde for the latter to sit on top of Jumbo and ride in street processions. If, instead of Wilde sitting on the elephant, Jumbo were to sit on Wilde, the result would be more satisfactory to the people, and it wouldn't hurt Jumbo much."

After a speaking engagement in Philadelphia, Forbes found himself staying in the same hotel as Wilde. This was dispiriting enough to his exaggerated sense of self-importance; even worse, his itinerary from the Carte office had him leaving for Baltimore, the site of his next talk, on the same train as Wilde. Colonel Morse's plan was that Wilde would attend and—this is what really irritated Forbes—help to publicize Forbes's lecture there, despite the fact that Forbes had been lecturing successfully for years and Wilde was a complete novice. Morse's plan also called for both men to attend a reception peopled with the elite of Baltimore society after Forbes's lecture. Then Wilde would take a train to his next engagement, in Washington, and Forbes would travel to his, in another city.

But the two men, seated in the same compartment on the train from Philadelphia, quickly began to insult each other. Forbes mocked Wilde's real-world "achievements"; Wilde boasted of his superior box-office receipts. Forbes spoke of his bravery in combat; Wilde dropped the titled names of his dinner-party conquests in London. On and on it went until the train reached Baltimore, where Wilde refused to get off, reneging on his commitment to attend Forbes's talk and the reception on his behalf. Instead, he traveled on to Washington. Forbes responded by demeaning Wilde that night in his lecture, drawing a mocking contrast between Wilde's clothing when meeting the American public, and Forbes's when summoned from a grisly battlefield in rural Russia to meet Czar Nicholas II in the imperial capital of St. Petersburg, a distance of 150 miles, which he had covered on horseback. "Now I wish it understood that I am a follower, a very humble follower, of the aesthetic ecstasy," Forbes told his audience, which tittered at this obvious untruth:

> But I did not look much like an art object then. I did not have my dogskin knee breeches with me nor my velvet coat, and my black silk stockings were filled with holes. Neither was the wild, barren waste of Russia calculated to produce sunflowers and lilies.

After seeing these words printed in several newspapers, Wilde told the *Washington Post* he had never planned to attend Forbes's lecture—

a lie—because, as he claimed, "Our views are wide apart. If it amuses [Forbes] to caricature me in the manner which he did last night, well and good. It may serve a purpose, and judging from the fact that his audience, as stated, came to see *me*, it is answering one very good purpose. It is advertising Mr. Forbes at my expense." This prompted Forbes to write a public letter saying that he had heard—from Wilde—that the twin purposes of his American tour were to enrich himself and to become famous (both of which were true). This in turn led the *Post*, which shared Forbes's disdain for instant celebrities, to express that contempt in a front-page article, illustrated with a cartoon depicting a sunflower-holding Wilde beneath a half-ape, half-human savage. "How far is it from this [the ape-man] to this [Wilde]?" asked the headline. Then came this text:

> We present in close juxtaposition the pictures of Mr. Wilde of England and Mr. Wild of Borneo, who judging from the resemblance, is undoubtedly kin. If Mr. Darwin is right in his theory, has not the climax of evolution been reached and are we not tending down the hill toward the aboriginal starting point again? Certainly a more inane object than Mr. Wilde of England has not challenged our attention.

A subsequent editorial in the *Post* mocked Wilde's "mushy face, his long and plastered locks, his leer, which stands, we fancy, for a smile, his untidy linen, his damnable posing, [and] his inane collection of words called a lecture." Wilde had come to Washington "to pose, to dawdle, to exhibit with vulgar emphasis his beefy limbs to extort dollars under the false pretense of having something to say," the editorialist wrote. "All true Englishmen will be glad if we can terrify him back to Britain so that they may kill him." These attacks, which originated with Wilde's spat with Forbes, wounded Wilde. But he was prepared to rise above any unpleasantness connected to a self-satisfied martinet he considered a boor. What Wilde didn't know was that he was about to be insulted again in Washington, and for the same reason, by someone he did respect.

The novelist Henry James, an American by birth but an Englishman by temperament—he had been living in Britain since 1876—returned to America for an extended visit at almost the same moment Wilde arrived for his lecture tour. James was a well-established literary figure on both sides of the Atlantic by this time, having published *Daisy Miller* in 1879, *Washington Square* in 1880, and *The Portrait of a Lady* a year after that. Unlike Wilde, he made a point of shunning the press, a policy he planned to continue in America. Wilde gave dozens of interviews after landing in New York; James was so determined not to do so that he entered the States through the "back-door," as he put it in a letter, via Canada, even taking the extra precaution of checking into hotels under the (pompous) pseudonym Harry Heliotrope. Though James and Wilde moved in similar circles in London, and had friends in common, there is no evidence that they had ever met.

But we know they did meet on January 22, at a reception held at the home of Judge Edward G. Loring and his wife in Washington. James had arrived more than a week before Wilde, staying at the home of two of the leading social figures in the capital, the historian Henry Adams (a descendant of two American presidents) and his wife Marian, known to virtually everyone as Clover. (Mrs. Adams is believed to be the model for two of James's most famous fictional characters, Daisy Miller and Isabel Archer.) A letter to a friend in Britain shows that James was enjoying his visit to the American capital—at first:

> I believe that Washington is the place in the world where money—or the absence of it, matters least. It is very queer and yet extremely pleasant: informal, familiar, heterogeneous, good-natured, essentially social and conversational, enormously big and yet extremely provincial, indefinably ridiculous and yet eminently agreeable. . . . The sky is blue, the sun is warm, the women are charming, and at dinners the talk is always general.

He altered his opinion when that dinner-table talk turned to the imminent arrival of Oscar Wilde. James, no stranger to self-importance (though he was not the pompous ass Forbes was), was, like Forbes, disheartened by the attention directed at Wilde, a "literary" figure who, in his view, had yet to produce anything of literary value. But what Wilde had produced—and this was something James envied (and perhaps resented)—was star quality. Washington society was abuzz at the prospect of mingling with the velvet-clad, lily-worshiping aesthete. It's possible, then, that James was not fully comfortable with the prospect of seeing Wilde at the Lorings' party. We know that days earlier, James's hostess in the capital, his old friend Clover Adams, one of the few prominent Washingtonians immune to Wilde's star power, wrote to her father: "I have asked Henry James *not* to bring his friend Oscar Wilde [to my home] when he comes; I must keep out thieves and noodles." It seems clear that "noodle" was Mrs. Adams's way of impugning Wilde's masculinity, a conclusion supported by this line from another one of her letters: "the sexes of my nouns are as undecided as that of Oscar Wilde." As has been pointed out by several of James's biographers, James's sexuality was the source of considerable psychic agitation for him, so it's probable he was not thrilled by Mrs. Adams's remarks, least of all by her assumption that he and Wilde—whose brazen efforts at self-promotion James found so distasteful—were friends.

The sight of Wilde in breeches and silver-buckled shoes, brandishing a yellow handkerchief in his lace-encircled hand as he charmed the Washingtonians who gathered around him at the Lorings' party, a fete attended by several United States senators, was apparently too much for James to take, so much so that he pretended it didn't happen. "I went last night to the Loring's [*sic*]," he wrote to his friend in Boston, the art collector Isabella Stewart Gardner, " . . . and found there the repulsive and fatuous Oscar Wilde, whom, I am happy to say, no one was looking at." But we have another view of that night—and of the relative merits of James and Wilde as party guests—from Harriet

Loring, the daughter of Judge and Mrs. Loring, who wrote, a few days after the party, to John Hay, the former assistant to President Lincoln and now an official at the State Department, about the just-concluded social season in Washington:

> One prominent feature has been the lions that have roared for us—first we had Mr. Henry James Jr. . . . He is always doing his level best and one can't help approving of him but longing for a little of the divine spark. Then we had Oscar. He . . . burst upon our view one Sunday—tights, yellow handkerchief and all. He is the most gruesome object I ever saw, but he was very amusing. Full of Irish keenness and humor and really interesting.

Though James had called Wilde "repulsive," he visited him two days after the Lorings' party, and a day after Wilde's Washington lecture, at Wilde's suite at the Arlington Hotel, a block from the White House, where Wilde had requested candles from management to illuminate his rooms, rather than using the available gas lamps. This meeting has puzzled biographers for decades. Perhaps, as the late Richard Ellmann speculated, James overheard Wilde praising his books at the Lorings' home and wanted to thank him. We know that a few months later Wilde said "no living Englishman can be compared to [William Dean] Howells and [Henry] James as novelists," and, as a reporter in Cincinnati watched, Wilde purchased some of their works so he could reread them.* But Michele Mendelssohn, a historian at the University of Oxford, believes it was homosexual attraction—implicit or explicit—that drew James to Wilde's hotel suite, where Wilde quickly showed he wasn't interested, whether James displayed his intentions or not.

---

* When speaking to a reporter from the *Boston Herald*, however, Wilde, ever aware of his audience, described *The Scarlet Letter*, by the Massachusetts native Nathaniel Hawthorne, as "the greatest work of fiction ever written in the English tongue.'

What is overlooked in both theories is the role of James's professional and personal envy of Wilde. Though James was a well-known writer, he was not a particularly well-compensated one. (Fortunately for him, he belonged to a wealthy family.) James's suspicion that Wilde was making more from speaking fees than James was earning from book royalties may have made him want to take a personal assessment of the man who had managed that feat. This curiosity was tinged with contempt and, more than likely, with fear. As a novelist, James saw himself as a member of an artistic elite that Wilde had no qualifications to join—at least not yet. But as James witnessed, the dandy in velvet and lace was celebrated in America not just by society swells but by persons of genuine achievement—senators, cabinet members, and the like—and, even more exasperating, was getting paid handsomely for it. When James looked at Wilde, he saw a repugnant and alien future: an age when the talent that mattered most wasn't artistic but narcissistic—a genius for self-puffery and public preening. To James, this was monstrous. Perhaps his intellectual curiosity, maybe even his sense of self-preservation, compelled him to meet the man who was calling that worldview into existence.

What we know for certain is that the meeting between the two men didn't go very well. (It's likely Wilde was just as nervous to meet James, a novelist of genuine standing, as James was to meet him.) James, making small talk, said, "I am very nostalgic for London." "Really?" Wilde said. "You care for places? The world is my home." Whether or not Wilde meant that as an insult, James took it as one. Hearing of Wilde's busy lecture schedule only made him more perturbed. Wilde bragged that he would soon be in Boston, the home of the aesthetic movement in America, to lecture on aesthetics. It's also possible he repeated something a star-struck woman had told him at a party in Manhattan: "Oh, Mr. Wilde, you have been adored in New York. In Boston you will be worshipped!"

Wilde had never been to Boston, of course, but he had a letter of introduction, he told James, from Wilde's dearest friend in England, the artist Edward Burne-Jones, to Burne-Jones's dearest friend in America, the Harvard professor of art Charles Eliot Norton. James, who knew both men, was neither impressed nor amused by Wilde's claim to be so well connected. When he returned from Wilde's hotel to Clover Adams's townhouse, James—who would later draw an unflattering picture of an effete, name-dropping, Wilde-like character (named Gabriel Nash) in his novel *The Tragic Muse*—told his friend and hostess she was right about the self-adoring Irishman. Wilde is "a fatuous fool," a "tenth-rate cad," and "an unclean beast," he said, opinions Mrs. Adams likely spread among her friends in Washington and beyond.*

Wilde would leave the capital before that happened, however, taking a train to New York and, after an overnight stay there, to Albany, where he lectured on January 27, and then another train to Boston, his precious letters of introduction in hand. It would be a while before he was fully aware of James's loathing for his fame-hunting ways. What he would find out a lot sooner was that, for reasons he never quite understood, the Harvard professor Charles Eliot Norton couldn't find the time to meet him there that winter.

BUT ONE OF Wilde's letters of introduction opened a very important door for him in Boston, where he arrived on January 28, checking into the Hotel Vendome, in the city's fashionable Back Bay district. Written by James Russell Lowell, the poet and former editor of the *Atlantic Monthly* now serving in London—where Wilde had met him at several parties—as America's ambassador to Great Britain, the letter was sent to Oliver Wendell Holmes, the poet, physician, and Harvard professor who was one of the giants of Boston's literary and social circles (and the father of the future Supreme Court justice, Oliver Wendell

---

* Wilde would strike back at James years later, in his essay "The Decay of Lying," in which he wrote: "Mr. Henry James writes fiction as if it were a painful duty."

Holmes, Jr.). "A clever and accomplished man should no more need an introduction than a fine day," Lowell wrote, "but since a stranger can no longer establish a claim on us by coming in and seating himself as a suppliant at our fireside, let me ask you to be serviceable to the bearer of this, Mr. Oscar Wilde, the report of whom has doubtless reached you and who is better than his report."

Holmes senior, a cofounder of the *Atlantic Monthly*, knew Lowell well, so he honored his friend's request by inviting Wilde to the Saturday Club, the preeminent intellectual gathering in a city many considered the intellectual capital of America. The Club, whose members included Ralph Waldo Emerson, William Dean Howells, the philosopher Charles S. Peirce (the founder of pragmatism), and the Harvard Divinity School professor James Freeman Clarke, met on the fourth Saturday of each month, which in January 1882 happened to be the day of Wilde's arrival. Emerson's health and memory were failing by this time, so it's unlikely he was still attending Saturday Club events. He would die, a few months later, in April 1882.

So Wilde changed his clothes (and, by doing so, made himself a more welcome guest at the Club than had the casually garbed Walt Whitman twenty years earlier) and took a carriage from his hotel to the Parker House, where the Saturday Club convened. It was surely an event filled with lively talk: Holmes, the unofficial chair of the group, was as famous in Boston for his conversational skills as Wilde was in London. Unfortunately, we have no transcript of the meeting, but Wilde must have been impressed with Holmes's wit. Eight years after they met in Boston, Wilde had Sir Thomas Burdon, a character in *The Picture of Dorian Gray*, remark, "They say that when good Americans die they go to Paris." What most of Wilde's readers didn't know was that Holmes had already written that line in 1858, in *Autocrat of the Breakfast Table*. (Wilde joked in *Dorian* that the opposite was also true: "And where do bad Americans go to when they die?" asks the Duchess of Harley. "They go to America," says Lord Henry Wotton.)

Another letter of introduction, this one from Wilde's favorite dinner host in New York, Sam Ward, to his sister Julia Ward Howe, led to an invitation to her Boston home, where she introduced Wilde to another assemblage of the city's social, academic, and civic elite that included the Harvard psychologist William James (the brother of Henry), the art patron Isabella Stewart Gardner (the friend of Henry), and Ebenezer Sumner Draper, a recent graduate of the Massachusetts Institute of Technology who would eventually become the governor of Massachusetts. Though Mrs. Howe made sure the Boston press was apprised of her party, she was no mere self-publicizing socialite. She had been a strong voice in Boston's abolitionist movement and wrote the lyrics to "The Battle Hymn of the Republic," the song that became the unofficial anthem of the Union cause during the Civil War. (A biography of Mrs. Howe, cowritten by her daughters, Laura E. Richards and Maud Howe Elliott, would win the Pulitzer Prize for Biography in 1917.)

We have an eyewitness account of Wilde's entrance to Howe's party, written by Alice Cary Williams, whose father, a Boston physician, had studied with Professor Holmes at Harvard. Williams was but a child at the gala, but she was savvy enough to grasp what she was seeing: an unforgettable show, presented by a one-of-a-kind showman.

"Suddenly a hush fell over everything, for Mrs. Howe had clapped her hands for silence," Williams wrote in her memoir, *Thru the Turnstile*:

The milling crowd moved back against the walls, leaving a clear space before the staircase. I sat on the floor, below the stairs. It was all so still, not a sound. Then, as I heard something above me, my heart began to pound. Raising my eyes, I saw coming down the stairs slowly, slowly, one step then another, a pair of patent leather shoes with silver buckles, then black stockings and above them green velvet knee breeches, and the knees were bending, bringing the figure down, nearer to me. . . . I looked up and saw a matching doublet, a ruffle running down its length, and beside it an arm and a hand, a pale white hand which held a lily. I gasped as I looked up into a face which had golden hair surrounding it, falling to the shoulders, and pale blue eyes fastened off on the ceiling above the guests, and this deathly white face began to speak in a high chanting voice. On it went and on, and when I thought it would never stop it gave a kind of shriek, lowered its eyes, and everyone clapped and shouted, "Bravo!" Then I heard Mrs. Howe's voice, "I don't need to introduce Mr. Oscar Wilde."

But it was another letter from Sam Ward that presented Wilde with the celebrity encounter he desired most in Boston. Ward sent this letter to his great friend, the poet Henry Wadsworth Longfellow. The two Americans—one so worldly, the other hardly at all—were unlikely but undeniable intimates, having met five decades earlier as foreign students at the University of Heidelberg, in Germany, where Ward was studying mathematics and Longfellow was preparing to take a professorship in modern languages at Harvard. Longfellow and Ward's shared love of poetry inaugurated their friendship, a bond that was surely strengthened when, years later, Ward arranged for the *New York Ledger* to pay his friend $4,000—roughly $80,000 in today's dollars—to publish Longfellow's "The Hanging of the Crane." No poet had ever been paid more for a poem (and probably has not since).

It's unlikely Wilde knew about that transaction, but he was definitely aware that Longfellow, the author of *Evangeline: A Tale of Acadie, The Song of Hiawatha,* and other best-selling poetry books, was the most widely read poet in the English-speaking world in 1882, certainly more popular than Walt Whitman and even more admired than Lord Tennyson. He also knew that Longfellow had entertained Charles Dickens, Thomas Carlyle, and William Makepeace Thackeray at his home—a list to which Wilde was eager to add his own name. This determination grew even stronger after he read these words from Longfellow, who had been asked to comment on Wilde's imminent arrival by a reporter for the *Boston Evening Traveler*: "Mr. Wilde has written some good verses. He cannot be an ignorant man."

This comment was all the more gracious considering Longfellow's poor health. A few weeks shy of his seventh-fifth birthday, the poet had been experiencing severe stomach pains for some time, a condition belatedly diagnosed as peritonitis. (Longfellow would die in March, a month before Ralph Waldo Emerson.) It appears his family had originally begged off Sam Ward's request to make the poet available to the traveling lecturer, but Ward—and Wilde—persisted. Finally, the Irishman was invited for breakfast. Longfellow was surely reluctant to disappoint his old friend. It's also likely that he remembered the kindnesses that had been shown him decades earlier by literary figures in Europe when he was studying there as a young man—at almost the same age as Wilde was now. Besides, Longfellow may have had some genuine curiosity to meet the young man whose mother, Lady Jane Wilde, a poet of some renown in both Ireland and England, had inaugurated a lively correspondence about poetry with Longfellow some years earlier.

The weather on January 30 was hardly conducive for traveling, not even for the relatively short distance between Boston's Back Bay and Harvard Square in Cambridge, where Longfellow lived in a grand old house, known locally as Craigie Castle, that once served as George Washington's headquarters during the Revolutionary War. Despite a heavy snowstorm and winds that diminished visibility, Wilde urged his driver onward, confident that his audience with Longfellow, a man who was as much a Boston landmark as Bunker Hill, would be huge news in the press the following day, the very day he would be speaking at Boston's Music Hall.

Though Wilde was certainly more celebrated for his wit than was Longfellow, it was the aging American who got the biggest laugh during their meal. This happened when Longfellow told Wilde of his encounter with Queen Victoria, who had invited him to Windsor

Castle when the poet was touring her country, giving readings, in 1868. The queen said a number of very kind things to her flattered guest, after which he expressed his shock and delight to find out he was so well known in Britain. "Oh, I assure you, Mr. Longfellow," the queen harrumphed. "You are very well known. All my servants read you."

Wilde would dine out on this story for years after his return to London. But first he had to deal with some fallout from his visit to Longfellow's home off Harvard Square. Apparently there were some students at Harvard, where Longfellow had taught for decades, who thought that revered institution of learning had been sullied by Longfellow's decision to receive the self-proclaimed Professor of Aesthetics, even if he had graduated with honors from a university as prestigious as their own. So the students hatched a plan that, much to the befuddlement of the sold-out crowd at Music Hall on January 31, resulted in dozens of empty seats in that auditorium, all of them at the front, just moments before Wilde was scheduled to begin speaking, at eight p.m. This mystery was solved when, just before that appointed time, a posse of Harvard students marched, noisily and ostentatiously, down the center aisle of the auditorium in pairs toward those empty chairs. This is how one Boston reporter described the scene:

> There were blond wigs and black wigs, wide-floating neckties of every hue and fashion, knee breeches and black stockings of "ye olden time," and in every hand the "precious loveliness" of the lily or the "gaudy leonine" glare of the sunflower. As the youths entered they assumed all sorts of poses, and held aloft or looked languishingly down on the circling petals of flowers. Then they took their seats, utterly pleased with themselves.

But Wilde had been tipped off about their prank. (In fact, some believe the entire episode was planned in advance by Colonel Morse as a publicity stunt.) So when Wilde took the Music Hall stage shortly afterward, he did so *without* his breeches, silk stockings, buckled patent-leather pumps, form-fitting velvet coat, or any finery from "ye olden time." He was in a conventional dinner jacket and trousers. Wilde then glanced down, as if by chance, on those who had gone to so much trouble to lampoon him. "As a college man, I greet you," he began. "I am very glad to address an audience in Boston . . . [where] I see about me certain signs of an aesthetic movement. . . . I am impelled for the first time in my life to breathe a fervent prayer: 'Save me from my disciples.'"

The rest of the audience at the Music Hall laughed, then burst into sustained applause. So did the editorial board of the *Boston Evening Transcript*, in print, the following day: "Mr. Wilde achieved a real triumph, and it was by right of conquest, by force of being a gentleman, in the truest sense of the word." He engineered a "thorough-going chastening of the super-abounding spirits of the Harvard freshmen. Nothing could have been more gracious, more gentle and sweet, and yet more crushing." Wilde tried not to gloat about his triumph and was partially successful. "Oh, I could sympathize with them, [When] I was in my first year at Oxford I would have been apt to do the same; but as they put their head in the lion's mouth, I thought they deserved a little bite," he told a reporter for the *New York Sun*. Word of Wilde's conquest soon reached the editorial staff of *Puck*, the humor magazine based in New York, which decided to spoof it in a piece that pitted Wilde not against a group of puny Harvard men, but against the burliest Bostonian of them all: John L. Sullivan, the celebrated bare-knuckles fighter who had defeated all (white) opponents (and would soon become heavyweight champion of the world).

"WILDE AND SULLIVAN / The Great Fight / *The Two Aesthetes Meet Near Concord*," read the headline. "The great contest between Oscar Wilde, of Dublin, and John L. Sullivan, of Boston, for the champion aestheteship of America took place yesterday," the piece began. "The ring was pitched in a remote [area] to avoid police interference, and the stakes and ropes were decorated with garlands of sunflowers and lilies. . . . ROUND FIRST—Both men displayed great caution until Wilde delicately planted lilies on Sullivan's frontal development, notwithstanding the Boston man's endeavor to parry the blows with peacock feathers. First tickle for Wilde. Time, ten seconds." On and on the fight went, *Puck's* man at ringside reported, until it was declared a draw after twelve exquisite rounds of aesthetic combat.

Despite the failure of the Harvard men to defeat Wilde, undergraduates at Yale tried a similar prank the very next night, when Wilde lectured in New Haven, as did students at the University of Rochester, in upstate New York, a week later. The students in Rochester even went so far as to convince a school janitor to don blackface and march down the center aisle of the auditorium in a swallow-tailed velvet coat with a huge sunflower pinned to its lapel, while waving to the crowd with his white-gloved right hand. (His other hand was left bare.)

George William Curtis, the author of the "Editor's Easy Chair" column in *Harper's Monthly* (and a well-known lecturer in his own right), criticized the actions of those undergraduates as "coarse and ungentlemanly." But he nonetheless thought Wilde a fitting target—*and* a clever self-promoter. "A man who wishes to show the worth of the modern renaissance is bound, first of all, not to make himself laughable," Curtis wrote. "The cheapest distinction is that which the tailor or barber can furnish.

> The "mission" of Mr. Wilde to this country has been quite lost under the accidents and incidents of his career. What kind of country did he suppose himself to be about to visit? If he had gone through England in knee-breeches and other oddities of apparel, he could hardly have hoped to win a more favorable audience for his views. . . . Had he lectured quietly in America, he would not have been relentlessly chaffed from one end of the country to the other. But nobody would then have heard of him, and no one would have gone to hear him.

One can almost sense a whiff of respect in that final line.

"What a tempest and tornado you live in!" Wilde's mother wrote from London, when reports of her son's encounters with mocking students and ambivalent editorialists reached the British press. (The brouhaha in Rochester was so disruptive that police had to be called.) But her son was far too confident of his growing celebrity—and the psychic armor it placed on him—to complain about such treatment. As far as he was concerned, his strategy was succeeding: by associating with American stars he was becoming a star himself, with all the pleasures and pitfalls that come with celestial status.

Don't worry about me, Wilde told his mother and any journalist who asked. "I am indestructible!"

CHAPTER FIVE

The Subject Is Always You

*B*efore he left Boston, Wilde remarked that the species of *Homo americanus* he had encountered most often in the United States wasn't the literary celebrity or the society hostess. It was the newspaperman. Nearly all those meetings, and there would be almost a hundred more before the year was over, took place in his hotel suite after he arrived in the city where he was scheduled to deliver a lecture. Wilde's appearance was publicized in advance by a Carte agency operative who notified the local press of his client's imminent arrival, placed advertisements for his speaking engagement in the city's most important journals, oversaw the hanging of posters on walls and streetlamps, and, when feasible, arranged for Wilde to take a tour of the municipality, an outing usually led by a star-struck civic official and covered by reporters. The journalists who came to interview Wilde at his hotel—most of whom had never conversed with a Briton before, and certainly not one with a double first from Oxford—came with notepads filled with questions about his mysterious "aesthetic mission," as well as his views of American poetry, architecture, painting, railway stations, food, novelists, fashion, and, on at least one occasion, hog butchering. One probing journalist asked him, "What is art?" and, later in the same interview, "What is civilization?" To the first, Wilde replied: "An artistic thing is anything which, independent of its practical use, pleases one by the beauty and delicacy of its form, the wonder of its design, or the nobility of its color." And to the second: "It is that condition under which man most completely realizes the perfection of his own nature. Civilization without art or beauty is an impossibility."

Even for someone who loved to talk as much as Wilde, this was a new and occasionally baffling experience. "Interviewers are a product of American civilization," he told a reporter sent to his hotel by the *Boston Globe*. "You gentlemen have fairly monopolized me ever since I saw Sandy Hook," he said, a reference to the spit of land in New Jersey near the entrance to New York Harbor. "In New York there were about a hundred a day. I had to leave my hotel and go to a private house when I wanted to push along my work. But I am always glad to see you." As he would later explain to a reporter from the *St. Louis Republican*: "We have no interviewing in England."

He wasn't exaggerating. The journalist credited with conducting the first interview in an English newspaper, William T. Stead, didn't do so until January 1884, when he asked a long series of questions of Gen. Charles (Chinese) Gordon, recently returned from Sudan—or *the* Soudan, as it was then known—at Gordon's sister's home in southern England. Stead's two-hour interview with the general, which focused on the political unrest in northeastern Africa, was published in London's *Pall Mall Gazette*, where Stead had recently become editor in chief. (Stead joined the *Gazette* in 1880, which means he was there in 1881 when the paper published several obviously fabricated letters mocking Wilde's impending lecture tour of the United States.) Stead's article on Gordon used no quotation marks, but much of it was written in the first person, the "I" clearly being the general. "During the three years that I wielded full powers in the Soudan I taught the natives that they had a right to exist. . . . I taught them something of the meaning of liberty and justice," Stead wrote, paraphrasing Gordon's responses to his questions. Stead claimed no ownership of his seeming journalistic innovation, however. He agreed with Wilde. "The interview is a distinctively American invention," he wrote later in a book he titled *The Americanization of the World.*

In truth, the newspaper interview was still something of a novelty even in America in 1882—and not an especially respected one. The *Oxford English Dictionary* cites the American magazine *The Nation* as the first journal to use the term *interview* in print, in this sentence, published in 1869: "The 'interview,' as at present managed, is generally the joint product of some humbug of a politician and another humbug of a newspaper reporter." Historians of journalism aren't in agreement as to which was the first interview to appear in America. A few point to a piece written in 1836 by James Gordon Bennett, the founding editor of the *New York Herald,* in which he questioned a brothel owner linked to the murder of the prostitute Helen Jewett, a crime that made headlines for weeks on end that year in New York. But most experts think the first published interview, as we understand that term today, was with the Mormon patriarch Brigham Young, conducted in 1859 and presented in question-and-answer format by Bennett's great rival, Horace Greeley of the *New York Tribune.* Either way, the consensus is that the interview did not become a regular feature of American journalism until the 1870s, when mass-circulation newspapers such as the *Herald* and the *Tribune* began to target a literate, but not especially learned, readership that expected to be entertained as well as informed by the penny press. The best way to reach that fast-growing audience, editors such as Bennett and Greeley agreed, was to present American life—the seemly and unseemly—as a never-ending show.

And like all shows, this one required stars. Public figures were now covered as personalities in stories that often used interviews to present those stars "as they really were"—or, at least, as they or the newspaper wished the public to think they were. Whereas it used to be an unchallenged axiom in journalism that the news made names out of newsmakers, now the reverse was equally true: names made the news, sometimes merely by opening the doors of their hotel rooms to answer questions. Most of those names came from the stage, the political arena, or the athletic field, but the demand for lively copy soon led editors to seek out traveling lecturers, speakers who, like newspapers, were expected to entertain as well as to inform their audiences. Mark Twain, better known in the early 1870s as a lecturer (usually on travel) than as a novelist (*The Adventures of Tom Sawyer* didn't appear until 1876, and *Adventures of Huckleberry Finn* not until 1884), was interviewed so often in this period, and by so many simpletons, that he lampooned the process—"all the rage right now," he wrote—in his 1875 essay "An Encounter with an Interviewer." In response to one question in that piece, Twain told his interrogator from the *Daily Thunderstorm* that the most remarkable man he had ever met was Aaron Burr, the former vice president of the United States who had killed Alexander Hamilton, America's first secretary of the treasury, in a duel in Weehawken, New Jersey, in 1804. He had made Burr's acquaintance—and talked to him at great length—Twain insisted, at Burr's funeral in 1836. (Making that assertion even more preposterous is the fact that Twain wasn't born until 1835.)

Because most nineteenth-century Americans read newspapers in their leisure time, the success of press interviews was usually measured by their entertainment value. Their function, more often than not, was to be amusing—and if that happened at the expense of the interview subject, so be it. This was the environment Wilde landed in when he arrived in America in 1882. An unfamiliar brand of journalism was ascendant here, one determined to use him for its own ends. It wasn't long before he made it work for his.

But at first he was caught off guard. When Wilde was accosted on the *Arizona* by a pack of reporters, he was the victim of a journalistic technique that would later earn the name "ambush interview." Wilde was both flattered and flustered by the attention; he felt like an important personage—and prey—simultaneously. This situation was one he suspected he would encounter again as he continued on his tour, so he decided to take control of it. He did this by recalling a truth he had learned from his extravagantly extroverted mother in Dublin: life is a performance. The reporters who met Wilde in hotel rooms as he crossed America surely thought they were conducting an interview with Wilde. But, in fact, the opposite was true. Wilde was conducting *them*, transforming those journalists into the section musicians in a symphony of self-glorification, an opera of opportunism that had but one soloist and star: Oscar Wilde.

Conceived and executed as a piece of theater, this presentation turned a hotel room into a stage and employed props, costumes, and a script. Today, when it is possible to read all of Wilde's interviews in one sitting, it's fascinating to see how closely he kept to his chosen text, to marvel at the effort he committed to arranging the proper setting for his arias on Art, the Artist, and (most of all) Himself, and to see the faithfulness with which he followed his own stage directions—despite the tiring rail journeys he had to endure between lecture stops. He was able to do this day after day without losing focus because he was a natural performer who enjoyed putting on a show. "I love acting," he would later write. "It's so much more real than life."

Few actors had ever undertaken such a long and arduous tour. No one, in America or anywhere else, was interviewed more often in 1882 than Oscar Wilde, who was questioned by more than a hundred reporters in fewer than three hundred days. Though he had never been interviewed before, he had the foresight to implement the rule that aspiring celebrities have adhered to ever since in interviews, no matter what questions they've been asked: "The Subject Is Always You." And as he demonstrated to all future fame-seekers, that subject can be communicated visually as well as verbally.

Reporters sent to interview Wilde would find him in his temporary lodgings, the finest available in their city, where he made it his business to embody—not just in dress, but in speech patterns and in impossible-to-miss mannerisms—a species of humanity rarely seen in the United States in 1882. When the journalist arrived, Wilde would nearly always be lounging on a sofa, reading a book of poetry (usually, but not always, his own), near a table upon which the remnants of a recently partaken multicourse meal were in evidence on fine china, next to a mostly empty decanter of claret, a porcelain teapot (preferably blue) with matching cups, and an ashtray filled with extinguished cigarettes and at least one cigar. There would be a collection of party invitations and letters from abroad in proximity, as well as a vase filled with fresh flowers—lilies and sunflowers, if available—overlooking several fountain pens, a stack of writing paper, and a pile of leather-bound books, most of them written by famous Britons whose names—Ruskin, Pater, Swinburne, et al.—Wilde would soon drop and, in most cases, claim as close friends. Upon the back of the sofa where he was musing and digesting, the journalists would see animal skins, embroidered fabrics, and other decorative items Wilde had brought with him from his flat in London, so that he could beautify his temporary surroundings in America and make them more palatable to his elevated European sensibility.

After Wilde's valet, reading from the reporter's business card, introduced the journalist by name, Wilde would rise out of his aesthetic reverie and onto his elegantly shod feet (he favored patent-leather pumps even when not on stage, but he sometimes put on a pair of velvet slippers), shake the interviewer's hand, and offer him a seat. As the journalist followed his directions, Wilde would remain standing in front of him for a moment, presenting his visitor with a full-length view of his *ensemble*. Years later, when writing of Jesus, Wilde would say that "an idea is of no value till it becomes incarnate and is made an image." He believed the same was true of himself. This is how a reporter for the *Chicago Inter-Ocean* described what he encountered in Wilde's suite at the Grand Pacific Hotel:

> The aesthetic young man had been reclining in a very utter and languid attitude upon a sofa which was drawn up before the blazing grate, and the sofa was covered with a fine wolf-skin robe and a tiger skin, while where his head had lain was a silk shawl of the color of old gold and soft as the sigh of a maiden. [Upon standing,] he was found to be a tall and strongly-built young, [but] not too strong, not enough to be gross in flesh or muscle. His long hair, which curls up on the ends, was parted in the middle and fell to his shoulders. . . . The ears are entirely concealed by these thick locks, which he ever and anon brushes back carelessly, yet with a lingering and caressing notion. Mr. Wilde was dressed in a coat of black velvet, scarlet necktie, and handkerchief of the same color protruding from the pocket, light pantaloons, slippers and red socks. He was smoking a cigar, and handled it with the grace which only comes from long practice.

A reporter from the *Cincinnati Gazette* found his interview subject in a "coat and natty vest of cobwebby grey velvet hue, with a cold gravy bloom; his trousers were light in color and loose and limp in make. His shoes were of patent leather, with buff gaiters, and his low-cut Byronic collar was encircled by a silk cravat that was tied in a sailor knot, and was between Dunducketty grey and a dull pink in color. In the left lapel of his coat was a beautiful rosebud, and he held another in his left hand, whose delicate exhalations he ever and anon inhaled with evident rapture." A writer for the *Cleveland Leader* shook Wilde's hand after the aesthete rose from a "tete-d'tete covered with a silk shawl of an old gold tint, and over this a bear skin. A small table had been brought out into the center of the room, and on this rested a small teapot, one of the impossible blue kind, in which the ladies of two centuries ago delighted. Mr. Wilde wore a tightly fitting sack coat of brown velvet, vest of the same material, and loose trousers of subdued tint but of very self-assertive cut. His throat was encircled by a pale green tie, and the corner of a handkerchief to match stood out in relief against the brown of the coat."**

In these elaborate, if (so far) silent, performances, the star of London's dinner-party circuit was inhabiting the character he had come to America to play. Not Bunthorne. Oscar Wilde. His flamboyant style of dress, Wilde understood, would be his visual signature as he crossed the country. Happily noticing how he was being noticed for his sartorial choices, he wrote a letter to the Carte agency in New York requesting bespoke reinforcements so that he could continue to visually express his subject matter without interruptions caused by such mundane matters as laundering. "Will you kindly go to a good costumier (theatrical) for me [in Manhattan] and get them to make . . . two coats," he asked Colonel Morse.

> They should be beautiful; tight velvet doublet, with large flowered sleeves and little ruffs of cambric coming up from under the collar. I send you design and measurements. . . .** Any good costumier would know what I want. . . . Also get me two pair of grey silk stockings to suit grey mouse-coloured velvet. The sleeves are to be flowered—if not velvet then plush—stamped with large pattern. They will excite a great sensation.

He was speaking from experience—and, to borrow another phrase from today, with the confidence of a successful brand manager.

---

* It's interesting to note how often Wilde's American interviewers disagreed on small (and not so small) details. To some reporters, the animal skins Wilde brought with him to his hotel suites were from a wolf or a tiger, to others from a bear or a sheep. Some described his eyes as blue; others as gray (or grey). Most said that he was more than six feet tall; others, incomprehensibly, that he was barely over five feet.

** Waist: 38 ½ inches; breeches: 30 inches to the top of the knee; sleeve: 32 inches; neck: 17 inches

When questioned by reporters, however, Wilde explained his sensation-making fashion choices not in marketing or sartorial terms, but with words more suited to moral philosophy. When the *Salt Lake Herald* asked him why he dressed the way he did, he said, "[It] is based on a principle, for poets have principles, and that is that one should do as one preaches. . . . [That is why] my coat is pearl gray velvet and my necktie Venetian green." He was preaching the gospel of aestheticism, even before he opened his mouth.

THIS IS NOT to suggest that Wilde wasn't eager to open his mouth. What is striking about his hotel-room soliloquies is how often he expressed of his aesthetic principles in the first person. For a man who claimed that his mission in America was to extol the aesthetic movement as a sweeping historical force for the advancement of all of human civilization, Wilde had a persistent habit of framing that movement as a personal journey.

His first task was to define that movement to journalists who had little knowledge of it—and, in many instances, even less interest. The worldview he had come to champion, Wilde told them, was committed to exalting the power of art and beauty to transform and elevate the human experience by being beautiful—but not, he insisted, by teaching any moral lessons. The movement sought to beautify the homes not just of the wealthy, but of everyone, by encouraging artistic values in the production of furniture, textiles, lamps, clothing, books, and so on. "I hope that the masses will come to be the creators in art," he told the *Sacramento Record-Union*. "[I hope] that art will some time cease to be simply the accomplishment and luxury of the rich, but the possession, as it is the rightful heritage of all, of poor and rich alike."

This democratic urge was mitigated, however, by a cultish—some might say snobbish—aspect. The appreciation of beauty was not something that could be learned in a classroom or even in a lecture hall, Wilde and his fellow aesthetes believed. It had to be revealed to a person by beauty itself, which could only happen to the person sensitive enough to appreciate it. Elaborating on that contradiction—art by and for the masses versus art by and for the connoisseurs—was pleasant duty for Wilde, because it enabled him to talk about himself. And even better, to have his thoughts recorded in the press, an ego-inflating situation he made sure to boast about in a letter to his friend and occasional rival within the "smart set" in London, James Whistler. "My dear Jimmy, They are considering me *seriously*," Wilde wrote from America to the American ex-pat painting and socializing in England. "What would you do if it happened to you?"

And reporters *were* listening, which only encouraged Wilde to talk at greater length about himself, occasionally following connections that were apparent only to him. "My philosophy . . . is the appreciation of the beautiful," he told the *Philadelphia Inquirer*. "I have always loved nature in its wild, magnificent beauty. When I can meet her in the wilderness amid towering cliffs and hanging cataracts, then I love her and become her slave. I have since I can remember been impressed by the intensity of nature; but, alas, for the past few years I have been unable to gratify my longing. I have been a London man and have been surrounded by naught but smoke and fog. It is in the midst of the city life that I first saw all the follies of the present society and the grotesqueness of modern customs. I admire the Middle Ages, because their social life was natural and unharassed by petty rules." (One can only imagine what a tenth-century serf would have made of that comment.) "I approve of the medieval costumes, because they are graceful and because they are beautiful. . . . I love flowers, as every human should love them. I enjoy their perfume and admire their beauty. . . . The surroundings of art enhance one's existence and make life worth living. . . . The cultivation of aestheticism is a grand idea, and I am ready to sacrifice my life, enmity, and amity in its successful development." Three months and three thousand miles later, Wilde's fondness for long, first-person monologues would be as pronounced as ever. At least so reported a journalist for the *San Francisco Examiner*, who described Wilde's conversational style in his suite at the Palace Hotel as "animated," "youthful," and "quite enthusiastic"—"especially about himself."

Wilde told the *New York Tribune* that "a boy could become learned in any scientific subject by the study of books; the knowledge of the beautiful is personal and can only be acquired by one's own eyes and ears." As it had been by him, which prompted yet another oft-delivered, self-referential monologue. "In 1873 [I] entered Magdalen College," Wilde told the *New York World*, where he lived, as he described it to the *Tribune*, in a "wonderful set of old wainscoted rooms overlooking the [Cherwell] river, near a graceful bridge which," he added with displeasure, "they are now pulling down for the sake of a tramway." In this environment of serene scholarship and graceful architecture, "the theory of the effect of beautiful associations began to manifest itself to my mind. [Oxford] was by far the most beautiful [town] that I had ever been in and I experienced its effect on myself. . . . In 1876 I visited Italy and went through all the churches there, drinking in everything of the beautiful in art, and its whole splendor was revealed to me by association as it never could have been from any mere description."

After Italy the nexus between Wilde's aesthetic epiphanies and his narcissistic career goals took palpable shape. "I came back to Oxford more confirmed than ever in the correctness of my theories, and it was then that I began to write my poetry and gradually gathered around me a group of young men; an aesthetic clique if you will," he told the *World*. "We were very enthusiastic young men, and, insensibly, as it were, we became extravagant in our expressions as compared with the common manner of converse. . . . [Soon] rumors began to reach us that this movement of ours, for such it might now be called, had reached London," where, after Wilde rented an apartment there in 1879, he "preached [his] theories in every salon" in that city. It wasn't very long, Wilde told the *World*, before "Du Maurier's first caricature" was published in *Punch*, and the nattily dressed, Dublin-born aesthete found, "very much to [his] astonishment," that he was "becoming famous."

Astonishment? Not likely, considering how hard he had worked to be noticed. Delight? Absolutely.

Wilde's claim that he was the irresistibly charismatic leader of an aesthetic clique in Britain was, to say the least, exaggerated. Some might even call it a lie—not that Wilde would have objected to that term. His lecture tour of America, as he saw it, was an ongoing piece of theater—what we today would call performance art. Its success as a work of art wasn't predicated on truth-telling. Far from it. In fact, the relationship between art and accuracy was a subject about which Wilde was convinced Americans needed to be enlightened, for the sake of their culture. "Facts . . . are usurping the domain of Fancy, and have invaded the kingdom of Romance," he would later write. "The crude commercialization of America, its materializing spirit, its indifference to the poetical side of things, and its lack of imagination and of high unattainable ideals, are entirely due to that country having adopted for its national hero a man who, according to his own confession, was incapable of telling a lie, and it is not too much to say that the story of George Washington and the cherry-tree has done more harm, and in a shorter space of time, than any other moral tale in the whole of literature."

Some of that passage, which appeared seven years after Wilde returned to Britain in the essay he titled "The Decay of Lying," clearly originated in "the domain of Fancy" (and self-servingly so, considering the commercial nature of Wilde's lecture tour of America). Perhaps, as a classics scholar, Wilde, in exaggerating his "leadership" status among English aesthetes, was following the lead of someone he had studied in the classroom at Oxford: Julius Caesar, who wrote (ca. 50 B.C.E.) what many now consider to be the world's first campaign autobiography, *The Gallic Wars*, chronicling—and, some would say, embellishing—Caesar's military exploits in Gaul so that the citizens of Rome would demand that he be their head of state.

In exaggerating his own achievements, Wilde knew precisely—and precociously—what he was doing. Decades before the birth of the

modern public relations industry, a twentieth-century invention pioneered by Ivy Ledbetter Lee (the image counselor who redefined the
robber baron John D. Rockefeller in the press as a friend of the poor)
and Edward Bernays (the nephew of Sigmund Freud who taught the
American presidents Woodrow Wilson and Calvin Coolidge how to
"engineer public consent" for their policies), Wilde understood that
perception is reality, and that image trumps the truth. He made this
awareness clear in his reply to an American reporter who asked him if,
as the British press repeatedly claimed—and as Arthur Sullivan had
memorably written in *Patience*—Wilde ever really "walked down Piccadilly with a poppy or a lily in his medieval hand." "To have done it
was nothing," Wilde said in January 1882. "But to make people *think*
one had done it was a triumph."

Which brings us to probably the most famous witticism arising
from Wilde's American tour: his allegedly telling the U.S. customs
agent in New York that he had nothing to declare but his genius.
What makes the quip work, beyond its obvious success as a pun, is
how cleverly it invokes the notion that genius, usually understood as
an intangible (and interior) quality, in Wilde's case was an object he
carried with him like luggage, a genius so great that he couldn't cross
international borders without calling attention to it. The quip also
suggests a brilliant grasp of one of America's core beliefs: the idea that
America is a place, maybe the only place, where one can invent or
reinvent oneself without the limitations imposed by a class system, just
as the American icon Ben Franklin, a great self-publicist in his own
right, did when he arrived in Philadelphia more than a century earlier—by his own reckoning, penniless and possessing only his wit, his
savvy, and his tireless determination to succeed.

But according to John Cooper, the independent Wilde expert who
runs the "Oscar Wilde in America" website and leads an informative
walking tour of "Oscar Wilde's New York," there is no evidence that
Wilde ever declared his genius to that customs agent. Cooper found no
mention of the quote in any New York newspaper in 1882—and the

press was there to meet Wilde—or in any of Wilde's letters. After making his search, Cooper was able to correct *The Oxford Dictionary of Quotations*, which had previously identified the earliest source of the quotation as *Oscar Wilde: His Life and Confessions*, written by Wilde's friend Frank Harris, and published in 1916. As Cooper has demonstrated, the "nothing to declare" quip first appeared in 1914 in *Oscar Wilde: A Critical Study* by Arthur Ransome, a man who never met Wilde. Ransome was aided in his book project by Robert Ross, who was an intimate of Wilde's, but not until several years after Wilde's American tour. It is possible Ross passed on to Ransome something Wilde had told him he had said—or *wished* he had said. As Cooper writes, "Much history, especially quotation, is apocryphal: too good not to have been said. . . . It would not be unlike Wilde to revel in the public's belief of a rumor about himself." But "lacking evidence, it is not possible to be definitive about whether the remark is genuine. [The] reasonable inference is towards doubt."

The final thought on Wilde's supposed waterfront quip—taking some authorial license—properly belongs to Wilde, who surely would have been tickled by the quip's immortality and especially his ownership of it: "To have [said] it was nothing. But to make people *think* one had [said] it . . ."

IT WASN'T LONG, however, before Wilde began to notice quotes attributed to him he was certain he had *not* said. At least, not in America in 1882. Sometimes he was amused. When a reporter from Rochester asked him if it was true that, after a woman in Washington said to him, "and so this is Oscar Wilde: but where is your lily?" Wilde had replied: "At home, madam, where you left your good manners." The exchange was "absolutely true," Wilde told the man from the *Rochester Democrat and Chronicle*, "with the exception that it happened in London and that the lady was a duchess." The same journalist also wondered if, after Wilde supposedly complained that there were no quaint ruins or curiosities in America, an American lady had really said: "Time will remedy the one, and as for curiosities, we import them." "Oh, yes," Wilde replied, "that it is an excellent story, [but] it was first told of Charles Dickens when he visited this country [in 1842]. I find every community has its lady who is remarkably bright in her repartee and she is always credited with the latest *bon mot* making the rounds. Those two stories are following me all over [America,] localized in almost every city."

When more serious errors were made, especially those that impugned his motives for coming to the States, Wilde tried to overlook them—at first. By doing so, he was following the advice of a highly accomplished, exceptionally well-dressed man he had met at several parties in London, the former prime minister Benjamin Disraeli, recently elevated by Queen Victoria to the House of Lords as Lord Beaconsfield, who had famously said of political criticism: "Never complain and never explain." Wilde thought so highly of Disraeli as a novelist—a career in which he had almost as much success as he did in politics—that Wilde brought several of Disraeli's novels with him to America. (He also brought novels, in the original French, by Balzac and Gautier.) It seems Wilde, consciously or not, tried to follow Disraeli's advice about critics when his kerfuffle with the lecturer Archibald Forbes reached its peak in late January, when Wilde felt he was consistently mistreated by the press, a situation that became almost unbearable when the *Washington Post* joined the discussion by mocking Wilde in a cartoon that declared him more simian than human.

This prompted the Carte office in New York to write a letter to the *Post* complaining that it had crossed the line. When Wilde saw that letter, he wrote to Colonel Morse to inform him of his displeasure. "I regard all caricature and satire as absolutely beneath notice. You, without consulting me, wrote a letter in which . . . you said [the cartoon] was an insult. . . . I regret that you took any notice." Not long afterward, Wilde told the *Boston Herald* he was ignoring the many falsehoods written about him—among them, that he was a charlatan and a plagiarist whose only knowledge of aestheticism came from others—as all great men must. "An artist should not listen to, nor heed, ridicule and abuse. . . . Shelley was abused, but he did not heed it."*

But Wilde, who was certainly flattering himself by comparing his situation to Shelley's, soon felt compelled by his vanity to complain *and* explain. He told the *St. Louis Republican* that "in New York they wrote entirely fictitious interviews with me after having called on me. I think that might at least have spared me the trouble of talking to them." He was especially piqued when reporters referred to aestheticism as a passing fashion. "Do *not* call it a craze," he told a reporter from the *Dayton Daily Democrat*, who just had done so. "You Americans have such a way of treating serious things as a joke. And yet you are not a joyous people. . . . I do not see happy men and women [around me.] Everybody has a troubled anxious look [because] everybody is pushing forward in some business project. [They] do not appreciate art, so they call it a craze."

Rather than spreading a fad, Wilde saw himself as fulfilling a priestly calling. "The best service of god is found in the worship of all that is beautiful," he told the *Sacramento Record-Union*. "Such a worshiper can do no wrong willfully." The press in America has "treated me outrageously," he said to the *Rochester Democrat and Chronicle*. "But I am not the one who is injured. It is the public. By such ridiculous attacks" and errors "the people are taught to mock what they should reverence." Apparently, preaching the gospel of aestheticism had transformed Wilde—at least in his own eyes—into a holy man. And like many holy men, he often found his message misunderstood. "When I read the papers and see what they say about me, I feel as if I [am] traveling about in a country of barbarians," he told the *Rocky Mountain*

---

* Shelley's advocacy of atheism and free love, his scorn for monarchy and inherited wealth, and his explorations of incest and parricide in several of his literary works made him extremely controversial during his lifetime (1992–1822).

News. "If you expect English gentlemen to come to your country, especially gentlemen of letters and art, you must improve the character of your journalism," he told the *New York Herald*. But Wilde's pique only enhanced his feelings of self-worth. "If I could live 10,000 years—and my poems may get me something like immortality—I might find time to write letters to editors and correct" all the errors that had been written about him, the *Herald* quoted him as saying.

A charge often made against Wilde—that he had come to America to expand not so much the aesthetic consciousness of Americans as the thickness of his billfold—was one he tried to ignore, but couldn't. Wilde was appalled by the eagerness of reporters to ask him about his financial arrangements, a line of questioning he considered rude, so he often responded with sarcasm. "I am extremely impressed by the entire disregard of Americans for money-making," he told the *Chicago Inter-Ocean*, whose representative admitted to dropping his pencil upon hearing those words. American journalists "think it is a strange and awful thing that I should want to make a few dollars by lecturing," Wilde continued. "Why, money-making is necessary for art. Money builds cities and makes them healthful. Money buys art and furnishes it an incentive. Is it strange that I should want to make money? And yet these newspapers cry out that I am making money!"

He told the *Salt Lake Herald*: "I am quite conscious that much of what I say may be annoying, but after all I came to America to say it, and so long as an audience with such breeding allow me to strut my brief hour upon the stage, I should be singularly stupid not to take advantage of the opportunities given me." The "strut my brief hour upon the stage" line was inspired by a passage from *Macbeth*. It's fascinating to note, however, that Wilde omitted the next line from Shakespeare's tragedy: "It is a tale told by an idiot, full of sound and fury, and signifying nothing."

Wilde wrote to friends, new and old, about his often frustrating encounters with the American press. In a letter to Joaquin Miller, a poet from California whom Wilde had dined with in New York, he described some of his interviewers as "Narcissuses of imbecility." He was thanking Miller for coming to his defense in a letter published in the *New York World*. It's not surprising the two men would see eye to eye on such matters. Miller (born Cincinnatus Hiner Miller) was every bit the self-created, self-publicizing media "star" that Wilde was hoping to become in America. Calling himself the "Byron of the Rockies," Miller declaimed his poetry—"Songs of the Sierras"—in a white buckskin suit, cowboy boots, and spurs, with an enormous sombrero on his head and a bearskin on his shoulder. He claimed—sometimes accurately—to have been a Pony Express rider, a gold rusher, an Indian fighter, a judge, a newspaper editor, and a convicted horse thief. Once, while touring England, Miller showed up at a dinner at the exclusive Whitefriars Club in London with a pair of bowie knives dangling from his hips. When that wasn't enough to make him the center of attention, he plunged his hand into a nearby fish tank, extracted a tropical fish, and quickly swallowed it, after which he announced: "A wonderful appetizer!" Audiences (and the press) couldn't get enough of him.

Wilde expanded on his "Narcissus of imbecility" theme in a letter to his fellow classics graduate from Oxford, the Honorable George Curzon, then serving the British government in India, where he would eventually become Viceroy. Wilde signed his letter, "Yours (from Boeotia)," a reference to a province of ancient Greece that was legendary for the stupidity of its inhabitants. It should come as no surprise, then, that years later, safely ensconced back in Britain, Wilde aimed one of his most famous epigrams at modern journalism: "In the old days men had the rack, now they have the Press."

Yet Wilde never stopped sitting for interviews as he traveled across America in 1882 and, as far as we know, never refused an interview request, with one possible exception. He described the incident to a reporter for the *St. Louis Dispatch*: "I was dressing in Washington for a dinner party when a card was brought to me . . . detail[ing] how many western newspapers the owner was a correspondent for. I think there were eleven in all. I was slightly flurried, as you may suppose. I said [to myself], 'Now here is the man who moulds the thoughts of the West; I must be on my best behavior.'" Moments later, "in walked a boy, positively not more than sixteen. 'Have you been to school?' I asked. The juvenile interviewer said he had. 'Have you learned French?' No, he had not. I told him if he wished to be a journalist he ought to study French, [I] gave him an orange and dismissed him. What he did with the orange afterward I don't know, but he seemed very much pleased to get it."

But ever mindful of the importance of press attention, Wilde often stooped to flatter his inquisitors, young or old. He told the *Cincinnati Enquirer* that "some of the brightest hours I have passed in this country have been with the gentlemen of the press who have interviewed me, and I have found them among the most intelligent men I have met here." He seconded this view to the *St. Louis Globe-Democrat*: "I have met [reporters who] . . . have talked with me of art and literature, and understood the subjects." It is unlikely, however, that Wilde would have repeated that compliment about the reporter who interviewed him for the *St. Louis Republican*, especially not after the journalist referred to Walt Whitman's *Leaves of Grass* as *Blades of Grass*.

The intelligence of journalists was not the only subject Wilde contradicted himself about while speaking with his interviewers. He told several of them that William Dean Howells and Henry James were the best writers America had produced, others that it was Walt Whitman and Ralph Waldo Emerson, others that it was Nathaniel Hawthorne, and still others that it was Edgar Allan Poe. He told the *Charleston News and Courier* that "upon the whole I'd rather travel through a country rapidly," yet he insisted to the *Boston Herald* that "no one sees a country by passing through it [quickly] by railway. The true way to see a country is to ride through it [slowly on horseback]. . . . I rode through Greece once, through the Peloponnesus, saw every little hill and tree, and knew it all." (This was, to say the least, an exaggeration.) Asked about the American national character, Wilde answered that, in eastern cities such as New York and Boston, he had trouble detecting one. "The greatest fault I have [found] with you Americans is that you are not American enough. You are all too cosmopolitan," he said, "a feeble reflection of Europe." Yet, when asked on another occasion about the places he had most enjoyed in America, he said: "The best cities have a very high cosmopolitanism."

In expressing such contradictory views, Wilde was claiming for himself the capacity for intellectual vastness that another poet had famously claimed, a poet with a genius for self-promotion that Wilde hoped to replicate. "Do I contradict myself? Very well then. . . . I contradict myself; I am large. . . . I contain multitudes," Walt Whitman wrote in "Song of Myself." In writing those signature verses, Whitman was declaring his own genius. Though Wilde's interviews hardly count as poetry, he was singing the same song.

Some reporters liked what they were hearing. "[Wilde] is scholarly, studiedly polite, a gentleman, shrewd, fearless, observant, self-possessed and of poetic temperament," a journalist for the *Sacramento Record-Union* wrote of him. "He has been considerably misrepresented and unduly ridiculed [in this country]. . . . He is, however, ludicrously odd to the American eye in personal appearance; is eccentric (or affected) in this regard, and lacks the manifestations of manliness in his countenance, and frequently in his manner. If he [is] more an object of curiosity than respect to Californians, it [is] due to the latter causes." Lilian Whiting, the Boston-based poet, journalist, and author of self-help books who spoke to Wilde in her home city for the *Chicago Inter-Ocean*, was respectful of her interview subject—up to a point. "The fact is [Wilde] has been greatly misrepresented, his individualities caricatured, his tastes exaggerated, his appearance burlesqued," she wrote. "[He] has more than the average intelligence, is a scholarly and sufficiently well-appearing young man, whose intellectual method is strongly flavored with the ideas of Ruskin, Swinburne, Morris [and] Rossetti. . . . He is not great enough to merit so much attention, [but] he is not necessarily an object of ridicule."

To know whether Wilde read these interviews, we have to rely on the writers of the articles, who were not reliable sources. According to the *Sacramento Record-Union*, Wilde said he rarely read them and, on the few occasions he did, quickly put them out of his mind, a statement that seems hard to believe, considering how often he complained about them. "I think nothing of [them]," he told the *Record-Union*. "The voice of folly is always shrill and very loud, but it passes away. Of one thing I am convinced, and that is: the fool has no influence." The *Rochester Democrat and Chronicle* quoted him as saying that he completely ignored his published interviews. "What possible difference can it make to me what the *New York Herald* says? You go and look at the statue of Venus de Medici and you know that it is an exquisitely beautiful creation. Would it change your opinion in the least if all the newspapers in the land should pronounce it a wretched caricature?" Yet the *St. Louis Post-Dispatch* insisted that Wilde said to its reporter: "Oh, yes, I read every line" of what is written about him. "When I come in at night, tired and weary, the reading of a good vigorous attack acts like dish of caviar."

WITH HINDSIGHT, IT'S tempting to see Wilde's experience with the press as a spooky portent not unlike his declaration to his friends at Oxford that "somehow or other [he would] be famous" and, "if not famous, notorious." While crossing America, Wilde at first charmed most of his interviewers, then disturbed them, a change that led to his being mocked, rejected, and, finally pilloried by them. This was a trajectory he would experience on a larger scale—and with far more disastrous consequences—just over a decade later in London.

But Wilde had no way of seeing the larger pattern or knowing it would be a microcosm of his career. He saw his encounters with American journalists as a necessary, if often exasperating, step toward accomplishing his personal and professional goals. To be sure, the audience for his self-referential and self-*rev*erential monologues had changed in his new venue, and hardly for the better. In England Wilde's audience had been artists, writers, and aristocrats at posh galas; in America it was a collection of mostly uneducated newspaper hacks and curious ticket buyers for his lectures, some of whom yawned in his face.

But so be it. No matter who was (or wasn't) listening, Wilde would push on with the business of Oscar Wilde, Inc. Long before the coining of the term *talking head*, Wilde understood that talking to the press was getting him closer to his other great goal: money. By mid-June, after nearly fifty interviews were published in American newspapers, an accountant for the Carte organization calculated the gate receipts for Wilde's lecture tour so far at $18,215.69. After a little more than $7,000 in expenses was deducted from that gross, Wilde was issued a check for his half-share of the net proceeds: $5,605, a sum equal to approximately $129,000 today. And there would be more to come, from the nearly fifty lectures he was yet to give.

Sure, the act of being interviewed was often an ordeal that brought him into contact with dullards who misrepresented his views. But these experiences only made Wilde more determined. He could see foresee his ultimate success—and the role of the press in making it happen. Several weeks before he received his first payment from the Carte office, Wilde said something to a reporter for the *Omaha Weekly Herald* that suggests he could envision the benefits that were coming his way, and that money was only part of it:

"I'm a very ambitious young man," he said. "I want to do everything in the world. I cannot conceive of anything that I do not want to do. I want to write a great deal more poetry. I want to study painting more than I've been able to. I want to write a great many more plays, and I want to make this artistic movement [I am leading] the basis for a new civilization." Though the reporter probably didn't know it, Wilde was echoing a comment he had made several weeks earlier in Boston. "The supreme object in life is to live. Few people live. It is true life only to realize one's own perfection, to make one's every dream a reality. Even this is possible."

Especially if one makes wise use of the press. Wilde's nonstop encounters with American journalists made him sense that America would be the Republic of Celebrity. He drew the first map of this heretofore unexplored territory in 1882, charting his pilgrim's progress from one hotel suite to another, as he talked his way to stardom.

Wilde's mother, Lady Jane Francesca Agnes Wilde, a poet, a fervent supporter of Irish independence, and the person who taught Wilde the importance of creating a public persona. (BETTMANN/CORBIS)

Wilde's father, Sir William Robert Wills Wilde, in court dress. Sir William was an accomplished surgeon with a notorious private life. (BRIDGEMAN ART LIBRARY)

Wilde's wife, the former Constance Mary Lloyd, with their son Cyril, in 1889. The Wildes were married in 1884. She took the name Holland after Wilde was convicted of "gross indecency." (RDA/GETTY IMAGES)

Wilde as an undergraduate at Oxford's Magdalen College, in 1876. (HILLS & SAUNDERS/NYPL)

Wilde (in second row, wearing a dark suit and bowler hat) with several of his Magdalen College classmates, 1876. (LIBRARY OF CONGRESS)

Rev. John Pentland Mahaffy, Wilde's
classics tutor at Trinity College, Dublin,
and the man who taught Wilde the social
importance of witty conversation.
(DOUGLAS MCCARTHY/MARY EVANS PICTURE LIBRARY)

Richard D'Oyly Carte, the English
theatrical impresario who sent Wilde to
America. (HULTON ARCHIVE/GETTY IMAGES)

Napoleon Sarony, the portrait
photographer Wilde sat for in New York,
in January 1882. (LIBRARY OF CONGRESS)

Portrait number 15 from the session with Sarony. The book in Wilde's hand is his first collection of poems, published in 1881. (LIBRARY OF CONGRESS)

Portrait number 25 (of 27) from the session with Sarony, January 1882. (LIBRARY OF CONGRESS)

A portrait of Wilde made in 1883, after he dropped the curtain on "the Oscar of the First Period." (NATIONAL PORTRAIT GALLERY)

This advertisement, which used Sarony's portrait of Wilde without his permission, led to the Supreme Court case establishing copyright protection for photographers. (LIBRARY OF CONGRESS)

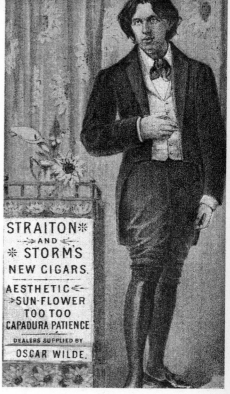

Wilde's image was used to sell products ranging from cigars to bust enhancers while he was in America.
(BRITISH LIBRARY; LIBRARY OF CONGRESS)

Poster for the original English production of Gilbert & Sullivan's *Patience*, 1881. (CREDIT TK)

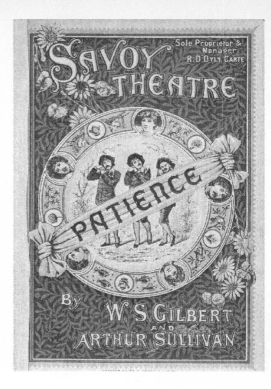

J. H. Ryley, as Bunthorne, in the authorized American version of *Patience* seen by Wilde in New York.

An 1881 drawing by Edward Linley
Sambourne in *Punch*, the English
humor magazine, depicts Wilde as
a sunflower. (BRIDGEMAN ART LIBRARY)

Wilde depicted as an aesthetic monkey on
the cover of *Harper's Weekly*, three weeks
after his arrival in America. (WISCONSIN

HISTORICAL SOCIETY)

Walt Whitman (who spent an afternoon with Wilde in Camden, New Jersey) in his favorite portrait. The "butterfly" on his finger was made of cardboard. (LIBRARY OF CONGRESS)

Robert Ross (said to be Wilde's first male lover) and Reginald Turner, ca. 1895. Ross and Turner were with Wilde when he died in 1900. (MARY EVANS PICTURE LIBRARY)

The actress Sarah Bernhardt, Wilde's great friend and mentor in self-promotion, photographed by Sarony in 1880. (LIBRARY OF CONGRESS)

John Douglas, the 9th Marquess of Queensberry. The Marquess, Lord Alfred Douglas's father, left an insulting card for Wilde at the Albemarle Club in February 1895. Wilde then sued him for libel.

Wilde and Lord Alfred Bruce (Bosie) Douglas, photographed in 1894, a year before their friendship led to three trials.

The *Illustrated Police News* (May 4, 1895) covers the close of Wilde's first trial at Old Bailey as a defendant, which ended in a hung jury. (BRITISH LIBRARY)

A drawing in *Frank Leslie's Illustrated Newspaper* (August 12, 1882) shows Wilde, between speaking engagements, in swimwear in Long Beach, New York. (CREDIT TK)

Wilde charming members of New York society at a party held in his honor in January 1882, as depicted in *Frank Leslie's Illustrated Newspaper* (LIBRARY OF CONGRESS)

Frank Leslie's Illustrated Newspaper repeats several comments attributed to Wilde during his stay in New York. (LIBRARY OF CONGRESS)

The author Henry James, who called Wilde a "tenth-rate cad" and an "unclean beast" after meeting him in Washington. (LIBRARY OF CONGRESS)

The poet Henry Wadsworth Longfellow, who told Wilde an amusing story about Queen Victoria at his home in Cambridge, Massachusetts.
(LIBRARY OF CONGRESS)

OSCAR WILDE ON THE PLATFORM.
THE FAMOUS AESTHETE POSING AND "MASHING" ON HIS SHAPE,
AT CHICKERING HALL, NEW YORK CITY.

A drawing in [journal TK] of Wilde presenting his first American lecture, at Chickering Hall, in New York, on January 9, 1882. (CREDIT TK)

The cover page of the sheet music for "Oscar Dear!" a song written about (and during) Wilde's American tour by M. H. Rosenfeld.

The actress Lillie Langtry, Wilde's sometime protégé, and the longtime mistress of the Prince of Wales. Wilde purchased this portrait, painted by Edward Poynter, in 1879. (JERSEY HERITAGE TRUST)

A drawing in the Natioanl Police Gazette of Wilde by his friend Sir Henry Maximillian (Max) Beerbohm, who wrote of Wilde: "Beauty had existed long before 1880, [but it] was Mr. Oscar Wilde who managed her *début*." (NATIONAL PORTRAIT GALLERY)

A snapshot of Wilde, probably taken by Lord Alfred Douglas in 1900, in Paris, a few months before Wilde's death.

Sir Edward Carson, a former schoolmate of Wilde's in Ireland and later the barrister who cross-examined him on the subtext of *The Picture of Dorian Gray*.
(LIBRARY OF CONGRESS)

Wilde's emergence as the aesthetic apostle to England's social elite was immortalized, as it was happening, in *A Private View at the Royal Academy, 1881*, painted by William Powell Frith. (CREDIT TK)

CHAPTER SIX

Promote Is Just Another Word for Provoke

Wilde's encounters with the press taught him a lot about how to be a celebrity, but there were other lessons he had to teach himself. One of the most important of these experiences had occurred on January 31, at the Music Hall in Boston. That was the night Wilde successfully mocked those who had come to mock *him*: the smug, lilies-and-sunflowers-carrying Harvard students who had danced down the auditorium's main aisle in their black wigs, wide-floating neckties, and knee breeches from "ye olden time" just as Wilde—who had cleverly chosen not to wear breeches—was about to begin speaking. The best defense against ridicule, Wilde taught himself that evening, is to go on the offensive. Not to *be* offensive; his arch put-down of the college men, "Save me from my disciples!"—a remark quoted with delight in the press—was gentle enough. But that wouldn't have surprised anyone who knew him. The quips that made Wilde such a welcome party guest in London were never cruel. Rather than being offensive, Wilde would achieve his goals in America by being something similar yet different: he would be *provocative*, making statements designed to trigger a response from the press. He would issue these declarations as often as he could, in the presence of whoever was listening, on stage or off. What Wilde came to understand as he moved his tour westward from the East Coast, putting himself on display at one event after another, was the rule that countless other celebrities have followed ever since: *promote* is just another word for *provoke*.

He soon put this credo into practice. After delivering an afternoon lecture in Buffalo on February 8—his seventh talk in nine days— Wilde took a train twenty miles north to Niagara Falls, even though he had no speaking engagement scheduled there. He was met at the railway station by "hundreds of starry-eyed women" whose male consorts were perplexed that such a "manless man" could "catch the eyes of their ladies," the *Niagara Falls Gazette* reported. A carriage took Wilde to Prospect House, the hotel closest to the falls. Checking in with Wilde were his new road manager, J. S. Vale, hired by Colonel Morse to oversee this portion of Wilde's tour, and an aide named Stephen Davenport. (This latter name is now believed to be that of Wilde's Negro—to use the then-current term—valet, who was never identified in the numerous stories about Wilde in the press.) The hotel registry, which survived after Prospect House was demolished several years later, suggests that the vaunted American sense of humor was just as well developed—or ill developed—in 1882 as it is now. On the same registry page signed by Wilde was this name and address: "Santa Claus, Alaska."

In deciding to see the falls, Wilde was following in the touristic footsteps of two of Britain's most venerated literary men. Charles Dickens had come to Niagara in April 1842, writing in *American Notes* of his experience there: "I was in a manner stunned, and unable to comprehend the vastness of the scene. . . .

Then, when I felt how near to my Creator I was standing, the first effect, and the enduring one—instant and lasting—of the tremendous spectacle, was Peace. . . . Niagara was at once stamped upon my heart, an Image of Beauty; to remain there, changeless and indelible, . . . for ever.

Twenty years later Anthony Trollope wrote of his visits to the falls, in *North America*:

> Of all the sights on this earth of ours which tourists travel to see—at least of all those which I have seen—I am inclined to give the palm to the Falls of Niagara. In the catalogue of such sights I include all buildings, pictures, statues, and wonders of art made by men's hands, and also all beauties of nature prepared by the Creator for the delight of his creatures. This is a long list; but, as far as my taste and judgment go, it is justified. I know no other one thing so beautiful, so glorious, and so powerful.

But now, twenty years after Trollope (and forty after Dickens), Wilde told a reporter for the *Buffalo Express*, "I was disappointed in the outline [of the falls]. The design . . . was wanting in grandeur." He would amplify on this opinion later, to the *New York Tribune*: "They told me that so many millions of gallons of water tumbled over the Falls in a minute. I could see no beauty in that. There was bulk there, but no beauty. . . . Niagara Falls seems to me to simply be a vast, unnecessary amount of water going the wrong way and then falling over unnecessary rocks." Later still he would write: "Every American bride is taken there, and the sight of the stupendous waterfall must be one of the earliest, if not the keenest, disappointments in American married life."

These remarks were intended to be noticed, and they were. Editorials across America denounced Wilde and, when reports of the rumpus reached Britain, the humor magazine *Fun*—making its point in a poem it called "Disappointed Again"—reminded its readers that Wilde had been equally unimpressed by the Atlantic ocean when he sailed to America.

> *UNIVERSE, you are a failure,*
> *   You're one masterly mistake;*
> *Firmamental glories, pale your*

Fires, and played-out old earth, quake.
You may teem with hidden treasure,
But we won't be reconciled,
Since you seem to take a pleasure
In disappointing Wilde. . . .

Perhaps you'd best endeavor
To improve your old design,
Make catastrophes more clever,
And phenomena more fine.
Dye Niagara rose-madder
Have the wide Atlantic biled;
Then he may feel somewhat gladder,
The disappointed Wilde.

As the fallout from his comments on the falls reached critical mass, Wilde stepped off a train in Chicago, then America's fourth-largest city, on Friday, February 10, after an all-night ride from Buffalo. His acts of provocation in upstate New York had had their desired effect: every seat was sold for his lecture at Central Music Hall. Despite Wilde's success at the box office, it's clear not everyone in the city was delighted by his arrival. The *Chicago Daily News* claimed to be speaking for most Chicagoans when it declared: "We like to look at Western mules, but not aesthetic asses."

Wilde had a weekend to kill before his lecture on Monday night. He filled some of that time with room service (consuming at one solitary feast a meal of brook trout, quail, salad, steak, peas, a baked potato, champagne, and a tray of sweets) and by attending receptions thrown by Chicago's social elite (at one of them meeting the department store magnate Marshall Field, the man credited with devising the marketing slogan "The Customer Is Always Right," a view Wilde did not always subscribe to—unless *he* was the customer). He also took an extensive tour of the city that had rebuilt itself after the Great

Fire of 1871. He rode on Chicago's first cable car, which had opened for business on State Street only two weeks earlier. He visited the huge Interstate Industrial Exposition Building, where in 1880 the Republican Party had nominated James A. Garfield for president. He toured the exhibits at the Art Institute of Chicago. And he crossed the hand-cranked drawbridge across the Chicago River to view the 154-foot tall Water Tower on North Michigan Avenue, a building revered by virtually all Chicagoans as a symbol of the city's strength and perseverance, as it had been one of the only public buildings to survive the Great Fire. Wilde was quiet during this tour. But he would express his opinions of the city soon enough.

The first jolt experienced by the nearly two thousand Chicagoans who arrived at Central Music Hall on February 13 was created by the title of the lecture they found on their programs. The press had announced that Wilde would speak on "The English Renaissance," as he had in New York, Washington, Boston, and Buffalo, but Wilde—perhaps bored with the subject (or noticing how many of his listeners had been bored with the subject)—had written a new lecture, "The Decorative Arts," which he would give for the first time. Wilde carried his text in a leather case when he emerged from the wings, attired, one Chicago journalist wrote, "in a neat-fitting black dress coat, a low-cut white vest showing a broad expanse of immaculate shirt-front," and "black trunks, tied at the knee with a small black bow." Wilde's hair was "thrown back from his face," the reporter added, "making him seem less womanish than when he is seen in private. . . . His hands were gloved in white. . . . His attitude was easy."

For a moment, anyway. After acknowledging the applause that greeted his appearance on stage, Wilde quickly aimed a punning put-down at one of the city's most respected institutions, the *Chicago Tribune*, edited by the former mayor Joseph Medill. Wilde did so in response to the editorial published in that paper that compared the real-world achievements of John L. Sullivan, who had just won the bare-knuckles heavyweight championship from Paddy Ryan in an eighty-seven-round slugfest held near Gulfport, Mississippi, to the real-world "achievements" of Wilde. (The paper came out in favor of the cultural significance of Mr. Sullivan.) Wilde acknowledged the futility of criticizing the "wicked and imaginative editor" who had written that editorial, he told his listeners, because he knew the conscience of an editor is "purely decorative."

Then he moved on to the decorative arts that he had actually come to Chicago to praise and discuss, declaring that all great art is decorative, but that not all decoration is art. To illustrate that second point in a manner that had nothing to do with editors, Wilde disdained the then-current American fashion for painting sunsets and other natural phenomena on china. Artists "might paint sunsets, but let them not do so on dinner plates," he said. Such artists "have chosen the wrong material. . . . These [sunsets], if beautiful enough, should be painted [on canvas], handsomely framed and hung on walls. Soup should not be ladled from them." Wilde then went on to declare that virtually nothing made by a machine could qualify as beautiful; that art is the result less of exuberant feeling than of excellent technique; that art schools should be housed in elegant buildings; and that craftsmen are more likely to produce beautiful things when surrounded by beautiful things themselves. Even the *Tribune* acknowledged that these teachings were received by an "orderly and appreciative" crowd that presented "not the slightest suggestion of rowdyism or ridicule."

Until Wilde spoke of the city's most beloved building. Apparently, Wilde hadn't given the exterior of the Water Tower much of a look before entering it; once inside, he was introduced to the massive waterworks housed within, an imposing metallic behemoth of pumps, gears, and tubing that struck him as "grand." But upon exiting the waterworks, when he gazed back at the Water Tower, he was horrified and now shared his opinion with the audience at Central Music Hall: "I was shocked, when I came out of the place to see the Tower—a castellated monstrosity with pepper boxes stuck all over it. I was amazed that any people could so abuse Gothic art."

In saying this, Wilde insulted Chicagoans much the way he might have had he told Washingtonians that the White House more resembled an oversize bunkhouse than a residence fit for a president. There was a moment of shocked silence in the auditorium after Wilde's remark, then an audible wave of angry murmuring. But Wilde pressed on with his lecture, finishing roughly thirty minutes later on a conciliatory note. The spirit of commerce—a spirit certainly embraced by Chicago, the capital of America's food-processing industry—was not necessarily the enemy of great art, he said. After all, men of commerce had built the most artistic cities in the world. (He declined to mention that all those cities were in Europe.) But the damage was done. "I didn't expect to learn anything, and I haven't," one audience member was overheard to say, after Wilde left the stage to tepid applause.

More provocative remarks would be forthcoming from the lecturer the next day. Before checking out of his hotel, he met a reporter for the *Tribune*, who asked: "Mr. Wilde, are you aware that you wounded the pride of our citizens by referring slightingly to our Water Tower?" "I can't help that," Wilde said. "If you build a water tower, why don't you build it for water and make a simple structure of it, instead of building it like castle, where one expects to see knights peering out of every part?" Then Wilde upped the ante by criticizing the entirety of Chicago's rebuilding effort after the Great Fire. "It seems a shame to me that the citizens of Chicago have spent so much money on buildings with such an unsatisfactory result," he said. "Your city looks positively dreary." Wilde was holding true to his high standards of taste, as well as his commitment to publicizing his speaking tour. But it's also possible his crankiness was the result of travel fatigue. Though he had been in America for just five weeks, he had already covered a distance greater than that from the southern edge of England to the Scottish border in the north. (And he had never even traveled that far in Britain.)

The *Chicago Daily News* rose to the city's defense, declaring that Wilde had "failed to note the degree in which" those recently constructed buildings "responded to the fundamental conception of art—economy and fitness," proudly adding that such basic concepts had, in Chicago, resulted in a modern metropolis packed with "comfortable houses, and warm and easy toilets." The *Duluth Tribune*, based nearly five hundred miles away in Minnesota, had sent a stringer to observe Wilde's movements in Chicago. This anonymous journalist had a witty take on what he had witnessed: "Oscar's knee-breeches and flowing hair were novel sights, and the audience [at Central Music Hall] feasted their eyes upon them, but the lecturer didn't seem to 'take' half as well as a vaccination. Oscar, of course, spoke of the 'beautiful in art,' and the 'joy in art,' and it was all Greek to the men and women who listened to him. Had he spoke of the 'beautiful in grain' or the 'joy in pork,'" he would have been understood and appreciated."

Wilde told his British friends that he *was* appreciated. "My audiences are enormous," he told George Curzon. "In Chicago I lectured last Monday to 2,500 people! This is of course nothing to anyone who has spoken at the [Oxford] Union, but to me it was delightful—a great sympathetic electric people, who cheered and applauded and gave me a sense of serene power.... I lecture four times a week, and the people are delightful and lionise [me].... I travel in such state, for in a *free* country one cannot live without slaves, and I have slaves—black, yellow and white."

WILDE AND HIS "slaves" left Chicago by train on February 14, headed for Fort Wayne, Indiana. His exit from the shores of Lake Michigan could not have come sooner for the editorial page of the *Chicago Daily News*. "Go, Mr. Wilde," it harrumphed, "and may the sunflower wither at your gaze."

Wilde's white slave, Mr. Vale, arranged for several interviews once his master was settled in his suite at the Aveline House, the best hotel in Fort Wayne. Wilde's room-service order was a subject of some fascination to the journalists who came to see him there, one of them noting that, rather than the "odor of the lily or the bloom of the sunflower, the supposed aesthetical diet," Wilde feasted on a large steak smothered in mushrooms, a dozen oysters, fried potatoes, and a bottle of champagne. Once he was properly nourished, Wilde took another swipe at the city he had just left. "Commercially, [Chicago] is a wonderful city," he told the *Fort Wayne Gazette*, "but I was surprised by its poor architecture. There are no artistically beautiful buildings [there]."

Wilde's controversial appearance in Chicago had already been noticed by the *Gazette*, which published two "shorts" touting Wilde's lecture in Fort Wayne in the same CITY NEWS column before he arrived. "Oscar Wilde tomorrow night," said the lead item, and then—after brief reports on the arrest of two drunks, an accident that injured a six-year-old boy, and other bits of local interest—came this final item: "Lilies are in great demand [here]. So are sunflowers—Oscar Wilde—tomorrow night, you know." These reminders enticed enough locals to fill most of the seats on February 16 for Wilde's lecture at the Academy of Music, a structure originally built as an roller-skating rink. But the *Gazette* was not wholly impressed with the man who drew that crowd. "His lecture is certainly a . . . beautifully worded piece of literature," the paper wrote. "But as for Oscar Wilde he is not an elocutionist; his voice is as effeminate as a school girl's."

Wilde left the next morning, traveling to Detroit, where the city's most influential newspaper, the *Free Press*, had freely expressed its antipathy to Wilde in an editorial declaring that "those people who go to see him will have the 'satisfaction' of knowing that they are contributing money to a Barnumic show," an allusion to the American huckster who got rich exhibiting the "FeeJee Mermaid" and other frauds to the public. It seems Detroiters heeded this warning, as barely four hundred of them showed up at the city's Music Hall, a venue that could seat nearly eight times that number, to hear Wilde on February 17. The *Free Press* decided to gloat: the few who did experience "the sickly atmosphere" created by Wilde inside the Music Hall, wrote a reviewer for the paper, "felt the bracing, vivifying air of common sense once more" when they left that building and reached the street outside. The paper also couldn't help wondering, if Wilde was serious about "obliterating all that is plain and homely" in the world, as he had frequently declared from the podium, "where, then, would Oscar Wilde be?"

The *Cleveland Plain Dealer* took a more welcoming tone regarding the man who would be lecturing at Case Hall on February 18. Upon learning that some locals were planning to reprise the "sunflowers and breeches" stunt pioneered in Boston (and just repeated in Fort Wayne), the *Plain Dealer*'s editorial page told those Clevelanders that such behavior would merely "advertise their inferiority to Wilde both in sense and manners." So there was no organized mockery at Wilde's talk, which was attended by approximately five hundred people, at one dollar per seat. Even so, Wilde left the city in a huff, and the *Plain Dealer* was to blame. It had publicized his $500 appearance fee, a disclosure that not only revealed that his local promoter had lost money, but was met with anger by many of Cleveland's working men, who were shocked to learn that their hourly wage was but a puny fraction of the princely sum paid to a grown man in short pants for merely talking.

Wilde arrived in Cincinnati on February 20, for a rare day off. Though he was hoping to rest in his suite at Burnet House, he agreed to take a guided tour of the city. Perhaps because a hard rain had begun to fall, or, more likely, because he hoped to get some fresh publicity, he made several provocative comments about Cincinnati on this tour. Dismayed at seeing a sign that said "NO SMOKING" at a local art school, Wilde, an enthusiastic smoker, grumbled, "Great heaven, they speak of smoking as if it were a crime. I wonder they do not caution the students not to murder each other on the landings." The shock of his guides at hearing these words only encouraged him. "You have no architecture, no scenery [here]. . . . I wonder no criminal has ever pleaded the ugliness of your city as an excuse for his crimes." Later that night, Wilde attended a performance of selections from *Aida*, sung by the renowned soprano Adelina Patti. He was seated with great fanfare in the director's box at Cincinnati's Music Hall, where he spent nearly the entire evening standing and shouting *Brava!* This adulation for Patti was genuine, but perhaps not truly spontaneous. Wilde knew he would be returning to Cincinnati to give a lecture three days later and that seats were still available; he also knew a man from the *Cincinnati Enquirer* was watching his every move at the theater. "The aesthetic young man" who would soon be speaking in Cincinnati "was a wrapt listener of the diva," the reporter wrote in the *Enquirer* the next day. "And he was the cynosure of all eyes."

Wilde departed by train the following morning, just as his comments on Cincinnati's architecture were being read in the press, for Louisville, Kentucky, for a lecture to be presented on the twenty-first. If Wilde was of two minds regarding his potential reception in that city, he had good reason. The *Louisville Courier-Journal* had praised the American edition of his *Poems* as "the best first book [of poetry] extant," "full of flash and promise," and declared that "Mr. Wilde has been called an ass and an 'idiot' but he is neither." Yet when the same paper sent a reporter to meet Wilde at his hotel in Washington, when he spoke there in January, the result was an article that said:

> [Wilde] has . . . an effeminacy of delivery best described as 'Sissy' . . . . He is neither a man nor a woman. He is between the two. He is not intellectual-looking, but he has brains. He is an ass with brains.

As Wilde sat in his rooms at the Louisville Hotel for interviews with the local press, the Carte organization placed an advertisement in the *Courier-Journal* touting its client's appearance as "THE AESTHETIC EVENT OF THE SEASON." Wilde faced stiff competition for ticket buyers in Louisville. On the same night he would be lecturing at the Masonic Temple Theater, General Tom Thumb (one of P. T. Barnum's top moneymakers) was presenting "A Unique Parlor Entertainment" at the Opera House; Joseph K. Emmet, the star of numerous Broadway musicals, was performing in *Fritz in Ireland, or the Bell Ringer of the*

Rhine and the Love of the Shamrock, at Macauley's Theater; and the comedy and minstrel group known as the "Original Big Four" was playing the Buckingham Theater, supported by "an invisible wire walker, a Dutch comedian, a quartet of Irish tenors, and a dog and monkey act." (Whether it was the wire, or the walker, that was invisible was not made clear.)

Despite that competition Wilde drew a nearly sold-out house. It is a tribute to his success as a traveling salesman that the most famous traveling salesman in America was at his lecture, sitting in the first row of the dress circle. This was the Kentuckian Joseph Mulhattan, who, while crossing the hinterlands representing several manufacturers based in Louisville, made a hobby of making up "news" stories, then placing them with gullible (or sleazy) newspaper editors. In one well-known hoax, Mulhattan claimed that after George Washington's tomb was opened for repairs, it was discovered that his corpse had transformed into rock. Washington's features, he wrote, were "perfectly natural, with the exception of eyes and ears, no trace of which can be seen. The body is of a dark leathery color, and [resembles] sandstone." In an equally oft-printed hoax, Mulhattan said he saw a young girl at the seashore carried away into the afternoon sky by a bundle of balloons she was holding in her hand—until a local sharpshooter, who just happened to be there with his rifle, shot the balloons one by one, enabling the screaming child to gently descend to Earth, unhurt. Maybe it's not surprising that Mulhattan was known as the "Liar Laureate of the United States."

There's no evidence Wilde and Mulhattan were introduced, but we know Wilde made the acquaintance of another Louisvillian while there—Mrs. Emma Speed (born Emma Keats), the daughter of George Keats, the brother of Wilde's poetic hero, John Keats. George Keats had emigrated to America in 1818, settling in Louisville a year later, where, after getting rich as a real estate developer, he built a mansion known locally as the Englishman's Palace. His daughter Emma was born in Louisville in 1823. After hearing Wilde praise her uncle's "delicate sense of colour harmonies" and other aesthetic virtues, Mrs. Speed came backstage, introduced herself, and invited Wilde to come to her home the next day. He accepted and spent several unforgettable hours with her, "reading the letters of [John] Keats to her father, some of which were at that time unpublished, poring over torn yellow leaves and faded scraps of paper, and wondering at the little [edition of] Dante in which [John] Keats had written those marvelous notes on Milton." Making this day even more pleasurable for Wilde was the contrast it posed to some of the reviews of his talk that appeared in the Louisville press that morning, articles filled with adjectives such as "monotonous" and "graceless." Striking a (slightly) more positive note, the *Courier-Journal* concluded that Wilde was "not a charlatan" but rather "a young man of showy, if not great talents, . . . worthy of being stared at and listened to."

Mrs. Speed had a more generous take. So moved was she by Wilde's reverence for her uncle that she wrote to the lecturer shortly after his departure, asking that he accept from her the original manuscript of Keats's famous sonnet beginning, "Blue! 'Tis the life of heaven." Wilde's gratitude was immense. "What you have given me is more golden than gold, more precious than any treasure this great country could yield me," he wrote back.

> It is a sonnet I have loved always, and indeed who but the supreme and perfect artist could have got more from a mere colour a motive so full of marvel: and now I am half enamored of the paper that touched his hand, and the ink that did his bidding, and grown fond of the sweet comeliness of his charactery, for since my boyhood I have loved none better than your marvelous kinsman, that godlike boy, the real Adonis of our age.

Wilde, who liked to think of himself as an Adonis, was soon forced out of this reverie by the demands of his tour. An engagement on February 22 at English's Opera House in Indianapolis attracted five hundred patrons, who sat so quietly through his lecture that the *Indianapolis Journal* described their response as "tumultuous silence." Wilde was happy to retire to the silence of his suite at the New Denison Hotel afterward, but this peaceful interlude was interrupted at around eleven p.m. by a knock on his door. Once opened, Wilde was face to face with his road manager, Mr. Vale, and a fast-talking aide to Indiana governor Albert Gallatin Porter. It seems that that night at the executive mansion the governor was hosting a party for Civil War veterans—those who fought on the Union Side—who were in Indianapolis for a convention, as well as for members of the recently formed Greenback Party, which was also holding a political meeting in the city. This reception, which was well under way, apparently had not reached the level of excitement the governor had hoped for, so when his aide suggested it might be a good idea to collect the famous Oscar Wilde and have *him* enliven the proceedings—either as a wit or, just as beneficially, as a freak—the governor quickly assented.

So did Wilde, who loved a party as few men before (or after) him ever have. He changed out of his robe and slippers and back into his breeches, tights, and buckled shoes and, minutes later, joined his two companions in a carriage that brought them to the governor's mansion, not far away. Perhaps Wilde wasn't in as much of a party mood as he thought he was, because he soon made a rare faux pas, referring at the reception to the farmers who made up much of the membership of the Greenback Party as "peasants." Nor did it help when, asked his opinion of the mansion's architecture, Wilde (according to the local press) replied: "No better than the Atlantic [Ocean]"—unaware the building had been designed by his host, Governor Porter.

Wilde left the next morning for Cincinnati, whose citizens had either forgiven him for his provocative remarks about their architecture, or were curious to meet the man who had made them. Either way, more than a thousand people, including Mayor William Means, took their seats at the sold-out Opera House for Wilde's lecture, on February 23. There was an audible sigh, however, when he took the podium. Whether because of a laundering issue, or because his talk was scheduled for two p.m., Wilde was not wearing his typical "evening" lecture wear, having replaced that ensemble with a more conventional one of trousers and a corduroy jacket with a red handkerchief drooping from its pocket that one reporter described as "cunningly arranged into a lily shape." After his lecture, Wilde was surrounded by a crowd of adoring women who thanked him for bringing his aesthetic message to their city. But the showman in him knew he had failed them. A few days later he admitted as much in a letter to Colonel Morse: "They were dreadfully disappointed at Cincinnati at my not wearing knee-breeches."

Wilde took an overnight train to St. Louis, arriving the next morning in a city that was partially flooded by the Mississippi River and where, later that night, he drew a crowd of fifteen hundred to Mercantile Library Hall. It was a large and profitable audience but not a particularly friendly one. When Wilde praised the city's beautiful streets, a group of hecklers began an ironic round of applause, lasting far longer than was merited; his call to Americans to adopt a "bright and simple" mode of dress was met with similarly scornful clapping. When his lecture was finished, Wilde complained to Vale backstage about the "villainous" treatment he had just received. But a few days later he remembered it differently, writing to a friend in London: "I send you a line to say that since Chicago I have had two great successes: Cincinnati . . . and St. Louis."

After appearing in several smaller midwestern cities, Wilde wrote to the English actress Mrs. Bernard Beere, sounding like an excited tourist. He had "seen Indians," he said, men whose appearance he likened to several London theater critics, and coal "miners who are nearly as real as Bret Harte's." (Harte, an American writer of western fiction, much of it about the Gold Rush, was then living in Britain, where he was extremely popular.) To Mrs. George Lewis, he wrote: "I don't know where I am: somewhere in the middle of coyotes and cañons: one is a 'ravine' and the other a 'fox,' I don't know which, but I think they change about. [A miner here] asked me if I was not 'running an art-mill,' and on pointing to my numerous retinue, said he 'guessed I hadn't needed to wash my own pans.'"

It was around this time that Wilde was asked to comment on reports that two well-known Britons—Lillie Langtry and Henry Labouchère (the outspoken member of Parliament who also edited the journal *Truth*)—were coming to America. These reports were only partly accurate: Mr. Labouchère wasn't coming; it was his wife, a retired actress now working as Langtry's acting coach, who was. (Wilde had recommended Mrs. Labouchère for that job to Mrs. Langtry several years earlier.) Unaware of the error made by the press, Wilde gushed at length about two people he considered dear friends. Of Mrs. Langtry, he said, "Beautiful women are quite indescribable." But that didn't stop him:

> The beauty of her face is in the extreme sweetness and loveliness of her expression and the wonderful delicacy and transparency of her complexion. The real wonder of her beauty to all of us who are artists is that whether one carves her in marble or paints her in color she is equally lovely, the lines of her face being as strong and as definite in outline as a Greek bronze, and yet so perfect in proportion that the effect is one of the simplest loveliness.

He said of Labouchère, who, along with his political career, was a man with whom Wilde had traded quips at many a party: "He is one of the most brilliant conversationalists in England. He is the only brilliant enemy I ever had [there]."

Thirteen years later that final sentence would come back to haunt him. But on March 11, Wilde was feeling a sense of relief. After speaking in yet another small midwestern town, he was returning to Chicago, to speak again at Central Music Hall. Because it was his second appearance there in less than a month, he prepared a new lecture, "The House Beautiful," in which he took it upon himself to teach his listeners how to transform their ordinary homes into aesthetic havens in a world of philistines. In detail:

"All ornaments should be carved; have nothing made by machinery," Wilde said. "You should not have cast-iron railings fixed outside the house, which boys are always knocking down, and rightfully too, for they always look cheap and shabby. . . . Within the house: the hall should not be papered, since the walls are exposed to the elements by the frequent opening and closing of the door; it should be wainscoted with beautiful wood. . . . Don't carpet the floor: ordinary red brick tiles make a warm and beautiful floor. There should be no pictures in the hall, for it is . . . a mere passageway. . . . A large painted oak chest is the best stand for cloaks; for hats, a pretty rack in wood to hang on the wall, such as I have seen in Greece and Turkey, though there it was used for guns. . . .

"Don't paper the ceiling [of any room]; that gives one the sensation of living in a paper box. . . . Have no great flaring gas chandelier in the middle of a room. . . . If you must have gas, let the room be lighted from side brackets on the wall, and each jet of flame should be covered with delicate shades or hidden by screens. . . . Wax candles are better still, as they give a softer light."

On he went for ninety minutes, offering the kind of advice that, a century later, would make a very rich woman of Martha Stewart. These interior decorating tips were listened to by an "appreciative" and "cultured" audience that filled two-thirds of the seats at Central Music Hall, the *Chicago Tribune* reported—a more-than-respectable turnout, the paper judged, considering "the disagreeable weather" outside, and Wilde's recent appearance at the same venue. Wilde was doubly delighted: he was swarmed by grateful female listeners after the lecture; and he was informed, shortly after that love fest, that it had been a successful evening at the box office.

Wilde arrived on March 15 in Minneapolis, where an editor at the *Minneapolis Tribune* had called him an "ASS-THETE" in a headline that morning, a "witticism" that would be repeated by other editors as

Wilde continued on his tour. Hours later he was even more dismayed to see that the mockery had been effective: only 250 people showed up for his lecture at the Academy of Music. He did far better the next evening in St. Paul—Minneapolis's rival across the Mississippi River—where, perhaps trying to prove theirs was the more sophisticated of the Twin Cities, a full house of one thousand took their seats at the Opera House to hear his lecture. Despite that turnout, Wilde, maybe still irked by the headline in the *Minneapolis Tribune*, told his audience that he was shocked by the mud on the streets of St. Paul. He would have the opportunity to be even more provocative the following night, when he appeared at the same venue for a St. Patrick's Day celebration convened by several local clerics of Irish descent.

Just being Irish was a provocative act in Minnesota, where the local power elite was composed almost entirely of Scandinavians and Anglo-Saxons. Wilde wasn't expecting to speak at this event, but, when asked, he agreed to say a few words. "Ladies and gentlemen," he began, "when I gave myself the pleasure of meeting with you tonight, I had not thought I would be called upon to say anything, but would be allowed to sit quietly and enjoy listening to the loving and patriotic sentiments I knew would be given voice. But the generous response you have given to the mention of the efforts of my mother in Ireland's cause has filled me with pleasure and pride.

> It is also a pleasure to me to speak to an audience of my countrymen, a race once the most artistic in Europe. There was a time before the reign of Henry II, when Ireland stood at the front of all nations of Europe in the arts, the sciences and general intellectuality. . . . But with the coming of the English, that came to an end, for [such achievements] could not live and flourish under a tyrant. But the artistic sentiment of Ireland was not dead in the hearts of her sons and daughters. It is that sentiment which has induced you to meet here tonight to commemorate our patron saint. It finds expression in the love you bear for every little nook,

every hill, and every brook of your native land. It is shown in the esteem you bear for the names of the great men whose deeds and works have shed such luster on Irish history. And when Ireland gains its independence, its schools of art and other educational branches will be revived, and Ireland will regain the proud position she once held among the nations of Europe.

These words were heartfelt, but it's possible there was another reason for Wilde's soaring mood. He had just learned that his travels through the Midwest (and all the provocative remarks he had made while being there) had paid off: the San Francisco impresario Charles E. Locke was offering $5,000—the equivalent of $117,000 today—if Wilde agreed to come to California for three weeks, beginning in late March, to deliver a maximum of twenty lectures. The Carte organization was probably reluctant, at first, to deal with Locke because he was the producer of the "pirate" edition of *Patience* that had just played in San Francisco, a production that, despite its success at the box office, had produced not a dollar in royalties for the organization's chief clients, Gilbert & Sullivan. (Because of deficiencies in U.S. copyright law, Gilbert & Sullivan's operettas were often mounted in America by companies not using the official score or script, and not paying any fees to its creators.) But the size of Locke's offer trumped all else. Wilde was almost as intimidated by the proposition as he was exhilarated. "Six lectures a week for three weeks seem to me enormous," he wrote to Colonel Morse. But he gave his assent.

He had a lecture to do first in Omaha, a city that made good sense logistically for his now-extended tour: it was the starting point for the westward half of the transcontinental railroad, completed in 1869. It was not, however, a hotbed of aestheticism. To the contrary, a sure way to defame a person in the 1880s in Nebraska was to liken him or her to any object linked to the aesthetic movement, as happened when the editor of the *Omaha Daily Bee* mocked a journalistic competitor by saying: "The biggest sunflower in America is planted in the editorial chair at the *Omaha Herald*." But a local women's group, the Social Arts Club, was intent on erasing Omaha's image as a cultural backwater, so it sponsored Wilde's appearance.

A crowd of nearly one thousand showed up at Boyd's Opera House on March 21 to hear Wilde speak on "The Decorative Arts." According to one historian, most "went with the sincere desire to hear and to learn," but others were "impelled by the same curiosity that would have induced them to buy tickets to see a five-legged calf [or] an educated Indian." Wilde was politely received, but there was trouble afterward, when it was whispered about town that, upon receiving an invitation to attend a party in his honor that night at the home of one of Omaha's leading citizens, he had demanded a $50 appearance fee.

There was no evidence to support the charge; even so, a reporter for the *Daily Bee* decided to take some revenge when he saw Wilde at the Omaha railroad station on March 22. Wilde told the journalist he was expecting a tedious train journey from Nebraska to California, but the reporter corrected him, saying that he would surely be entertained by the sight of numerous wild animals through his window. "You will see flocks of aesthetic jackrabbits," he said, as well as equally aesthetic herds of antelope and buffalo. Wilde, not realizing he was being mocked, replied, "How lovely." The reporter further insulted Wilde in his article in the next day's paper by comparing his physical appearance to that of "Big Nose George," the notoriously ugly bandit who had been lynched a few months earlier by a mob in Rawlins, Wyoming, after which he suffered the additional (if posthumous) indignities of having the top part of his scull sawed off—it was later used as an ashtray—and a pair of shoes made from his skin.

AFTER BOARDING A train bound for Sacramento, some fifteen hundred miles away, Wilde was told he was riding "express." He would soon learn, however, how imprecise that term was in 1882. The train came to a halt every thirty minutes or so to take on coal, water, mail, and additional passengers. Fortunately, he was traveling first class, which meant that, during the day, he sat in a reclining plush velvet seat and, at night, slept in a private pull-out berth—a few dozen yards (but a world away) from the traveling salesmen, farmers, miners, cowboys, card sharps, and prostitutes who sat and slept, cramped and uncomfortably, in the noisy second-class cars.

At first, Wilde was often induced to step out of the train during its many stops and wave to the crowd of gawking locals who had been informed of his presence on the train by the press. Though Wilde loved to preen, he eventually tired of these command performances. There was a ready solution available to him, however, right there in the first-class car. This was the actor John Howson, a member of the Conley-Barton Opera Troupe, traveling to San Francisco to mount the production of *Patience* authorized by the Carte organization. Howson was playing Bunthorne, so he had a long-haired wig, a pair of breeches, black silk stockings, and so on, which, on several occasions, he happily donned to greet the cheering groups hoping to see the famous aesthete from abroad. When the train stopped in Corinne, Utah, forty citizens of that town, many of them holding a sunflower, arranged for a brass band to greet Wilde. What they didn't know was that the man effusively thanking them for their efforts was Howson.

In a letter to Norman Forbes-Robertson, Wilde described what he was seeing from his window when the train was moving: "At first grey, gaunt desolate plains, as colourless as waste land by the sea, with now and then scampering herds of bright red antelopes, and heavy shambling buffaloes, rather like Joe Knight"—a London theater critic—"in appearance, and screaming vultures like gnats high up in the air, then up the Sierra Nevadas, the snow-capped mountains shining like shields of polished silver in that vault of blue flame we call the sky, and deep canyons full of pine trees . . . and at last from the chill winter of the mountains down into eternal summer, groves of orange trees in fruit and flower, green fields, and purple hills, a very Italy, without its art.".

Finally, on March 26, four days after he left Omaha, a connecting train from Sacramento took Wilde to Oakland, where—dressed in brown trousers, a white shirt, a puce-colored tie, a black velvet frock coat, yellow leather gloves, and a wide-brimmed felt hat—he was met by Charles E. Locke and his minions, by journalists from all the major newspapers in San Francisco, and by hundreds of curious "civilians," who moved (quietly and respectfully, the *San Francisco Examiner* reported) wherever Wilde moved at the train terminal, so as to stay close to the "Bard of Beauty" as he walked to the ferry that would take him across the bay to San Francisco.

A reporter for the *San Francisco Chronicle* wrote that Wilde spent most of that ferry trip in the open air on deck, "poised on one leg like the decorative fowl of aestheticism," as he gazed with enthusiasm at his destination across the water, a metropolis whose streets, at this distance, gave the appearance of bleached ribs on a gigantic skeleton. San Francisco was then the ninth-largest city in America—and the largest and wealthiest by far in California. (Los Angeles didn't even rank in America's top hundred cities by population, according to the 1880 census.) The contract with Locke surely elevated Wilde's mood; the scent of money was in the air, what the writer Ernest Lehman would later call "the sweet smell of success."

But soon there was another odor, this one from the tons of human waste flushed into the bay by San Francisco's sewer system, "churned into aggressive life by the ferry boat" and "borne on the wings of the western wind," as the *Chronicle* reporter put it. So overtaxed were Wilde's delicate sensibilities by this olfactory intrusion that the master of provocation was provoked to bolt from the deck. The journalist eventually found him in the ferry's cabin, burying his face in a floral bouquet that had been presented to him hours earlier by the women of Sacramento, when he changed trains there. Perhaps it's just a coincidence but, years later, in *The Picture of Dorian Gray*, Wilde would have his title character investigate the "psychology of perfumes," driven to do so, Wilde wrote, by his appreciation of the power of "sweet-smelling roots" and "scented pollen-laden flowers" to "expel melancholy from the soul." One thing is for certain: Wilde wanted to be at his best when he arrived in the city that had exended him such a lucrative invitation.

CHAPTER SEVEN

Keep Yourself Amused

*O*scar Wilde and San Francisco. Today it seems a perfect, even inevitable match, but the link hardly seemed obvious in 1882. San Francisco was not then the unofficial capital of gay America; nor was Wilde the revered martyr/icon of gay culture in America or anywhere else. Even so, there is no doubt that the time Wilde spent in and around San Francisco ranked among the most enjoyable portions of his lecture tour. "A really beautiful city," he called it the following year in "Impressions of America," using an adjective he rarely used to describe any other American locale. He would restate his affection for the place, albeit ironically, with these words spoken by Lord Henry Wotton in *The Picture of Dorian Gray*: "It is an odd thing, but everyone who disappears is said to be seen in San Francisco. It must be a delightful city, and possess all the attractions of the next world."

Wilde wasn't trying to disappear; he preferred the grand entrance. And as he described it in a letter to his friend Norman Forbes-Robertson, he got what he wished for on March 26, when (he said) he was met at the San Francisco waterfront by four thousand people who lined the streets to cheer and wave as he traveled in an open carriage pulled by four horses to the city's newest and largest hotel, the Palace. Wilde was a chronic exaggerator in his letters, and it's interesting to note that none of the journalists who docked with him in San Francisco after accompanying him on the ferry from Oakland mentioned this exuberant throng in their articles on his arrival. Perhaps the pressure of their deadlines forced them to leave the scene before the crowd had fully formed.

But another source lends credibility to Wilde's account, a cartoon titled "The Modern Messiah" that appeared in the San Francisco weekly *The Wasp*. Drawn by George F. Keller, "Messiah" depicted Wilde with a halo of flower petals around his head, holding a giant sunflower in his hand as he sits in an impossibly pompous posture on a braying jackass while riding through San Francisco surrounded by a worshipful crowd of sunflower-carrying citizens of that city, many of them—including Mayor Maurice C. Blake and Colonel Alexander G. Hawes, the president of the Bohemian Club, the most prestigious social organization in town—clearly recognizable to the paper's readers. Also impossible to miss in Keller's cartoon was his rendering of the face of Wilde's local promoter, Charles E. Locke, on a large padlock encircling the jackass's neck, and the drawing of a bulging money bag tied to the beast's tail marked "$5,000," the sum Locke was said to be paying Wilde for coming to California. The editor who published this cartoon was a Civil War combat veteran from Indiana in his second stint as a journalist in San Francisco. His name was Ambrose Bierce.

No matter how many San Franciscans actually turned out to see Wilde on the twenty-sixth, we know that the *San Francisco Examiner* published a poem eleven days before his arrival welcoming the news that Locke was bringing him to the West Coast, and welcoming Wilde himself with this doggerel:

> *Hail! Brother, hail! From o'er the seas,*
> *How glad am I to greet you!*
> *Although your pants but cap your knees,*

I'm highly pleased to meet you.
Although your locks to some give shocks,
*   To you I now extend*
A hearty hand of fellowship,
*   My brother, poet, friend.*

We also know the *Examiner* and its journalistic rivals had kept San Franciscans well informed of Wilde's triumphs, troubles, and faux pas as he crossed America. The lecturer's tour-opening, sold-out talk at Chickering Hall in New York was reported on at length, as was his one-upping put-down of the Harvard undergraduates in Boston, his face-to-face (and knee-to-knee) meeting with Walt Whitman in Camden, his humiliating night before the sarcastic audience in St. Louis, and his oft-repeated criticisms of American architecture, whether built by man (the Water Tower in Chicago and the entire city of Cincinnati) or by Mother Nature (Niagara Falls.) This coverage increased, in column inches and in excited anticipation, as Wilde's train approached California.

"Oscar Wilde is at hand," said the *San Francisco Chronicle* on March 25. "He is undoubtedly to be the lion of the hour, and his lecture on Monday at Platt's Hall is already sold out. . . . The furore touching his appearance [in this area] has spread to Oakland [where] . . . he will . . . deliver a lecture in the Armory on Tuesday, a fact which shows how widely the interest in him is spreading." In fact, that interest had spread 6,500 miles away to New Zealand, where a nearly two-thousand-word piece headlined, "Wilde in San Francisco: The Aesthete's Reception," would appear in the *Auckland Star*. The *Chronicle* weighed in again on March 26: "An Irishman whose natural love of the fair sex has led him into flights of passionate fancy, and whose appreciation of the beautiful in all forms . . . has carried him into the realms of eccentricity, now offers a show for the curious." This show, the *Chronicle* noted with approval, was being offered by "an educated man . . . imbued with the appreciation of art . . . of which he is the high priest."

It's likely Wilde's road manager, J. S. Vale, collected such press clippings and presented them to Wilde soon after he alighted from his carriage in the semicircular, graveled driveway that served as the entrance to the Palace Hotel, at the corner of Market and New Montgomery Streets. Designed by the New York architect John P. Gaynor for the San Francisco financier William C. Ralston (the founder of the Bank of California), the Palace, completed in 1876, was said to be the most luxurious hotel in the world. It was surely among the costliest. Ralston spent $5 million—more than $117 million, in today's dollars—on the project, some of it to buy an entire forest in the Sierra Nevada Mountains to furnish oak and other woods for his seven-story, 755-room hotel. He also contracted with fifteen marble factories to supply the stone for eight hundred fireplace mantels, nine hundred washbasins, and nearly fifty thousand square feet of flooring. The hotel had its own orchestra, which played every afternoon in the music pavilion, often choosing selections from Gilbert & Sullivan's oeuvre. Its guests could choose to dine at any of thirteen dining rooms.

One sign these elegant surroundings elevated Wilde's mood was the friendly banter he exchanged with the reporters who came to see him at the Palace on the afternoon of his arrival. Aware of the vexing time Wilde had recently experienced in St. Louis, a journalist for the *Examiner* asked if he was "disappointed with America and Americans." To the contrary, said Wilde, laying on the charm: "There is much here to like and admire. The further West one comes, the more there is to like. The western people are much more social than those of the East, and I fancy that I shall be greatly pleased with California." It is worth noting that, at this point in time, Wilde had yet to socialize with any "western people" in California, other than Mr. Locke and his aides, railroad conductors, ferry personnel, reporters, and the staff of the Palace.

Wilde toured the San Francisco Institute of Design the next morning; then it was on to the Bohemian Club on Pine Street, near the Barbary Coast—San Francisco's redlight district—for lunch. It seems that location, and the name of the club, gave Wilde a false set of expectations: "I never saw so many well-dressed, well-fed, business-like looking Bohemians in my life," he later said. This was not an overstatement. Though the club was founded in 1872 by journalists from the *Chronicle* as a drinking place for reporters, pressmen, and, as its charter said, "gentlemen connected professionally with literature, art, music, the drama, and those who, by reason of their appreciation of these objects, [are] deemed eligible," members of the city's business establishment, whether they appreciated the arts or not, were soon invited to join because their wealth enabled the club to cover its operating expenses.* One thing the membership always agreed on, in the early years of the Bohemian Club, was that any visiting literary man of note (or, in this case, notoriety), whether he be an established author such as Mark Twain and (later) Rudyard Kipling, or a hardly established author such as Oscar Wilde, would be invited to the club for a meal.

Several hours after that meal Wilde took the stage for his first talk in California—he resurrected a revised version of "The English Renaissance" for the occasion—which the *Chronicle* covered in a piece that began: "Oscar Wilde's lecture . . . last night was the means of filling Platt's Hall with the most fashionable audience that any entertainment could attract in this city. The doors of the hall at 8 P.M. were fairly besieged by the beauty and wealth of San Francisco, as the face of Manager [Charles E.] Locke, beaming at the crowded portals where [he saw] the slow-moving mass of respectability worth $1 a head, was as joyous as a full blown sunflower." (Actually, reserved seats went for $1.50.)

After that rich, good-looking mass was seated, and Wilde made his entrance in his Bunthorne garb, a reporter for the *Examiner* found that "as soon as the first feeling of anxious wonder at the lecturer's appearance had passed away, [the audience] caught the infection of his enthusiasm . . . and exhibited their interest by marked attention." In his hourlong speech Wilde told his listeners that there was "no poetry

---

* This trend accelerated so quickly in the twentieth century that the Club became a social bastion for corporate CEOs and leaders of the Republican Party, and remains so today.

in the steam engine," that a child's education should be about "beauty, not the record of bloody slaughters and barbarous brawls . . . they call history," and that the "value of the telephone" is only "the value of what two people use it to say," a remark (not unlike what some would say about Twitter and other Internet platforms 130 years later) that led to a crescendo of tittering caused by Wilde's pronunciation of that new tool of communication as "teel-a-phone." Despite that phonetic error, Wilde left the stage to a hearty round of applause, after which he went, as the guest of the Bohemian Club, to the opera, where, as the *Chronicle* reported, "he gallantly threw a bouquet at the prima donna."

Ambrose Bierce tossed no bouquets at Wilde. The corrosive wit who would later, in his book *The Devil's Dictionary*, define *air* as "a nutritious substance supplied by a bountiful Providence for the fattening of the poor," had this to say in *The Wasp* about the lecturer who had just spoken at Platt's Hall:

> That sovereign of insufferables, Oscar Wilde, has . . . mounted his hind legs and blown crass vapidities through the bowel of his neck, to the capital edification of circumjacent fools and foolessses. . . . The ineffable dunce has nothing to say and says it . . . with a liberal embellishment of bad delivery, embroidering it with reasonless vulgarities of attitude, gesture and attire. There was never an impostor so hateful, a blockhead so stupid, a crank so variously and offensively daft.

This was harsh stuff, even for a committed hyperbolist such as Bierce (and especially for a man who hadn't even attended the lecture). Bierce's loathing for Wilde wasn't personal—the two hadn't met—but it was genuine. To Bierce, a mostly self-educated son of a failed farmer/shopkeeper, Wilde was a privileged, posturing, overeducated phony who had never worked a day in his life. Even worse, he was a privileged, posturing, overeducated phony who had never worked a day in his life *from abroad*.

Wilde ferried across the bay the next day to Oakland, where Armory Hall, a building usually filled with soldiers, was on this occasion filled with flowers in honor of the evening's lecturer. Despite the efforts of the *Oakland Tribune*, which had defended "the poem in breeches," as it called Wilde, and attacked his critics as those who "laugh at what [they] cannot understand"—perhaps a reference to Bierce—Wilde was not able to duplicate the large crowd of ticket buyers he had attracted in San Francisco. He did, however, attract a huge nonpaying crowd the next afternoon when he went to San Francisco's Chinatown. "Mobbing the Esthete," read the subheadline in the account of this visit published in the *Chronicle*, which reported that "a scene of considerable excitement occurred yesterday afternoon when Oscar Wilde ventured out in search of Celestial handiwork and called at a store on Sacramento Street." (*Celestial* was an adjective often used by the jingoistic press as an ironic synonym for *Chinese*.)

> No sooner had he been seen to leave his carriage than a general rush took place, and in a moment the street in front of the store was utterly impassable, and it required the best efforts of Officer Curtis to prevent the spectators from precipitating themselves into the store. His purchases completed, Oscar Wilde advanced through the passageway that had been cleared and entered his carriage. . . . The blinds were pulled down, but the spectators, bent on seeing the esthete at closer quarters, crowded forward and pulled aside the curtains, revealing the apostle leaning back and convulsed with laughter.

Wilde returned to Platt's Hall that night for a second lecture falsely promoted, one has to assume by Locke, as Wilde's "positively final" appearance in San Francisco. Locke, a man who valued hype almost as much as he did exclamation points, announced Wilde's topic as "Art Decoration! Being the Practical Application of the Esthetic Theory to Everyday Home Life and Art Ornamentation!" apparently thinking

"The House Beautiful" too staid. Wilde found the auditorium at Platt's less full than it had been for his first appearance there, but his instructions for tasteful home design were listened to, the press reported, with respect. The same could not always be said, however, for his fashion advice. Women in the hall gasped when Wilde disdained the "ridiculous bonnets" and "tight, flimsy dresses" favored by American women, and men laughed when he urged them to examine paintings of George Washington to "see how a great and brave man arrayed himself"—and then use that breeches-wearing president as their sartorial role model.

Chances are Wilde gave that second bit of advice with a wink, which reveals another lesson he had learned while on his speaking tour: the importance of amusing him*self* as a means of retaining his focus. Wilde, who had never given a single lecture in England, had now presented nearly fifty of them in America. This was not merely a new experience for him, it was an extremely challenging one: the pressure to keep things fresh—for himself as well as for his audience—was significant, all the more so as he sometimes lectured six times a week. Wilde treated his fame-creation project in the States as work, but he came to grasp that it was more likely to succeed if it was also fun, as it had been in England, where he had amused himself (and others) at posh parties with his near-endless supply of epigrams. Hence his "fashion advice" that the men of San Francisco dress like George Washington. Such "impromptu wheezes" had certainly worked for him in London.

He also came to realize that many of his focus-enhancing moments of fun in America would happen *off* the lecture stage. After completing his second talk at Platt's on March 29, Wilde returned to Chinatown with Messrs. Vale and Locke, two San Francisco policemen, and a reporter from the *Examiner*, for an extended "insider's" tour of the district Wilde so wished to experience again, in all its titillating and exotic splendor. This is from the account in the *Examiner*, published the next day:

Last night, after the close of his lecture, Oscar Wilde . . . made a thorough inspection of the Chinese quarter of the city, Mr. Wilde having expressed a wish to see all the inner secrets of Chinatown, no matter at what cost to his olfactory and optical nerves. [His] experienced guides fulfilled his desire to the utmost of their ability. Joss houses, Chinese hospitals in Ellick Alley, theaters, lodging houses, underground burrows, Murderers' Alley, the hunts of the highbinders, the holes of rag pickers, opium dens, gambling houses, places of the most questionable character, restaurants, slaughter houses, offal depositories, merchants' residences, pawnbrokers' stores, junk stores, fish and hog markets, and all the thousand and one queer haunts of the Celestial people were thoroughly explored.

(There was no Chinatown in 1882 in London.)

It was everything Wilde had wished for, but he expressed his delight with a mixed geographical metaphor. "This is just like a chapter from *The Arabian Nights*!" he gushed to his guides.

We don't know how many opium dens he visited that night. There were more than two hundred of them in San Francisco in 1882, usually announced by a red a sign above the door saying, in Chinese calligraphy, PIPES AND LAMPS ALWAYS CONVENIENT. But we know that Wilde's introduction to such places was something he never forgot, as evidenced by a passage, written nearly a decade later, in *The Picture of Dorian Gray*: "There were opium dens," Dorian knew, "where one could buy oblivion. . . ." Three pages later, Wilde described one:

At the end of the hall hung a tattered green curtain that swayed and shook in the gusty wind which had followed [Dorian] from the street. He dragged it aside, and entered a long, low room. . . . Shrill flaring gas jets, dulled and distorted by the fly-blown mirrors that faced them, were ranged round the walls. Greasy reflectors of ribbed tin backed them, making quivering discs of light.

The floor was covered with ochre-coloured sawdust, trampled here and there into mud, and stained with dark rings of spilt liquor. Some Malays were crouching by a little charcoal stove playing with bone counters, and showing their white teeth as they chattered. . . .

At the end of the room there was a little staircase, leading to a darkened chamber. As Dorian hurried up its three rickety steps, the heavy odour of opium met him. He took a deep breath, and his nostrils quivered with pleasure. When he entered, a young man with smooth yellow hair, who was bending over a lamp, lighting a long thin pipe, looked up at him, and nodded in a hesitant manner. "You here, Adrian?" muttered Dorian. "Where else should I be," he answered, listlessly.

No one could accuse Wilde of being listless in California. On Thursday, March 30, he toured the art gallery and library on the campus of the University of California, in Berkeley, where the account of his visit published in *The Berkleyan,* the student literary magazine, shows that "snark"—usually said to be a journalistic creation of the twenty-first century—was very much alive in 1882. "Under the guidance of his brilliant young local apostle" (William Armes, then a senior) "the prophet of High Art . . . visited the University yesterday. The news of his approach rapidly spread, and the general interest in the Library suddenly increased. . . . One thing, however, surprises us. Knowing the considerate nature of his youthful [guide], we did not expect that he would inflict upon his guest the gratuitous cruelty of a visit to the Art Gallery. But the deed was done, and the look of anguish with which the crushed lily gazed on the frescoes would have melted a harder heart than ours."

After dining with Armes in Oakland, Wilde gave a second, better-attended lecture at the Oakland Armory. He traveled by train the next day to Sacramento, some ninety miles away, stopping briefly en route in the town of Livermore, where he waved to a few locals—not that the

Livermore Herald was impressed. "Oscar Wilde, the apostle of beauty, has been to Livermore," its reporter wrote. "But he didn't stay long.

> He was dressed in his regulation suit—mouse-colored velvet coat, black velvet cape, loose, baggy, light, poetic pants, patent leathers, and a regular "Buffalo Bill" hat. . . . He sat in his seat about as utterly graceful as a sack of flour. He is not handsome, has large features, no beard, and looks like anything but a poem. We have seen finer looking restaurant waiters.

When Wilde reached Sacramento, he lectured at the Congregational church, where the church organist had entertained the audience with solos on the grand organ for nearly an hour, owing to Wilde's tardiness. The crowd was small but sincere in its appreciation of what Wilde had come to say on home decoration; so was the *Sacramento Daily Union.* At least so it seemed—or maybe not. "Mr. Wilde's lecture was one of clear-cut English, bold, incisive, poetical, graceful and almost winning in the beauty of his sentences and the delicacy of his periods," a reporter for the paper wrote. After returning to San Francisco early the next morning, Wilde found the stamina to give a "special afternoon lecture" at Platt's Hall on "The House Beautiful," which, though not a sellout, was well attended by a mostly female audience.

Then it was time for fun. Wilde had been invited back to the Bohemian Club in San Francisco for a night of "High Jinks," to begin shortly after his matinee lecture. What the guest of honor didn't know was that the Bohemians' plan was that the fun would be at his expense. (It was April Fool's Day, after all.) The plotters' weapon of choice was alcohol, which they poured again and again into the tumbler sitting before Wilde at the club. The idea was that Wilde would be rendered senseless and, more to the point, defenseless, after which the Bohemians would take turns mocking him to his face. But Wilde downed drink after drink until it was the Bohemians who were senseless, many of them falling asleep at the table; they snored and/or slobbered while Wilde remained as erect and alert as when he arrived, finally leaving the club under his own power in the early morning hours, returning in a hansom cab to the Palace, after thanking his few remaining conscious hosts for an absolutely wonderful time. A few days later a delegation of Bohemians called on Wilde at his hotel suite and asked—as an act of contrition and as a symbol of his victory over them—if Wilde, now revered as a "three-bottle man," would sit for a portrait to be painted by one of the club's members, the artist Theodore Wores, which would be exhibited at the club, once it was finished. Wilde proudly accepted.

After a day of rest on Sunday, April 2, Wilde traveled on the third to San Jose, where the *Daily Morning Times*, commenting before his arrival on the fashion advice he had just given to the men of San Francisco, wondered: "Why not go further back [than George Washington] and look at a painting of Edward the Black Prince, with an iron pot on his head, and coat and breeches made of the same soft material, and use that as an argument for Spring fashions in cast iron?" Despite that sarcasm, nearly four hundred ticket buyers showed up to hear Wilde lecture on "The English Renaissance" at the California Theatre. After an overnight stay, Wilde moved on to Stockton, eighty miles to the northeast, where he spoke on "The House Beautiful" before a similarly sized crowd at Mozart Hall.

Aware of Wilde's enthusiastic reception at a St. Patrick's Day event held weeks earlier in Minnesota, his California promoter, Mr. Locke, scheduled a fourth—and this time truly final—lecture in San Francisco for him on April 5. No interior decorating or fashion tips this time; the topic was "Irish Poets and Poetry of the Nineteenth Century." Though the audience at Platt's Hall was "only fair" in size, according to the *San Francisco Call*, Wilde spoke as if it were a packed house, with great feeling, vigor, and insight, prompting the *Chronicle* to note that this lecture "elicited the most applause of any which [Wilde] has delivered here."

"The poetry and music of Ireland are not merely the luxury of the rich, but the very bulwark of patriotism, the very seed and flower of liberty," Wilde said. "The Saxon took our lands from us and left them desolate. We took their language and added new beauties to it," he added, before reading selections from verse written by his mother, Thomas Davis, Gavin Duffy, William Smith O'Brien, Daniel O'Connell, John Francis Waller, and others. So moved was the audience by Wilde's reading, the *Call* reported, that, when he finished, a young woman rushed the stage and presented him with a "fragrant bouquet of violets, whereat the audience again applauded and Oscar," nearly overcome by emotion, "bowed in thanks."

With a rare break in his lecturing schedule, Wilde spent much of the next two days socializing. He attended an afternoon party on Friday, April 7, at the artist's studio on Montgomery Street shared by the painters (and Bohemian Club members) Jules Tavernier and Joseph Dwight Strong. Apparently Wilde was so enchanted by the paint-stained floor, the unfinished works parked on easels, the brushes soaking in solvent, and so on, that he exclaimed: "This is where I belong! This is my atmosphere! I didn't know such a place existed in the whole United States."*

Strong's wife Isobel wrote an account of Wilde's visit in her memoir, *This Life I've Loved*, which shows us what delightful company Wilde could be, in the right environment: "I think he was a little nearsighted, for he nearly tumbled against" a mannequin upon which her husband would place clothing owned by a sitter, so as not to force that sitter to be in the studio when he was painting that clothing. (Her husband had given the dummy the name "Miss Piffle.") After Wilde bowed to the "quiet lady," Mrs. Strong wrote, he apologized and made some casual remark. "It may have been our watchful attitude that gave him an inkling of the situation, for without changing his voice he began a conversation with Miss Piffle...."

---

* Actually he did. Wilde had spent several hours posing for the Bohemian Club member Theodore Wores at *his* studio.

He told her his opinion of San Francisco, and incidentally of the United States and its inhabitants; he replied to imaginary remarks of hers with surprise or approval so cleverly that it sounded as though Miss Piffle were actually talking to him. It was a superb performance, a masterpiece of sparkling wit and gaiety. Never before, or since, have I heard anything that compared to it. When he left we all felt we had met a truly great man.

The great man was the guest of honor that night at a party at the home of W. J. Callingham, a San Franciscan who had made his fortune in the insurance industry. According to a reporter for the *Call*, Wilde—as he had done in New York, Boston, and other cities—made sure that the "the jollity was kept up till the wee sma' hours." He left San Francisco for good the next day, in a first-class compartment (with his valet and Vale) on a train headed east toward Salt Lake City, stopping along the way to deliver a second talk in Sacramento. If Wilde had time to read the *Call* before he left, he would have been pleased to see that the paper pronounced his visit to San Francisco a "palpable hit" with audiences and declared that his appearances had been more successful there "from a managerial point of view" than in any other place Wilde had visited in the United States. The first verdict was subjective; the second is a fact. Though Wilde had honored only fifty percent of his agreement with Locke—presenting ten lectures in twelve days in and around San Francisco, rather than twenty in twenty-one days—that number was greater by far than the number of lectures he had delivered in any other metropolitan area in America. He had bolstered his own bank balance—and Locke's as well.

THE PRESS IN Salt Lake City was divided along sectarian lines regarding Wilde's imminent visit. The *Deseret News*, owned by the Mormon Church, was skeptical, wondering what a "so-called aesthete" could say of value to the residents of Salt Lake. It would later report, with some glee, that when Wilde arrived at the city's Walker House hotel on April 10 he entered through the ladies' entrance. Another Mormon paper, the *Salt Lake Herald*, refrained from openly mocking Wilde but nonetheless deemed him a personage unworthy of serious scrutiny. The *Salt Lake Tribune*, the city's largest independent paper, urged its readers to treat Wilde with respect and as someone who probably knew more about the subject he was speaking on—the arts—than they did. Even so, the *Tribune* delighted in reporting the story, perhaps apocryphal, of how Wilde was shocked to see, while riding the train to Salt Lake, that an enterprising youngster was selling his collection of poetry for ten cents. "Is it possible my poems have reached such beastly figures as that?" Wilde was said to have exclaimed, before confronting the boy: "Do you know, my dear sir, that you are lending your countenance to a hellish infringement on the right of a British author!" "Do you s'pose the feller that wrote the book cares?" the boy is said to have replied. "I am that man," Wilde supposedly said, to the laughter of everyone else on board.

After reaching his destination, Wilde, in what was a rare honor indeed, was given a personal tour of Salt Lake City by the president of the Church of Latter Day Saints, John Taylor, an Englishman who had emigrated to Canada before settling in America, where he joined the LDS Church, soon becoming one of founder Joseph Smith's most trusted aides. (Taylor had been with Smith when he was murdered in Carthage, Illinois, in 1844; Taylor was wounded in the attack.) Wilde had nothing but praise for the city's abundant gardens, clean streets, and views of the nearby mountains, while touring with Taylor, who considered himself not merely "God's vice-regent upon the Earth and the religious dictator to the whole world," but the "Poet Laureate of Zion." Taylor wrote one of his most famous poems, "The Upper California," when he, and many other Mormons, believed they would be building Zion in northern California, rather than Utah:

The Upper California—Oh, that's the land for me!
It lies between the mountains and the great Pacific sea;
The saints can be supported there,
And taste the sweets of liberty
In Upper California—Oh, that's the land for me! . . .
We'll burst off all our fetters and break the Gentile yoke,
For long it has beset us, but now it shall be broke:
Nor more shall Jacob bow his neck;
Henceforth she shall be great and free
In Upper California—Oh, that's the land for me!

Wilde's opinions of Taylor's poetry, if he expressed any, are lost to history. But we do have a record of what he really thought of Salt Lake. In "Impressions of America" he described the city's most famous building, the Tabernacle, as a "soup kettle" and, to a reporter from the *Denver Tribune*, called it "the most purely dreadful building I ever saw," with an interior "suitable for a jail." He would also have some fun at Taylor's expense. "The building next in importance [to the Tabernacle] is called the Amelia Palace, in honour of one of Brigham Young's wives," Wilde said in "Impressions." "When [Young] died the present president of the Mormons"—Taylor—"stood up in the Tabernacle and said that it had been revealed to him that he"—not Amelia Young—"was to have the Amelia Palace" and that "on this subject there were to be no more revelations of any kind."

The Salt Lake Theatre, built at the direction of Brigham Young, who had a rocking chair installed in the center of the first row for his personal use, was nearly filled to its fifteen-hundred-seat capacity on April 11, for Wilde's talk on "The Decorative Arts." (Included in the audience were Taylor, five of his seven wives, and more than a dozen of his children.) Considering that seats in the dress circle cost $2.75, this was a good night for Wilde and the Carte agency. The reviews, however, were poor. The *Deseret News*, predictably, declared Wilde ridiculous and unoriginal. The *Salt Lake Herald* asked, and then answered, its own question: "How is it that a man so strikingly awkward, so sorry at elocution, so ugly, so vulgar of front teeth, so painfully dreary . . . should be the highest card in the pack of current lecturers?" it wondered, before noting that "the clown is usually the most intellectual . . . and best-paid man about the circus." On this night the Oxford-educated Wilde laughed all the way to the bank.

He also made sure to laugh at the Mormons, later telling a reporter from Colorado that Salt Lake City had interested him chiefly "because it was the first city [in the world] to give a chance to ugly women"—a slighting reference to polygamy. Though he probably didn't know it, Wilde, in saying this, was echoing a joke made by Mark Twain, who had remarked in *Roughing It*, published in 1872, on the "pathetically homely" state of Mormon women and declared that "the man who marries one of them has done an act of Christian charity"—and the man who married *more* than one "had done a deed of open-handed generosity so sublime that the nations should stand uncovered in his presence and worship in silence."

Because of a train delay, Wilde arrived so late at his next stop, Denver, that he was forced to take a carriage through a snowstorm from the railway station directly to his lecture venue, the Tabor Grand Opera House, built by the Colorado mining magnate Horace A. W. Tabor, whose declared intention had been to give Denver a theater the equal of anything to be found in Europe or America. It was hard to argue he had failed. The Tabor Grand had marble floors, a rotunda in the entranceway roofed with stained glass, a domed ceiling above the auditorium painted with frescoes depicting a gracefully clouded sky, hallways and stairways covered with thick crimson carpeting, banisters made of mahogany and cherry wood, and fifteen hundred mohair seats.

Most of those seats were filled on April 12 when Wilde, who had changed into his breeches on the train, arrived at the theater, stopping first in his dressing room, where he quickly downed half a bottle of champagne. Suitably fortified, he walked onto the hall's impressive stage, where he found a single lily drooping in a glass on a wood table, next to a decanter of drinking water. Without an introduction, he launched into "The Decorative Arts," occasionally stopping to brush his hair off his face in "an ingenious manner as if realizing something amusing had just been said," noted a writer for the *Denver Tribune*. When Wilde finished his address, he bowed to the polite applause and quickly returned to his dressing room where he finished the bottle of champagne.

Then he was taken by carriage, though it was only a few blocks away, to the Windsor Hotel, a magnificent building in Denver's business district owned by a consortium led by Tabor, then Colorado's lieutenant governor, as well as its richest man. The hotel's best suite was occupied by Tabor's political office—he was planning a run for governor—so Tabor had instructed the hotel staff to redecorate another suite for its famous art-loving guest. A fresco depicting "The Genius of the Renaissance" had been hastily painted on the ceiling over Wilde's bed; the walls of the bedroom and his sitting room were covered with pink and green wallpaper, flocked with lilies; and statues of Venus and Cupid were moved into his private bath. While dining in his refurbished suite, Wilde was interrupted mid-mutton chop by the arrival of Tabor, who asked Wilde if he was happy with his rooms. After Wilde said he most certainly was, Tabor asked if he would be interested in visiting the source of his great wealth. This was the legendary Matchless silver mine, which generated upward of $100,000— more than $2 million today—per *month*, located some one hundred miles away in Leadville, Colorado, a city both men knew to be the next stop on Wilde's lecture itinerary, and where Wilde would be speaking in another theater built by Tabor. Wilde declared he would be delighted: "Of all things that which I most desire to see," he said, "is a mine." Of course, if that was really Wilde's most fervent desire, he could have visited one of the hundreds of mines in Great Britain before he came to America. So it's hard to know how seriously we should take him on this point, even though several weeks earlier he had told the *Chicago Inter-Ocean*: "I want to see Leadville immensely. . . . Those new forms of life—new attempts at civilization that have sprung up in your [American] mining cities—are objects of the keenest intellectual interest to us in Europe."

It is also hard to know what he meant by "attempts at civilization." Leadville was one of the most dangerous places in America, a boomtown—its population had jumped from about 300 to roughly 30,000 after silver was discovered there in 1878—filled with prospectors and those who preyed on them. By 1879 the total value of the silver ore mined in Leadville was estimated at $10 million; three years later it had almost doubled. Unfortunately, many came to Leadville to get rich without ever swinging a pickax or going underground. "The ominous command, 'Hold up your hands,' accompanied by the click of a pistol, was heard almost nightly" in Leadville, one journalist wrote in 1879. "Men were robbed within the shadows of their own doors [or] stripped of their valuables in their own bed chambers." Those who resisted—and even those who didn't—were often murdered. "The charge was frequently made that the police were in league with these criminals," the reporter added. A survey taken that same year found that Leadville had eighty-two saloons, thirty-five houses of prostitution, twenty-one gambling rooms, and three very busy undertakers.

In "Impressions of America" Wilde would say that he had been fully aware of Leadville's dangers, claiming that "I was told that, if I went there, they would be sure to shoot me or my traveling manager. I wrote them and [said] nothing that they could do to my traveling manager"—Mr. Vale—"would intimidate me." He also asserted to an American reporter—no doubt facetiously—that he had "practice[d] with [his] new revolver by shooting at sparrows on telegraph wires from the [railroad] car window" before leaving Denver for Leadville. "My aim," Wilde bragged, "is as lethal as lightning."

DESPITE ALL THE train traveling he had done in America, Wilde was unprepared for the rigors of the noisy, rattling, six-hour-plus train journey from Denver to Leadville, which climbed five thousand feet up the Rocky Mountains on a narrow-gauge track. In truth, he was luckier than he realized: the railroad had reached Leadville only in 1880; before then, the final portion of the trip had to be made in a wagon pulled by mules. There was no welcoming committee, or crowd of curious onlookers, at the Leadville station when he arrived. Vale escorted him through falling snow to the city's finest hotel, the Clarendon, of which Horace Tabor was part owner, and which was next to the theater where Wilde would be lecturing that night, the Tabor Opera House, which Tabor owned outright.

Born in Vermont, Tabor had arrived in the mining regions of Colorado in the 1860s, moving from camp to camp in a (so far) fruitless search for a big strike, supplementing his income by operating a general store wherever he settled. In 1877 he came to Leadville and opened a store where he also had a post office and an informal bank. In May 1878 two German immigrants, August Rische and George Hook, came to Tabor for "grubstaking" support. In return for $17 worth of supplies, Tabor got a one-third interest in whatever the Germans found. He later provided a wheelbarrow, a hand winch, and other tools to the pair, bringing his outlay to around $64. On Fryer Hill, about a mile from Tabor's store, Rische and Hook struck a vein of silver ore at around twenty-seven feet below the surface. Before long, this mine, now called the Little Pittsburg (*sic*), was generating $8,000 a week. In 1879 Tabor sold his interest in the mine for $1 million and used his position of prominence—he had been elected mayor—to turn Leadville from a mining camp into a real city. He organized a fire department, created a municipal water system, founded the Bank of Leadville, and helped to fund schools, hospitals, and churches. But he hadn't lost his interest in mining. In 1879 he took a portion of his proceeds from the Little Pittsburg and became the sole owner of the Matchless, a mine that had been open for months in Leadville without producing much of note. In January 1880, after chronic flooding problems at the mine were resolved, so much silver ore was found in the Matchless that Tabor's personal take rose upward of $2,000 per day.

Tabor wasn't in Leadville when Wilde arrived on April 13—he was living in a mansion he had built in Denver—but many of his employees and associates were. One of them, the house physician at the Clarendon Hotel, was called to attend to Wilde shortly after the lecturer took possession of his suite at the hotel. Apparently the altitude—at 10,152 feet, Leadville was, and still is, the highest incorporated city in America—had left him dizzy and nauseous. The doctor diagnosed the condition as "a case of light air" and sent Wilde's valet out for medication. (We don't know what it was, but it very well could have been laudanum, a tincture of opium used to treat all sorts of disorders in the late nineteenth century.) "Prescription $1," Wilde later wrote in the expense log he kept for the Carte agency.

By eight p.m., a crowd described by the *Leadville Daily Herald* as "a whole house of curiosity seekers" had assembled—those in reserved seats paying $1.25—at the Tabor Opera House, built in 1879 by Tabor, who immediately declared it to be the finest theater between St. Louis and San Francisco. (The Tabor *Grand* Opera House, in Denver, wasn't built until two years later.) The official opening of the Leadville auditorium in 1879 was memorable, but not for the reason Tabor wished. A pair of criminals named Frodsham and Stewart had been lynched by vigilantes the night before, and their bodies were still hanging from the beams of a partially completed building across the street. Pinned to Frodsham's corpse was a note saying, "Notice to all thieves. . . . This is our commencement, and this shall be your fates. We mean business, and let this be your last warning. [Signed] Vigilantes' Committee. We are 700 strong." According to one historian, far more locals came to see the two dead men dangling than came to opening night at the Opera House, and attendance that evening for *Serious Family!*, a comedy starring Jack S. Langrishe, was poor, though the show did sell out the rest of its run.*

As reported in the *Herald*, Wilde, after keeping his audience waiting for several minutes, "stumbled onto the stage"—the medication, perhaps?—"with a stride more becoming a giant backwoodsman than an aesthete," wearing his "low-necked knee-pants costume," and immediately began speaking. His topic was "The Decorative Arts," and he urged his baffled listeners to have their rapidly growing but still primitive city follow the lead of sixteenth-century Pisa, where artists were inspired by "brilliantly lighted palace arches and pillars of marble and porphyry, noble knights with glorious mantles flowing over their mail riding in the sunlight, groves of oranges and pomegranates, and through these groves the most beautiful women that the world has ever known, pure as lilies, faithful, noble, and intellectual." Apparently one listener couldn't contain himself, shouting: "We live in adobes in this country!" At the moment when Wilde was instructing his audience that "there is no better way of loving nature than through art," a baby in the crowd began to wail. "I wish the juvenile enthusiast would restrain his raptures," Wilde said, before the infant was transported out of the hall in the arms of its mother.

In "Impressions of America" Wilde said that, because there were many silver miners in his audience, he "read them passages from the autobiography of Benvenuto Cellini," the celebrated silversmith of the Renaissance, "and they seemed much delighted." But . . .

---

* Langrishe had previously run a theater company in another dangerous American city, Deadwood, South Dakota. In the TV series *Deadwood*, Langrishe was played by Brian Cox.

I was reproached by my hearers for not having brought him with me. I explained that he had been dead for some little time which elicited the enquiry, "Who shot him?"

Wilde dropped another name from the Renaissance, and one from his own era, in a story he told in a letter to Mrs. Bernard Beere, aware that she would repeat the tale in London. "My audience [in Leadville] was entirely miners . . . in red shirts and blonde beards," he wrote.

I described to them the pictures of Botticelli, and the name . . . seemed to them like a new drink. . . . I approached modern art and had almost won them over to a real reverence for what is beautiful when unluckily I described one of Jimmy Whistler's "nocturnes in blue and gold." Then they leaped to their feet and in their simple grand way swore that such things should not be. Some of the younger ones pulled their revolvers out and left hurriedly to see if Jimmy was "prowling about the saloons" or "wrestling a hash" at any eating shop. Had he been there I fear he would have been killed.

After his lecture Wilde returned to his suite at the Clarendon Hotel, where he changed into a pair of long pants, donned a slouch hat, and threw on his favorite coat, the bottle-green wool one with the collar made of seal fur. (It was surely below freezing outside, even in April, owing to Leadville's elevation.) Now it was time to experience first-hand the "new attempts at civilization" that had "sprung up" in America's most famous mining city. His guides were friends and/or employees of Mr. Tabor. Wilde's group headed for State Street in the heart of Leadville's entertainment district, not far from the hotel, where Wilde quickly learned that the link between old and new civilizations was alcohol.

The wooden sidewalks on each side of the street were lined with saloons, some with ironic names—the Board of Trade, the Chamber of Commerce, and the Little Church (which had a mock chapel front, through which patrons entered looking not for salvation, but for booze, gambling tables, and prostitutes)—and others with more typical ones: the Red Light, the Bon Ton, and so on. The "French section" of the street was populated by businesses featuring prostitutes said to be from Paris, which made them, the owners of these pleasure pits insisted, the most "artistic" of all the women on offer in Leadville.

It wasn't unusual for a saloon to have a barker and/or a small brass band outside to lure patrons inside, often promising "female bathers, daring tumblers and other dramatic attractions." (It was even less unusual to have to step over a prostrate drunk to enter.) Here's how the journalist Ernest Ingersoll, who had studied zoology at Harvard with Louis Agassiz and was probably the only visitor to Leadville who could match Wilde in academic achievements, described the "dramatic attractions" he found on State Street, not long before Wilde arrived: "In Leadville at night there is wildness and wickedness to satisfy the most insatiate seeker of excitement," Ingersoll wrote in *Scribner's Monthly.*

The floor is packed with men hidden under broad umbrella-like hats. All are smoking and drinking. On either side are tiers of boxes, for admission an extra price is charged, and where it is expected you will buy so-called wine at five dollars a bottle. The stage is a scene of constant buffoonery and broadly vulgar jokes; but the final act, at one o'clock of the morning, beggars description for all that is vile. Even the bedizened girls in the boxes turn their back for shame. Yet the drunken crowd hoots with glee— mainly, I believe, at the effrontery of the show, and now and then shower silver dollars on the stage in place of bouquets.

Ingersoll didn't mention the name of the saloon he was describing, but it was probably the most famous of all the saloons in Leadville— Wyman's (also known as Pap's), a place we know Wilde visited. Its proprietor, Charles (Pap) Wyman, made some peculiar requests of, and some equally strange offers to, his patrons. PLEASE DO NOT SWEAR was emblazoned on a clock behind his lengthy bar near an open Bible, which sat on a slanted mahogany shelf on the bar and which all patrons were invited to read, in between rounds of rotgut. Another sign in Pap's caught Wilde's attention so memorably that he mentioned it in "Impressions of America"; it hung above a musician and read PLEASE DO NOT SHOOT THE PIANIST. HE IS DOING HIS BEST. Wilde called this "the only rational method of art criticism I have ever come across" and would later expand on the point, declaring: "I was struck by this recognition of the fact that bad art merits the penalty of death, and I felt in this remote city . . . the aesthetic implications of the revolver." Yet another sign at Wyman's invited patrons to stop and visit with Pap, who deemed himself as essential to his establishment's decor as the gaudy chandeliers and garish wallpaper. Pap loved to talk, but he was a man of action. It was said that he had killed several men and that he carried his coins in a purse made from a human scrotum.

Wilde, with his long hair hanging out of his wide-brimmed hat, looked like a typical pleasure seeker on State Street and, in some ways, acted the part as well. He was more than willing to down a shot or two at the bars he visited and, according to some reports, tried his luck at a few gaming tables. So it went until after midnight, when Leadville's mayor, David H. Dougan, who had been acting as one of Wilde's guides, suggested a visit to the Matchless Mine, about two miles from the city's nightlife district, where a late supper would be served. Before long a horse and buggy took Wilde and his new friends up Fryer Hill to the Matchless, where they were met, inside the mine's shaft house (a large wooden structure designed to keep weather out of the mine below), by Charles Pishon, Horace Tabor's mining superintendent.

After welcoming Wilde to Leadville's most famous mine, Pishon told Wilde he would need to change his attire to go down into the mine and handed him a "complete dress of India rubber," as Wilde described it—Pishon surely would have called it a rubber *suit*—which

Wilde put on, declaring, when he finished, that it "reminded [him] of the togas worn by Roman senators." But he didn't stop there. To have been truly authentic, he said, the lining of the slicker should have been made of "purple satin and there should be storks embroidered upon the flaps, with fern embroidering around the edges." The expertise of the Oxford-educated classics scholar on such matters apparently sailed over the heads of his listeners, who merely laughed at his appearance: the rubber suit's legs were clearly too short for his six-foot-three-inch frame. As Wilde would soon see, every miner at the Matchless, which was far below the water table, wore protective gear, as water was almost always dripping into the mine from above.

Then, after Wilde tucked his hair into the headgear handed him by Pishon, the dandy was transported down mineshaft number three, considered to be the driest of the entrances to the Matchless, while standing in a metal ore bucket that came up to his waist. It was lowered by a rope-and-pulley system to the floor of the mine, more than a hundred feet below. The trip took a full minute, all of it in darkness.

Wilde would later claim, in a letter to Mrs. Bernard Beere, that he had steadfastly held true to his aesthetic principles while traveling in that bucket and had exhibited nothing but grace and elegance the entire time. In truth, he was visibly frightened and held steadfast to the thick braided rope that was slowly lowering him to his destination. Pishon stood next to him in the bucket, holding a small candle in his hand, as the primitive conveyance descended into the deep hole, which measured barely four feet across but was large enough, if need be, to lower a mule to the bottom of the mine, after its legs were properly bound with rope. (Once untied, the mule would pull cartloads of crushed rock to the shaft leading to the surface, where, after being loaded into the ore bucket, the rock fragments would be hauled up.)

After they reached the bottom, Pishon used his candle to point out the differences in the silver ore thus illuminated, some of it high grade, some low, but all of it valuable. Wilde expressed his surprise that a substance so lucrative and, once it was transformed by silversmiths into jewelry, so beautiful, could look so ordinary on a mine wall. Even so, he later described the silver deposits as "the finest sight in the world."

Another fine sight awaited him in a small room at the bottom of the mineshaft, for there Wilde was met by a dozen miners. All of them were seated on stools at a wooden table, each with a liquor bottle in front of him, in a musty, damp space with an earth floor, its ceiling and walls supported by wooden struts and planking. This room, redolent of crushed rock and the aroma of recent dynamite blasts, was lit by candles, held vertical by steel spikes hammered into the mine's walls. (Judging from photographs taken in this period, it's likely that several of those miners had removed a candleholder from the mine wall and attached it to their hats.)

It was customary in Leadville, Wilde was informed, for each bottle to make the rounds of the table, with appropriate toasts, and before long every bottle was empty. Was food consumed? No menu survives for us to examine, but we do have this comment from Wilde, who described his meal at the bottom of the Matchless in "Impressions of America": "The first course [was] whisky, the second whisky, and the third whisky." But he also wrote, in his letter to Mrs. Beere, that, after he had proved to his hosts that "art and appetite could go hand in hand"—which suggests there *was* food—he had lit a "long cigar," the smoking of which the miners "cheered till the silver fell in dust from the [walls of the] room on our plates." (If there was food, it would have been lowered by ore bucket from the surface; there were no kitchen facilities at the bottom of the Matchless.)

Moments later, receiving an honor almost as great as getting a tour of Salt Lake City from the president of the Mormon Church, Wilde was handed a large, somewhat unwieldy jackhammer by Pishon, who invited him to use it to open a new vein of ore in a tunnel not far from the Matchless's "dining room," in a wall marked with deposits of silver carbonate. "I brilliantly performed, amidst unanimous applause," Wilde told Mrs. Beere, and the vein was christened "The Oscar." "I had hoped that in their simple grand way they would have offered me shares in 'The Oscar,'" he wrote, "but . . . they did not."

Despite that disappointment, Wilde's fellow supper guests reported that he "chatted incessantly" after returning to the banquet table, giving a soliloquy on Cellini and other metalworking artists of the Renaissance that lasted nearly till sunrise. And as he had at San Francisco's Bohemian Club, Wilde proved he could more than hold his liquor. When the Matchless's ore bucket, after making several trips down and then up, deposited the last reveler on the surface as dawn was breaking, it was Wilde who was the least fatigued and the least intoxicated of them all, giving effusive thanks for the hospitality to Superintendent Pishon, before climbing into the buggy that would bring him back to the Clarendon. As newspaper readers across America would soon learn, the most memorable performance in the history of Leadville took place not at the Tabor Opera House, but at the bottom of a mine.

CHAPTER EIGHT

Go Where You're Wanted
(and Even Where You're Not)

*W*ilde was so moved by his encounters with Leadville's miners—above ground and below—that he dashed off a reference to them, which he added to his lecture on "The House Beautiful":
"In all of my journeys through the country, the only well-dressed men
I have seen in America were the miners of the Rocky Mountains.
They wore a wide-brimmed hat which shaded their faces from the
sun and protected them from the rain, and their flowing cloak, which
is by far the most elegant piece of drapery ever invented, may well be
dwelt upon with admiration. Their high boots too were sensible and
practical. These miners dressed for comfort and attained the beautiful." Wilde's spirits probably sank a bit, however, when he saw the
empty seats at his next lecture venue, the Colorado Springs Opera
House, on April 14. The social leaders of that spa town, intent on
establishing their home as the state's cultural capital, had decided
Wilde was "an advertising dodge," one good enough to fool the rubes
of Leadville and Denver perhaps, but not them. Had an authentic aesthete, a man such as John Ruskin, come to speak on the decorative
arts, the *Colorado Springs Daily Gazette* wrote, the lecture surely would

have sold out. Wilde ignored the insult and traveled north after his poorly attended talk for a return engagement in Denver, where he spoke on "The House Beautiful," on April 15, before a sizable crowd at the Tabor Grand Opera House.

By this time the editor of the *Leadville Herald* was aware of the aspersions that had been cast upon his hometown, and his neighbors in Denver, by the elitists of Colorado Springs, so he decided to double down on those slurs and, by doing so, mock his mockers. He did this in a "Special Dispatch" in the *Herald* that purported to chronicle the barbaric events that occurred after Wilde took the stage for his second appearance in Denver:

> Oscar Wilde, whose name is now a household word, . . . opened his lecture promptly at fifty minutes past eight o'clock, and had talked for about four minutes, when a committee appointed by the city council entered the stage and informed the gentleman that the sheriff of Arapahoe was waiting outside in a carriage to escort him to the county jail, on a charge of obtaining money through false pretenses. The citizens [of Denver] believed the lecture delivered there [three days] earlier, for which Wilde received one thousand dollars, was worth about half the time the audience was compelled to listen, valuing that time at a nickel every forty-five years.

The worst was yet to come:

> At two o'clock last night a band of masked men entered the jail, grabbed the eloquent gentleman by the collar and hung him from an old cottonwood tree. . . . The only reason the mob gave for acting as they did . . . was that while visiting Leadville he failed to visit the Pioneer billiard hall and drink some of their two-hundred-and-fifty-year-old Tom and Jerry.*

---

* A cocktail made from rum and brandy.

Just as the folks in Colorado Springs would have expected their uncivilized neighbors to behave.

Had Wilde seen the article, he might have anticipated the remark later made by Mark Twain who, after reading a similar article about himself, announced to the world that the report of his death was "an exaggeration." But there were moments in the next week when he might have wished he *had* been hanged. The Carte agency had booked him for a grueling series of stops in Missouri, Kansas, and Nebraska—seven in eight days—where interest in what he had to say was often weak and scorn was offered with vigor. The *Kansas City Star* wrote on April 17: "Oscar Wilde, the long-haired what-is-it, has finally reached Kansas City, and the aesthetic noodles and blue china nincompoops are in the seventh heaven of happiness." The *Kansas City Journal* noted that the lecturer's arrival coincided with that of P. T. Barnum's circus, a parallel it deemed perfect: "Oscar Wilde and a circus today. You pay your money and you take your choice."

Wilde checked into the Coates House Hotel at Tenth and Broadway, next to the Coates Opera House, where he would be speaking that night. Both buildings had been built by Wilde's local promoter, Kersey Coates, the founder of the Kansas City Chamber of Commerce and a man determined to elevate his city from its status as America's "Cow Town." Turnout was poor for the lecture, but Coates took some solace in knowing that, according to the *Journal*, the small crowd included many of the city's "most prominent citizens." Apparently, for the rest of Kansas City's citizens, the lure of seeing Zazel (real name: Rosa Maria Richter), a sixteen-year-old girl shot out of a cannon nightly at Barnum's circus, was impossible to resist.

There was competition of a different sort at Wilde's next stop, in St. Joseph, Missouri, where, on the day of his arrival, April 18, the town was still buzzing with the news that the brothers Charles and Robert Ford had pleaded guilty to first-degree murder, had been sentenced to death by hanging, and had been pardoned by Missouri governor Thomas T. Crittenden—all within a few hours—in St. Joe the previous day. This bizarre adjudication followed the assassination, committed by the brothers two weeks earlier, of a man known to his neighbors in that town as Thomas Howard, but to the rest of the world as the outlaw Jesse James. At the time of his death, accomplished by a bullet to the back of his head, he had been standing on a chair in his living room attending to a framed picture on the wall with a feather duster. Wilde knew nothing of these events when he checked into the World's Hotel a few hours before he was slated to lecture at Tootle's Opera House. What he also didn't know—though it would have amused him—was that the *Chicago Times* had published a story on the outlaw's death that referenced *him*. No one who knew James, the *Times's* correspondent wrote, believed the circumstances of his demise. "Jesse ain't no Oscar Wilde," one of them told the *Times*. "You would hardly expect [him] to be standing on a chair and knocking dust off a picture on the wall. . . . He wasn't that kind of man."

The *St. Joseph Evening News* predicted that "a big crowd at the opera house" would turn out for Wilde—not to hear him speak, but "to see the fool who has cheek enough to run around among women with breeches coming down only to his knees." But the news about the Ford brothers muffled the drumbeat for Wilde, so Tootle's was less than half-filled. The next day Wilde understood why. "Outside my [hotel] window," he wrote to a friend in England, "about a quarter mile to the west there is a small yellow house surrounded by people. This is Jesse James's house, and the people are relic-hunters." The door-knocker was sold yesterday by public auction and the man who sold it has retired on a large income. . . . Today the foot-scraper and the dust-bin are to be raffled, and [James's] favorite chromo-lithograph"—the one he was dusting?—"has already been disposed of at a price in Europe only a Titian or an authentic Michael Angelo can command."

Wilde's audiences were even smaller after he crossed the Missouri River into Kansas. Only sixty of Leavenworth's sixteen thousand residents showed up for his talk on April 19, and the *Leavenworth Daily Times* reported that many of them fell asleep, "dreaming of a long, dry sermon, that being the only way to sit it out." Wilde left the next day for Topeka, where the *Topeka Capital* opined that his appearance that night at Crawford's Opera House was "too universally commented upon to require lengthy mention." Apparently an assigning editor at the paper didn't get the message, because a reporter was sent to interview Wilde. "He is a very pleasant conversationalist, has a wonderful command of words, and expresses himself in a very clear lucid manner, much contrasted with the utterances of his burlesquers," the reporter wrote of his subject. After those compliments, however, the journalist showed himself to be a believer in the "science" of physiognomy:

> [Wilde] is narrower, by a good deal, at the top than the sides of his head, and his cranium, surrounded by a heavy shock or mane, parted in the middle, is a vivid sight. . . . His face is a broad expanse of anything save alert intellectuality; in fact, it expresses inert consciousness of having a fat thing in the lecture business more than anything else.

Wilde's "fat thing in the lecture business" turned out to be thinner than the reporter thought. The turnout in Topeka was poor, below three figures in total. Nor did things improve at Wilde's next stop, Lawrence, where another tiny audience showed up. It got even worse the night after that, April 22, in Atchison, where only thirty ticket buyers came to hear Wilde, despite (or maybe because of) the fact that the local promoter had hired a boy to lead a burro through town with a sunflower tied to its head, as it carried signs on either side of its body with the message, "I lecture at Corinthian Hall tonight."

As the thirty people in that hall awaited Wilde's entrance, a rumor spread that he would cancel rather than appear before such a small crowd. But Wilde did appear. He did so because he had learned an important lesson about the kind of show business he was in: one must *always* show up. After four months on the road, Wilde, who had no "show" other than himself, realized that if your goal is to be talked about, you have to remain in the public eye, no matter how small that public might be on a given night, and no matter how painful the experience might be in the short run. Today we would call it "paying your dues," which is why fledgling rock bands perform at terrible venues, and rookie comedians in run-down coffee shops. Wilde came to understand in 1882 that the quest for fame requires commitment: you go where you're wanted, and even where you're not.

He had also learned a truth about the institution that did most of the talking about him: the press is just as ready to cover a flop as it is a triumph. And as Wilde grasped long before anyone else, bad publicity is still publicity. "Oscar Wilde Disgusted" was the headline in the *Louisville* (Kentucky) *Courier Journal* after the debacle in Atchison, above this text: "Oscar Wilde lectured in Atchison, Kansas, last night to thirty people. He is disgusted and proposes to start East in a few days." That this item appeared in a journal six hundred miles from where the incident took place shows how successful Wilde was in making a story out of any event, flattering or not. Sure, he was disappointed at the poor turnout in those small Kansas towns, but he wasn't disgusted. In the only letter he wrote from that state, sent to Norman Forbes-Robertson, his mood was upbeat: "The summer is just breaking in Kansas, and everything looks lovely; I took a long drive yesterday afternoon and had a delightful time in what they call a 'spider buggy and a fly-up trotter.' No one knows the pleasure of driving till one drives an American trotter. They are absolutely perfect!"

Knowing that perception shapes reality, Wilde did his best to mold the narrative that would be told about him back home. While in Kansas, he sat for an interview with the *Manchester Examiner and Times*, based in England's second-largest city, conducted by an Englishman who was so taken with Wilde that he referred to him, with only a tad of irony, as "Oscar the Great." "In the eastern cities of America Wilde's photograph is most conspicuous, and Mr. Wilde told me that the demand for it far exceeded any possible supply," the reporter wrote. "He was enthusiastic about the kindnesses he had received in many of the western towns, particularly Cincinnati . . . and San Francisco, and spoke most highly of the . . . intelligence of the leading people he had met in those cities.

> In New York he had a reception given to him such as in England is rarely given to a prince. . . . In the West people traveled long distances and waited weary hours at railway stations to see him pass. He was compelled, even when fatigued, to show himself on the platforms, and . . . the farmers went back to work cheered and refreshed by the phantom of delight on which they had feasted their hungering eyes.

Wilde would soon hear from his mother (hardly an impartial source) that his plan to impress his neighbors in England was working. She wrote to say he was "the talk of London—cabmen ask me if I am anything to Oscar Wilde—the milkman has bought your picture! And in fact nothing seems celebrated in London but you."

His next stop was Lincoln, Nebraska. "I have come here from Atchison," Wilde told an interviewer on April 23, omitting to mention the paltry number of his listeners there, after "having lectured in Topeka, Denver and other points in Kansas and Colorado. My trip to the Pacific coast has been one of supreme gratification to me. . . . I lectured [in San Francisco] four times, and at Oakland twice, having large and enthusiastic audiences . . . [as I did] in San Jose, Stockton and Sacramento. I lectured twice at Denver and once at Leadville, at the latter place addressing an immense crowd of miners. The theme of my lecture there was 'Handicraft,' and I . . . won their entire good will." After listening to this ode of self-adoration, the reporter, identified at the bottom of the article as "Argus," described Wilde as "a man of great intellectual strength" who is "certainly brainy enough to tell Nebraskans a great many things worth knowing." Apparently the headline writer at the paper disagreed: the headline above the piece read "Argus and the Ass."

The brainy "Ass" had a day to kill before his lecture the next night at Lincoln's Old City Hall, so he went to morning chapel at the University of Nebraska where he gave a brief talk to the assembled undergraduates on his aesthetic mission. The *Hesperian*, a student newspaper, reported that Wilde was "quite taken with the pretty faces on the right side of the chapel. 'If we fellows at Oxford had young ladies there—well, we'd never study. Can *you* study with such attractions?'" he asked. Wilde had been introduced to several professors before the service. He recognized the name of George Woodberry, an instructor of rhetoric, having heard it in Cambridge, Massachusetts, where Woodberry had made a name for himself at Harvard as a promising poet. Wilde invited Woodberry to join him that afternoon, when Wilde was slated to tour the Nebraska countryside with the local journalist Clement Chase. Chase, for reasons that remain a mystery, took Wilde and Woodberry to the state penitentiary a few miles outside town. Wilde described what he saw there in a letter to his friend Helena (Nellie) Sickert:

> Poor sad types of humanity in hideous striped dresses making bricks in the sun. . . . Little whitewashed cells, so tragically tidy, but with books in them. In one I found a translation of Dante. . . . Strange and beautiful it seemed to me that the sorrow of a single Florentine in exile should, hundreds of years later, lighten the sorrow of some common prisoner in gaol.

In a grim irony, Wilde—who would reread all of Dante's *Divine Comedy* as a prison inmate in England—had glimpsed his own future.

Along with Wilde's portentous letter, we have one from Woodberry, sent to Charles Eliot Norton, his former mentor at Harvard:

> [Wilde] is the first artistic man I have ever seen—the first one in whom the artistic sense is mastering. . . . He has the eye, whether for natural or spiritual objects; speaking generally, he has not the

heart. He stops at surfaces—for beauty is a surface, and he sees only that. . . . But he was most amiable, pleasant and obliging. I enjoyed his company and talk, and . . . I liked to see a young man of enthusiasms, sincere I think and trying to make his faith prevail.

These enthusiasms were put to the test when Wilde headed east, stopping to preach his Gospel of Art before modest audiences in Des Moines, Iowa City, and Cedar Rapids, Iowa, followed by larger, if not fully appreciative, crowds in Dayton and Columbus, in Ohio. Wilde's talk was a "vain imagining of a morbid brain striving for an Arcadian existence," the *Columbus Daily Times* wrote. Finally, after stops in Harrisburg, Pennsylvania, and Freehold and Newark, in New Jersey, Wilde arrived in Philadelphia, a place he was excited to be returning to because of its proximity to Camden, New Jersey, where he visited Walt Whitman again. Unlike their first meeting, Whitman did not give an interview afterward about this second encounter with his new disciple—nor did Wilde—so we don't know what was discussed in Whitman's den on Stevens Street, or how intimately the two men bonded. But years later, when Wilde was living semi-openly as a gay man in London, the homosexual rights activist George Ives said that Wilde had told him: "The kiss of Walt Whitman is still on my lips."

After returning to Philadelphia from Camden on the afternoon of May 10, Wilde stopped at the home of the American aesthete Charles Godfrey Leland who, after spending a decade studying arts and crafts in Europe, had returned home to establish the Philadelphia Industrial Arts School. Wilde was wearing his fur-lined green coat and black slouch hat when he arrived from Whitman's, which Leland wrongly took as an attempt to mimic the garb of American cowboys. After changing into his breeches, Wilde was taken by carriage to Association Hall, on Chestnut Street, to deliver his lecture, in which he took a moment to praise Leland's educational work. The next day Leland wrote to thank him: "You made a great sensation. . . . As soon as your lecture ended a flock of young artful females . . . came directly to [my] school which they had never visited before. Nothing since my return to America has gratified me as much."

There was gratification in store for Wilde the next day, May 11, when he returned to New York, where his tour had begun, for a matinee lecture at Wallack's Theatre. For there, sitting in the front row of that famous venue on Broadway, was a man who knew quite a bit about shows and showmen, and how to use the press to advance one's goals—in fact, a person who had grown fabulously rich demonstrating his peerless expertise in such matters: P. T. Barnum. That America's greatest impresario was moved to see the traveling aesthete proved that Wilde's plan to make a "name" for himself was working. The aspiring dramatist was equally thrilled with the theatrical setting for Barnum to witness his success. There was "not an empty seat" in the house, he wrote to a friend in London, and, when Wilde took a bow at the end of his talk, a woman seated in a box stood up to toss him a solitary white lily, after which a rival admirer, also female, outdid her with a cascade of red roses. Best of all, these acts of adoration were recorded by reporters from virtually every newspaper in the city.

NEW YORK WAS supposed to be the final stop on Wilde's tour. But he had received an offer to continue lecturing in Canada for two weeks, which he accepted, bragging to James Whistler: "I have already civilized America—*il reste seulement le ciel*!" (all that's left is heaven). After arriving in Montreal, Wilde sent an equally self-puffing letter to another friend, describing what he said he saw from his hotel window: "I am now six feet high (my name on the placard), printed it is true in those primary colours against which I pass my life protesting, but still it is fame, and anything is better than virtuous obscurity." Lest his friend be unable to imagine that sign, Wilde made a drawing of it.

The man who would civilize heaven wanted to look divine in Canada so, before leaving New York, he arranged for a tailor there to freshen his wardrobe. This tailor, a savvy self-promoter in his own right, gave an interview to the *New York World* in which he described what he would be creating for his demanding new client:

> I am making two suits for Mr. Wilde according to his order and drawings. One is to be of black velvet and the other of the shade of a lake glistening in the moonlight. The shade is called *"couleur du lac au Claire de la lune"* or mouse-color. . . . [Each] suit has a plain velvet doublet fitting tight to the body, without visible buttons, . . . the lower part of the sleeves being of embossed velvet, with embroidered field-flowered designs and fitting tight to the arm. The upper part of the arms is to be in large puffs of the same material, only of a larger pattern, and the body of plain velvet. The sleeves are of two designs of brocaded velvet edged with a delicate ruffle of *mousseline de soie*. Around the neck is also a narrow frill in three rows of the same material as that which edges the sleeves. The breeches are to come to the knee and to be tight fitting, with two small buttons at the bottom.

Wilde was happy with the tailoring. So were his audiences in Ontario and Quebec, who delighted in the dandy's sartorial presentation. But Wilde was unhappy with the price, writing to Colonel Morse to say that "$50 for a jacket is ridiculous. . . . Try to get [the tailor] to abate the bill." (That $50 charge would be equal to nearly $1,200 today.)

While in Canada, Wilde accepted another offer to continue lecturing. The Memphis businessman Peter Tracy was paying huge appearance fees, but another reason Wilde said yes was that he would be speading in the American South, the losing side in the recent Civil War. As a child, Wilde had been taught by his mother that individuals linked by tradition, history, and common interests have a right to independence and a mandate to fight for it. Lady Wilde had been speaking of Ireland's struggle to free itself of English rule, not the attempt of the slave-owning American South to secede from the United States. But her son saw the parallels between them.

Six hundred Memphians attended his talk on June 12 at Leubries Theater, where Wilde stood on a stage arranged to resemble a Victorian drawing room: sofas and chairs formed a semicircle around his lectern, and framed pictures hung from a curtain behind him. Midway through his speech Wilde was startled by the appearance on the stage, surely arranged by Tracy, of a three-year-old girl named Mary Teresa McCarthy. She was carrying a basket of flowers that she presented to the speaker, who expressed his delight at having such a young and lovely convert to the aesthetic cause.

After his talk Wilde headed south in a Pullman car on which Tracy had placed a large sign, described by the *Memphis Public Ledger* as "a flaming white canvas with the great Aesthete's name printed on it in big black letters." Wilde was accompanied by his valet and the new road manager for his southern tour, Frank Gray. Their destination was Vicksburg, Mississippi, where, after checking in to the Washington Hotel, Wilde met with local dignitaries and toured the city's cemetery for Confederate Civil War soldiers. Though June 14, the night of Wilde's lecture on "The Decorative Arts," was described in the *Vicksburg Daily Herald* as "a scorcher," the city's Opera House was packed with a "large and recherché audience," which responded with pride and audible approval when Wilde referred to the South as a "land of art," a "home of song," and the "cradle of beauty" in America. Two days later an editorial in the *Daily Herald* said of Wilde: "He is a fine scholar, a talented poet; as a companion, he is sociable and entertaining, and in a business way sharp and shrewd. The press in this country has evidently done him a great injustice."

While traveling to New Orleans, Wilde observed a bit of southern "justice" that might have led him to rethink his views of the region. When his train stopped in Bonfouca, Louisiana (now part of Slidell), on the northeastern shore of Lake Ponchartrain, some thirty miles from New Orleans, he and his fellow passengers were eyewitnesses to a lynching. According to press reports, "Oscar Wilde ran across a lynching" this week "in Bonfouca, La. The negro assailant of a white woman had been taken out of jail by a mob, and Oscar saw the hanging from a [Pullman] car window. The negro was a preacher, and his wild eloquent appeals for mercy moved the aesthetic traveler greatly, but did not effect [sic] the lynchers, who quickly suspended him from a railroad bridge."

Wilde made no mention of this incident in any of his letters to London; nor did it interfere with his busy schedule in New Orleans, the largest city in the former Confederacy, where he arrived on June 16. After checking into the St. Charles Hotel, he entertained the press, again praising the South—despite what he had just seen—as the place where he had "encountered more that was agreeable and courteous in manners" than in any other section of America. He said such courtesy was, in his view, the rule in "warm countries and may be the result of climatic effects"; he also declared that "art belongs in hot countries" and that Sarah Bernhardt had told him that steamy New Orleans was "the one city [in America] where the people thoroughly understood and appreciated her." But when informed by a reporter that the Art Union of New Orleans, the city's leading art school, had recently improved its financial footing by organizing, selling tickets to, and overseeing wagering on a mule race, Wilde said: "A mule race! That is sad, very sad."

He was given a tour of the French Quarter by the former Confederate general Pierre Gustave Beauregard, the man who ordered the first shot fired in the Civil War, at Fort Sumter, in the harbor of Charleston, South Carolina, on April 12, 1861. Beauregard was now the president of the New Orleans, Jackson, and Mississippi Railroad and a towering figure in the city's social aristocracy. After escorting Wilde back to his hotel, Beauregard returned later to accompany him to his speaking engagement at the Grand Opera House, where seven hundred ticket buyers awaited his lecture on "The Decorative Arts."

Wilde left the next morning by train for Galveston, then the biggest city in Texas, roughly four hundred miles away. He was awe-struck by the scenery en route, telling a reporter that he was enthralled by the cypress trees, with their streamers of gray moss fluttering in the wind in the swamps of western Louisiana, and the sleepy alligators that sprawled on the muddy banks of the bayous. But as the reporter listening to him put it—rather shockingly, to our ears today: "Nothing in the way of animal life, however, seemed to please the art reformer so much as the young negroes." To prove this assertion, the journalist quoted Wilde as saying: "I saw them everywhere, happy and careless, basking in the sunshine or dancing in the shade, their half-naked bodies gleaming like bronze, and their lithe and active movements reminding one of the lizards that were seen flashing along the banks and trunks of the trees."

An editorialist in the *Galveston Daily News* encouraged the city to have an open mind about the man from London who was coming to speak to them about beauty. "We Americans are a busy, money-loving and money-getting people, and . . . we do not trouble ourselves much about 'the beautiful and the true' in our personal and home surroundings," he wrote. "If the visit of Oscar Wilde shall tend in any measure to . . . raise our conceptions and instincts to a more truly artistic standpoint, he will have done us a good deed." The *Daily News* was proud that the Pavilion Opera House was nearly sold out for Wilde's talk on June 19, but the newspaper was disappointed by what happened after he began speaking. The electric power for the hall's lighting malfunctioned, causing the lights to flutter on and off, then fail altogether. Even worse, some young men in the back of the hall did their best to distract Wilde by stamping their feet as he spoke. Had he been so inclined, Wilde might have "arrested" them: he told a reporter he had been made a colonel in the Texas Rangers while in Galveston. (When telling the same story upon his return to England, Wilde upped his rank to general.)

He left the next day for San Antonio. Though he arrived several hours later than anticipated, a large crowd had stayed to greet him at

Union Depot, a building freshly festooned, in his honor, with sunflowers. He was then taken by carriage to the Menger Hotel, where he was met the next morning by a writer for the *San Antonio Evening Light*. Much to Wilde's surprise, the reporter was an Englishman he knew, Henry Ryder-Taylor, who had worked for the *Telegraph* in London. Wilde was delighted to see a familiar face and happily joined Ryder-Taylor for a tour of San Antonio, where Ryder-Taylor had settled a year earlier. While on this tour, Wilde was moved, apparently erotically, by the grace of the old missions, built when Texas was part of Mexico. "Those old Spanish churches, with their picturesque remains of tower and dome, and their handsome carved stonework standing about the verdure and sunshine of a Texas prairie, gave me a thrill of strange pleasure," he said. But he was horrified to see how the city's most famous structure, the Alamo, had fallen into disrepair, telling Ryder-Taylor it was "monstrous" that such a "noble" building was so neglected. (He wasn't exaggerating: in 1882 the Alamo was a dry goods store, after years of being used by the United States Army as a grain storehouse.)

A crowd of four hundred awaited Wilde at Turner Hall on June 21. In truth, they waited longer than they anticipated: a pianist had been hired to play while the crowd was taking their seats for the eight-thirty lecture; he couldn't be enticed to leave the stage until nine. Wilde spoke for an hour, but not everyone could hear him because several members of his audience, as Ryder-Taylor noted in the *Evening Light*, found the aesthete's lecture "too long between drinks" and the "squeaking of the new boots of the[se] thirsty ones going out for refreshments" often drowned out the speaker. One person who *was* able to hear Wilde was the reviewer for the *San Antonio Express*, and he was impressed—all the more so because he hadn't expected to be:

> The original and only genuine Oscar Wilde, the much talked of
> and extensively advertised English lecturer on aesthetic and per-
> sonal adornment, appeared before a very fair audience last eve-

ning at Turner Hall . . . [where] he impressed upon his hearers the necessity and utility of inculcating in the minds of our rising youth a love of the beautiful . . . and gave it as his opinion that there were other and greater pleasures to this life than the American plan of pursuing unceasingly the struggle of money-getting. . . . Outside of his personal appearance, we can recall nothing to ridicule, even though we were so disposed.

Wilde had a nearly identical experience in Houston. His lecture venue there, Gray's Hall, sat atop a saloon where one patron, apparently displeased by what was happening in the auditorium above him, persisted in ringing a large gong in that saloon as Wilde was speaking, which was heard throughout the hall. Gray's could hold eight hundred patrons, and it was far from filled on June 23; many of those who were there seemed bored. Even so, the *Houston Post* came to Wilde's defense on its editorial page:

He may insist too roundly upon the necessity of the decorative principle, but . . . there can be no doubt that Mr. Wilde's ideas of the beautiful should prevail. . . . A young community must grow into an appreciation of those principles and if Wilde has stirred any latent sentiment in those who have ignored the value of those principles, we should thank him heartily.

FROM HOUSTON, WILDE and his retinue returned by overnight train to New Orleans, where he had a second lecture scheduled for June 26 at Spanish Fort, a former military base on the southern bank of Lake Ponchartrain. Wilde had two free days before his talk; perhaps motivated by the sight of the "half-naked" Negroes he had seen en route to Texas, he spent the night of June 24 at a voodoo ceremony in New Orleans, where former slaves were marking—in an all-night celebration with drums, dancing, and, in all likelihood, an animal sacrifice or two—St. John's Night, ostensibly the birth date of John the Baptist. Wilde's guide was the New Orleans author George W. Cable, who had written several well-received novels about the city's Creole population.

Wilde also met with journalists at the Charles Hotel. His trip to Texas was one topic of conversation, but the main subject on the minds of his interviewers was the news that, after his lecture, Wilde would be traveling to Biloxi, Mississippi, where he would be dining at Beauvoir, the home of Jefferson Davis, the former president of the Confederate States of America. This wasn't just breaking news; it was shocking news. The reaction of the *Selma* (Alabama) *Times* was typical: "It seems incredible that [Wilde] is to be the guest of Davis. The President of the Confederacy is the last person we should suspect of taking an interest in the laughing stock of the day. He is so modest, retiring, elegant in his dignity, that we would have not thought it possible for the self-asserting, sight-seeing, pseudo-fanatical, long-haired aesthetic humbug to have penetrated the quiet home of the grand Southerner. . . . Surely this [report] is a mistake."

But it was not. According to Hudson Strode, the author of a highly sympathetic, three-volume biography of Davis, the visit was the result of an interview Wilde gave in June, in Memphis, to *Meriwether's Weekly*. That journal was owned by a friend of the Davis family, which had lived in Memphis following the Civil War. The man from *Meriwether's* noted that Wilde's hotel suite was "in disorder, with magazines and photographs strewn on the floor, and on the table were the two volumes of Jefferson Davis's *The Rise and Fall* [*of the Confederate Government*.]" The journalist expressed surprise that Wilde was in possession of that work and was even more astonished by his response: "Jefferson Davis is the one man I would like most to see in the United States," Wilde supposedly said, after which he declared it remarkable that it took "Northern armies numbering three million soldiers four years to whip him." The interviewer then wrote that Wilde asked him where Davis was now living. When told he was in Mississippi, four hundred miles away, Wilde said: "That's a long way to go to meet anyone, but not too far to go to see such a man as Jefferson Davis." This article was read by Davis's daughter, Margaret Davis Hayes, then still living in Memphis, who sent a copy of the magazine to her mother, Varina Davis, at Beauvoir. Not long afterward Wilde received his invitation.

Several of the words in that article—especially the "four years to whip him" part—sound much more like something an American southerner would have said rather than Wilde. But when Wilde was interviewed by the *New Orleans Picayune* two weeks later, he was quoted as saying this, which sounds like something he *would* say: "[Davis's] fall, after such an able and gallant pleading of his own cause, must necessarily arouse sympathy. . . . The case of the South in the Civil War was to my mind much like that of Ireland today. It was a struggle for autonomy, self-government for a people. . . . People must have freedom and autonomy before they are capable of their greatest result in the cause of progress. This is my feeling about the southern people as it is about my own people, the Irish. I look forward to much pleasure in visiting Mr. Jefferson Davis."

But first Wilde had an appearance to make, on June 26, at Spanish Fort, which was sold out for his talk on "The House Beautiful." The *New Orleans Daily Press* had done its part to encourage that turnout: "It is feared that Oscar Wilde will not be heard very well in the hall at Spanish Fort, but he can be seen—and this alone is worth the money." Wilde left the next morning for the ninety-mile trip to Biloxi, where the local press was still in shock over his plan to dine with Davis. "It's like a butterfly making a formal visit to an eagle," wrote an editorialist for the *Booneville* (Mississippi) *Pleader*.

Wilde was received at Beauvoir by Davis, then seventy-five and somewhat frail, his lively fifty-seven-year-old wife Varina, their eighteen-year-old child Varina Anne (Winnie) Davis, and a visiting cousin, Mary Davis. According to Strode, the dinner was an unpleasant experience for Mr. Davis, who sensed something so "indefinably objectionable" about Wilde that he excused himself early from the dinner table, pleading a slight illness. ("I did not like the man," Davis was said to have told his wife the next day.) It's possible that Wilde, who often praised the beauty of the South, had offended Davis at dinner by telling a story he would later repeat in "Impressions of America" about the doleful nostalgia he said he encountered so often in the former Confederacy. According to Wilde, he had once remarked to a man standing next to him on an elegant veranda somewhere in the South, a lovely garden and a grove of magnolia trees in full bloom spread before them: "How beautiful the moon looks tonight," to which the Southerner replied, "Yes, but you should have seen it before the war."

We don't know for certain what caused Davis's discomfort. Strode's sources were not at the dinner; they were friends of Mary Davis who said Mary had told them of Mr. Davis's contempt for his guest. The scholar Ellen Crowell has an intriguing take on what might have been the cause of Davis's early departure: it was widely believed in the North that Davis had donned women's clothing while trying to elude capture by the victorious Union Army in 1865; this "evidence" of effeminacy was used by northern newspapers to heap scorn on the supposedly unassailable notion of southern manhood. "The modern androgynous figure in dandyish dress knocking at the door of Beauvoir repelled Davis because in Wilde he saw embodied the very gender indeterminacy of which he and men of his class stood accused," Crowell has written.

But it's more likely Davis's discomfort was caused by future shock. After spending time with his elaborately costumed, self-adoring guest, a man who (unasked) would leave behind an autographed photo of himself when he departed the next day, Davis—as Henry James had before him—realized with revulsion that he had a met a citizen of a new world in which he knew he didn't fit. The photo left by Wilde, number five from his session with Sarony, showed him standing, wearing his fur-lined wool coat over his velvet doublet and holding gloves in his left hand. He is wearing trousers, rather than breeches. It was signed: "To Jefferson Davis in all loyal admiration from Oscar Wilde, June '82—Beauvoir."

From Beauvoir, Wilde traveled to Mobile, Alabama, where on June 28 he lectured at Frascati Park, a resort and zoo located on Mobile Bay where, several months earlier, the Wallacks, a well-known entertainment troupe of the era, performed comedic sketches, Shakespearean monologues, and excerpts from operas, culminating in an attraction the Wallacks called "THE EIGHTH WONDER OF THE WORLD: A SILENT WOMAN." The three hundred seats for Wilde's talk at Frascati's open-air pavilion—located near a cage of screeching monkeys—sold out quickly, and, according to the *Mobile Register*, "extra horse-car facilities" were put into service to accommodate those ticket buyers; "even the mules pulling those cars were aesthetic, having sunflowers stuck in their headgear."

Similar anticipation was building for Wilde in Montgomery, Alabama, the first capital of the Confederacy, where the *Daily Advertiser* wrote on June 29: "OSCAR WILDE—This world famous man will arrive today, and deliver his great lecture entitled 'The Decorative Arts,' in McDonald's Opera House. . . . Mr. Wilde draws big crowds of only the best and most refined people. . . . No lady has heard of him that is not anxious to see and hear him, and, 'tis said, he 'adores the fair sex.'" This excitement was not shared by a reporter for the *Union Springs* (Alabama) *Herald*, however, who claimed to have witnessed Wilde's arrival in Montgomery. "Something in the shape of a man but more like a specimen of the high order of a baboon descended from the [railroad] car," he wrote.

> Yes, it was the veritable ass-thetic Oscar. . . . He was dressed in a suit of white silk, wore a flaming red cravat, a Derby hat, and carried a huge palm leaf fan which he used vigorously while passing to the hack. It is a sad commentary upon the good sense

and intelligence of . . . the American people who have placed themselves in the ridiculous role of paying court to this bundle of conceit.

After a tour of Montgomery, which included a visit to the building where Davis had been sworn in as president of the Confederacy, Wilde spoke before an audience of three hundred. (The *Daily Advertiser* kindly referred to that smallish group as "select.") Wilde left Alabama the next morning for Georgia where, beginning on June 30, in Colum-bus, he delivered five lectures in the next seven days. Turnout in Columbus was low, partly because Wilde's arrival was overshadowed by the news that President Garfield's assassin, Charles Guiteau, had been executed earlier that day, by hanging, in Washington. Wilde's audience wasn't much larger in Macon, where a reviewer for the *Macon Telegraph*, writing about the man who would later be acknowledged as perhaps the greatest comic dramatist in the history of the theater, declared that Wilde's "utter absence of that essential to all lecturers—humor—put an air brake to anything like applause."

Wilde pulled into Atlanta on July 4, meeting with the *Atlanta Constitution* after checking into the Markham Hotel. Atlanta was decades away from becoming the metropolis of the New South—its population, according to the 1880 census, was 37,400, making it just the forty-ninth-largest city in America. Even so, more than enough revelers were parading outside Wilde's hotel room, several of them tossing firecrackers, for him to complain to his interviewer: "Oh, the patriots, the patriots. Let's shut down the window and shut out the noise."

Actually, Wilde adored parades, just not this one. "I don't think anything so fine as the Declaration of Independence should be cele-brated at all if it cannot be celebrated in a noble manner," he said. "Amongst the most artistic things that any city can do is to celebrate by pageant the great eras in its history. . . . It shows [the city's residents] what otherwise they would not have a chance of seeing—noble costumes, beautiful colors, and sculpturesque groupings. . . . But I am afraid the only pageants that most Americans have a hope of seeing are the glaring processions of their traveling circuses." The reporter quickly changed the subject to Jefferson Davis. "He lives in a very beautiful house by the sea," Wilde said. "He impressed me very much as a man of the keenest intellect. . . . We in Ireland are fighting for the principle of autonomy against empire, for independence against centralization, for the principles for which the South fought. So it was a matter of immense interest and pleasure to me to meet the leader of such a great cause. Because although there may be a failure in fact, in idea there is no failure possible. The principles for which Mr. Davis and the South went to war cannot suffer defeat."

Wilde would soon learn (for the second time) that one of those "principles"—racism—had not suffered defeat. After boarding the first-class sleeper car with his valet Stephen Davenport for the trip to Savannah, Georgia's second-largest city, Wilde was met by an agent for the railroad line who told him it was "against the rules of the company to sell sleeping-car tickets to colored persons." (Davenport had not been there when the tickets were bought.) As was reported days later in the *New York Times*, "Mr. Wilde said that he had never been interfered with before [regarding the travel arrangements for Davenport], and persisted in having his darkey (sic) retain his sleeping-car ticket." The railroad company employee then approached the black porter working on that car, who spoke to Davenport directly, telling him that, if he stayed where he was, he might be lynched when the train stopped to pick up first-class passengers in Jonesboro, Georgia, if those passengers found a black man sitting in the whites-only car. Davenport agreed to move. (Of course, all Wilde's appearances in the South were for whites only, if not by law, by "custom.")

Two days later, when writing to his American friend Julia Ward Howe, Wilde expressed his delight in knowing that his southern tour was nearing its end. After speaking in Charleston, South Carolina, he lectured in Richmond, Virginia, a city of nearly 64,000, where he attracted a crowd of just two hundred, described by the *Richmond State* as composed of "some of our best citizens and a residuum of small potatoes of the male sex." Wilde was eager to reconnect with Howe in Newport, Rhode Island; his letter also gave him an opportunity to express his true opinion of the region he had spent so much time praising in public:

> I write to you from the beautiful, passionate, ruined South, the land of magnolias and music, of roses and romance: picturesque too in her failure to keep pace with your keen northern intellect; living chiefly on credit, and on the memory of some crushing defeats. And I have been to Texas, right to the heart of it, and stayed with Jeff Davis at his plantation (how fascinating all failures are!)

Wilde reached Newport, the summer home of the Astors, the Vanderbilts, and several other of America's richest families, on July 13, accompanied by his friend from New York Sam Ward (Julia's brother) and Stephen Davenport, all of them staying at Mrs. Howe's farm on Aquidneck Island. (The farm was Howe's summer retreat; she spent the rest of the year in Boston.) The arrival of Davenport in this preserve of the wealthy (and white) in New England was almost as much of a shock as it had been on that sleeping-car train in Georgia. According to Mrs. Howe's daughters, their mother's house was "thrown into a flutter by the advent of Wilde's valet. It was one thing to entertain the Aesthete, another to put up the gentleman's gentleman." In a letter written from Newport to the Harvard professor Charles Eliot Norton, Wilde said: "I have just returned from the South and have a three-weeks holiday now . . . and find it not unpleasant to be in this little island where idleness ranks among the virtues." But it wasn't all idleness for Wilde. After attending a polo match on July 15, he spoke that night to a sold-out crowd at the Newport Casino Theatre, a sumptuous hall designed by the celebrated New York architecture firm McKim, Mead & White. Then he attended the Casino Ball, one of the highlights of Newport's summer season, and had late supper on board the U.S. Navy battleship *Minnesota,* docked in Newport Harbor.

Mrs. Howe organized several dinners for her guest at her home as well. At one of them, Wilde, wearing a salmon-colored kerchief, out-talked two of the greatest talkers in New England: Oliver Wendell Holmes and his brother-in-law, Thomas Appleton, the man many believe Holmes had been quoting when he wrote, "Good Americans, when they die, go to Paris"—a line Wilde liked so well he "borrowed" it twice: in *The Picture of Doran Gray* and *A Woman of No Importance.* When asked by his fellow diners how he had spent his morning, Wilde said he had filled it with strenuous literary work—going over a proof of one of his poems, from which, after long deliberation, he removed a comma. And in the afternoon? he was asked. "I put it back in again." (Wilde may have borrowed this quip from Gustave Flaubert.)

From Newport, Wilde traveled to other vacation spots in the Northeast—first to the Catskills, where he dined at the summer home of the famous Brooklyn-based minister Henry Ward Beecher. Then he went to the New Jersey Shore where, in Long Branch, he was intro-duced to the former president of the United States Ulysses S. Grant, the man who had accepted the surrender of Robert E. Lee, marking the end of Jefferson Davis's Confederacy. (One can only wonder if there was anyone else in America in 1882 who had met, within a period of weeks, both Grant and Davis.)

Wilde gave a lecture on August 7 in Long Beach, New York, where his visit to the ocean, in swimming wear, was commemorated in a drawing published in *Frank Leslie's Illustrated Newspaper.* This popular American journal was run by Leslie's widow Miriam who, nine years later, would wed Oscar's brother Willie, a marriage based in New York that would last only two years. (In a decision that surely made Oscar chortle, the newlyweds honeymooned at Niagara Falls.) This marriage, and the illustration in her magazine, wasn't Mrs. Leslie's first link to the Wilde family. It is believed she was the unnamed friend of Helen Lenoir, the manager of the Carte agency in New York, who suggested to Lenoir in 1881 that it might be a good idea to send "a real aesthete" to America to publicize *Patience*.

From Long Island, Wilde traveled to upstate New York, speaking before good crowds in Saratoga and nearby Balston Spa; he was the subject of some ribbing at a breakfast held in his honor in a restaurant atop nearby Mount McGregor. The toastmaster praised Wilde as a "lover of the beautiful. He loves America. He loves our eagle. He especially loves our double-eagles," a slang term in 1882 for the $20 gold piece. (No one laughed louder at this than Wilde.) After lecturing in Sharon Springs and Cooperstown, he headed south, speaking again in Long Beach on August 16. From there, Wilde made a second swing through coastal New Jersey, lecturing in Sea Bright (on August 21), Long Branch (August 22), Spring Lake (23), Asbury Park (24), Atlantic City (25), and Cape May (26)—not that the *New York Tribune* was impressed. Wilde was just another shabby entertainer in those beach towns, the paper sniffed, following "in the wake of the professional mind reader, the ventriloquist, the bird-charmer and the actor who reads selections from *Othello*, *Macbeth* and *Lear*, all for a slight consideration."

Wilde took much of September off, returning to New York where, on the twentieth, he made his first public appearance in weeks—not to lecture, but to visit the New York Stock Exchange. His guide was the socially connected broker H. K. Burras. "It was about 2 o'clock in the afternoon when [Burras] brought his charming charge downtown," said the account of this visit in the *Washington Post*. "Oscar looked his sweetest. Finest black broadcloth wrapped a form pleasantly suggestive of corsets, and a shiny stovepipe sat with an exquisite grace just above a delicate ear. The flowing tresses of the philosopher were fresh from the oil jar, and rainbow stockings tucked into dapper knee-breeches were the only drawbacks to the pretty picture." When those working on the floor of the exchange took notice of this well-dressed visitor, the *Post* reported, "business came suddenly to a standstill:

> A brass band at a country fair never wrought more startling effects. About 1,000 messenger boys . . . crowded close around the aesthete. . . . Exchange rules counted for nothing, and the boys made the hallways and the galleries of the Exchange ring with their enthusiasm. [Soon] the brokers caught sight of Burras and his companion was recognized. Then there arose a shout which was a tempest, compared with which the cries and hootings of the messenger boys were but as pleasing murmurings.

Perhaps inspired by this fan frenzy, Wilde returned to the road, lecturing in Rhode Island, Massachusetts, and Maine before entering Canada's Maritime Provinces, for nine talks in ten days. Finally, on October 15, he arrived back in New York, never to leave again until his return to Britain. His friends in London expected him to immediately book passage home, but Wilde surprised them, remaining in New York for ten more weeks, living in hotels, then taking private rooms in Greenwich Village. He was staying in New York to greet his friend and protégé Lillie Langtry, who was arriving on October 23 to begin rehearsals to play Hester Grazebrook in a five-week run of *An Unequal Match*, a play written by Tom Taylor, who also wrote *The American Cousin*, the play Abraham Lincoln was attending when he was assassinated. "I would rather have discovered Mrs. Langtry than have discovered America," Wilde told the New York press, explaining his decision to remain in America to meet "the New Helen": "It was for such a lady that Troy was destroyed, and well might it be destroyed for such a woman."

Before the sun rose on October 23, Wilde, along with several journalists—all of them having just consumed a breakfast of oysters and champagne furnished by Langtry's producer, Henry Abbey—boarded a small boat that brought them to the ship carrying Mrs. Langtry (by coincidence, the same one that had brought Wilde to America, the SS *Arizona*) anchored at the quarantine station in New York Harbor. According to the reporter from the *New York Times*, whose vision may have been altered by that mostly liquid breakfast, Wilde, carrying a giant bouquet of lilies, was "dressed as probably no man in the world was ever dressed before. His hat was of brown cloth not less than six inches high; his coat was of black velvet; his overcoat was of green cloth, heavily trimmed with fur; his trousers matched his hair; his tie was gaudy and his shirtfront very open." What that reporter didn't know was that Wilde was repeating a performance he had given in Britain when meeting Sarah Bernhardt upon her return from her tour of the United States in 1880—and for the same reason: to make *himself* as much a part of the story as the woman he was ostensibly there to worship.

After Langtry moved into her hotel, Wilde took charge of her social schedule. He urged Sam Ward and Mrs. John Bigelow, the wife of the former ambassador to France, to be her sponsors into New York society. He also took her to Sarony's studio on Union Square. Newspapers claimed the portraitist paid Langtry a $5,000 sitting fee—more than three times what he had paid Bernhardt two years earlier. True or not, the session didn't go as well as either participant hoped. Sarony said of Langtry afterward: "She has a fine figure, good height, head well balanced, good features and a good expression—when she pleases." Langtry, after looking at proofs from the session, told Sarony: "You have made me pretty. I am beautiful."

As Langtry's rehearsal schedule became more intense, making her unavailable to Wilde, he was forced to seek other social engagements. On October 28 he attended a dinner at the Lotos Club. The toastmaster was Whitelaw Reid, the editor of the *New York Tribune*, a paper that had regularly expressed its skepticism of Wilde's mission to America. Wilde was not scheduled to speak, but Reid called him to the podium, where it seems Wilde's pique with the *Tribune* was something he felt compelled to express. "I thought that I should see a nation not so ready to mock as this nation has shown itself," he said. "I think that I have been the first source of income to many ink-stained lives." He also said he "found it difficult, at first, and even now, to realize that between Art and the [American] public there has arisen a mist of folly" rooted in philistinism and fanned by an ill-informed press. The notion of sculpture held by most Americans, Wilde said with equal parts scorn and dismay, "is derived from the figures in front of the tobacconists' shops."

These remarks were met with some laughter and even more grumbling. One listener, William H. Hurlbert, the editor of the *New York World*, somehow decided that no one was better suited to review Mrs. Langtry's performance in her American stage debut on November 6 than her "creator," Oscar Wilde. So despite his clear link to the actress, Wilde did review her work in *An Unequal Match*. Well, not her work as a performer; he reviewed *her* as a work of art. "It is only in the best Greek gems, on the silver coins of Syracuse, or among the marble figures of the Parthenon frieze, that one can find the ideal representation of the marvelous beauty of that face which laughed through the leaves last night as Hester Grazebrook," he wrote.

> Pure Greek it is, with the grave low forehead, the exquisitely arched brow; the noble chiseling of the mouth, shaped as if it were the mouthpiece of an instrument of music; the supreme and splendid curve of the cheek; the augustly pillared throat which bears it all; it is all Greek, because the lines which compose it are so definite and so strong, and yet so exquisitely harmonized that the effect is one of simple loveliness purely.

But if Wilde was expecting gratitude from Langtry for his review, he was disappointed. Rather than spending her free time with him, she was spending it with Freddie Gebhard, an American playboy and heir to a huge real estate and manufacturing fortune, who was happy to spend vast sums to keep her entertained and by his side.

Wilde had spent considerable time that autumn trying to interest the American actress Mary Anderson in taking the title role in a tragedy he had yet to finish writing, *The Duchess of Padua*, which he hoped would be the inaugural presentation at a new theater in New York. As the negotiations with Anderson dragged on, Wilde tried to interest another American actress, Marie Prescott, to take the title role in a New York production of *Vera; or the Nihilists*, his first finished play, the debut of which had been canceled at the last minute in London in 1881. When these efforts seemed headed for failure, the *Tribune* couldn't hide its glee, publishing this exchange between Wilde and one of its reporters:

"'Have you made any arrangements to produce your play?'" the *Tribune* reporter asked, referring to *Vera*, after arriving at Wilde's rented rooms on West Eleventh Street.

"'Why do you ask?' said Wilde.

"'The public might like to know.'

"'Oh!'

"Mr. Wilde closed his eyes and yielded himself to up to thought.

"'To persons of no reputation,' he presently began, 'small paragraphs are doubtless an advantage. But, really, I don't care for them.'

"'But the production of your play might be a matter of a long paragraph.'

"'Oh!'

"Mr. Wilde closed his eyes again.

"'Well, I have made no arrangements as of yet.'"

Surely hoping to add to Wilde's displeasure, the *Tribune* headlined the interview: "Oscar Wilde Thoroughly Exhausted."

But he wasn't so tired that he lacked the energy to get himself into trouble a few weeks later, after Langtry (and Gebhard) departed for Boston. On December 14, as Wilde was walking near Union Square, he was approached by a well-dressed young man. "Excuse me, Mr. Wilde," he said, "I am the son of Mr. [Anthony J.] Drexel, of the firm of Drexel, Morgan & Co., the Wall Street bankers. Having seen you once or twice in my father's office, I hope you will pardon me for introducing myself." Wilde had been to that office but had no memory of seeing the man there. Even so, he agreed to lunch with him at a nearby restaurant, during which young Drexel told him how, on a lark, he had purchased a lottery ticket and now, to his delight, he had learned it was the winning ticket, worth $500. He then proposed that Wilde accompany him to an address not far from Union Square to get his cash. There Wilde found himself in an office where several men were throwing dice, eight at a time, near a black cloth marked with numbers. After a cashier gave Drexel his winnings, Drexel joined in the game, apparently giving a small portion of his money to Wilde, so that he too could play, if he so desired. He did.

And at first he was glad he did, winning a tidy sum. But this was "banco," which the author Luc Sante, in his book *Low Life*, called "the most famous sucker game" in New York in the late nineteenth century. Before long, Wilde had lost more than $1,000 in the rigged game, writing three checks to cover his losses. He soon suspected he had been swindled and insisted on leaving. Young Drexel, obviously a coconspirator in the scam, claimed to Wilde that he too was outraged with the treatment his new friend had just received and left with him, promising that he would return to the site of the crime to regain Wilde's checks. After Drexel departed, Wilde took a cab to his New York bank, where he stopped payment on those checks; then he went to a police station, where he met Capt. Alexander S. Williams. "Captain Williams, in your long and varied experience as an officer of police, I presume you have occasionally met with persons who make fools of themselves?" Wilde asked. The captain nodded. "Well, I have just made a fool of myself." After listening to the details of Wilde's misadventure, Williams pulled out a book of mug shots, which Wilde flipped through. Within minutes he realized that "young Drexel" was actually the con man known to the police as "Hungry Joe" and/or "Paper Dollar Joe" and whose last name, depending on his mood, was Lewis, Sellick, or Astorhous.

Having "fallen into a den of thieves," as Wilde put it in a letter to a friend, the aesthete decided it was time to return home to England. Colonel Morse convinced the *Tribune* and the *Times* to hold their stories about Wilde's encounter with the banco scammers—the papers had learned of it from the police—until after Wilde's departure. But one reporter for the *Tribune* who knew of Wilde's duping, but was unaware of the deal his superiors had made, found Wilde lunching with two friends at Delmonico's on Christmas Eve. "Mr. Wilde, is it true that you have lost $1,100 in a banco game?" he asked. According to the journalist, Wilde "was cool and imperturbable," lighting a cigarette and "blowing a cloud of smoke into the air," before responding: "I have heard the report."

"Then I understand you to deny the story?" the reporter asked.

"It does not concern me enough to either deny it or affirm it," Wilde said, after which he took another puff. Then he said: "I should very much object, indeed, to losing $1,100, but I should not object to having it *known* that I had done so." As he had taught the world: the only thing worse than being talked about . . .

ON THE MORNING of December 27, 1882, nearly a year after he landed in New York, Wilde arrived at the Hudson River dock where the SS *Bothnia* was moored, awaiting the passengers it would carry to England. Wilde was accompanied by Helena Modjeska, then playing Camille at Booth's Theatre on West Twenty-third Street, in a performance the *New York Times* called "brilliant." Two years earlier, when Modjeska made her London debut in the same role, she had often come into contact with an Irishman who was eager to call attention to himself with his eccentric clothing and ironic epigrams. "What has he done, this young man, that one meets him everywhere?" she had asked one of her hosts of Oscar Wilde, then just two years removed from Oxford. "He does nothing but talk. I do not understand." Now she did. And so did America, not that the *New York Tribune* was willing to concede the point. "Oscar Wilde took a sorrowful leave of America yesterday," it declared in an editorial that ran nearly one thousand words:

> He confessed before his departure that his mission to our barbaric shores had been substantially a failure. He came here to reform our taste and dress, but we paid little heed. . . . He has gone back [home] with his knee—breeches, his long lank hair and his sunflower, leaving us to our fate. . . . The [American] public never took any interest in him save as a curiosity, and that was satisfied long ago. . . . If we benefitted little by his visit, he has . . . gained much valuable information for the enlargement of his own mind. He knows a good deal more about the world than he did when he arrived here.

There's no evidence Wilde declared his American tour a "failure" to the *Tribune* or to anyone else. But the paper was correct in saying that he left America a wiser person. Wilde had learned to be responsible, to deal with boredom and hostility, and to entertain a wide range of audiences while remaining true to his vision of his future. He had come to America a boyish twenty-seven-year old; he was leaving a twenty-eight-year-old man.

But what the *Tribune* did not see was that Wilde had *arrived* in America knowing something that the *Tribune* did not: that the world was rethinking what it meant to be a celebrity and, equally important, the ways in which one could achieve that status. In fact, Wilde, with his success in America, had hastened that process of redefinition into motion. And he had enjoyed himself immensely while doing so.

He had stepped off the SS *Arizona* a virtual unknown, a writer who had written one unproduced play and a self-published book of poems that had sold a few hundred copies in Britain and even fewer in the United States. If his name was readily familiar to any Americans in January 1882, it was only to the small number who subscribed to

British humor magazines such as *Punch*, and to the even smaller group who had been educated in England. But by the time he left, Wilde was the most written-about Briton in the United States, covered in the American press more than prime minister, Mr. Gladstone—even more than Her Royal Highness Queen Victoria. Wilde had come to make a household name of himself, and he had succeeded in households all across America, traveling some fifteen thousand miles and seeing more of that vast country than probably any living American save presidential candidates.

Though Wilde did most of that traveling by train, it is useful to think his tour with a metaphor from a more adventurous mode of nineteenth-century transit: ballooning. The balloons that floated in the skies over Europe, where the sport began, were not merely flying machines. They were publicity machines, calling attention to themselves—the balloons were often extravagantly decorated—and to the person flying them. With his flamboyant dress and soaring rhetoric about art, Wilde's arrival in (and descent into) an American town wasn't just an appearance. It was an event. Because of his understanding of public relations and public spectacle, his nearly 150 lectures on aesthetics and interior decoration—"the most determined and sustained attack upon materialistic vulgarity that America had ever seen," according to his biographer Richard Ellmann—filled halls on both coasts of America and many in between. His message wasn't always warmly received; even so, the remarks made about Wilde in the *Tribune*, intended to belittle him, only confirmed the size of his triumph. If he really was such a negligible figure, why take notice of him at all? And at such length? The *Tribune* not only failed to understand Wilde's purpose in coming to America; it failed to see he had achieved it. He had perfected the role of the "modern" celebrity. He was famous for being famous.

He had worked diligently to accomplish that goal, in the process devising a formula for creating fame that other modern celebrities—all of them far more shallow than he—are using today, whether they know it or not. (Among them: Paris Hilton, Drew Pinsky, Heidi Montag, Spencer Pratt, Nicole Richie, Kelly and Jack Osbourne, Meghan McCain, and the entire Kardashian family.) Clearly no one before Wilde had used the press so skillfully to establish a claim to renown. If not the inventor of the self-glorifying hotel room interview, he was its first great practitioner, sitting for roughly one hundred interviews in three hundred days—a record never approached before him and rarely matched in the years since. And he never forgot that, no matter what the question, the purpose of the answer was to increase the fame of Oscar Wilde. He was the first interview subject to grasp that a memorable interview is also a visual performance, the impact of which can be enhanced by props and a costume; he was the first to consistently present himself to reporters as a work of art, both theatrically and sartorially; and he was the first to conceive of the resulting verbal give-and-take with his interviewer as an opportunity for a monologue delivered by that subject *about* the subject, which was himself.

He also understood the infectiousness of celebrity, rightly intuiting that proximity to famous people would make *him* famous. Though he was eager to meet men such as Whitman and Longfellow because of their literary achievements, he was even more determined to spend time with them because they were public icons. Long before the advent of the "V.I.P. Room," Wilde grasped that celebrity enables one to join an elevated elite, and that the whole point of joining that elite is to be observed there. From below.

Actors, sportsmen, singers, and politicians had used photography to enhance their celebrity and to formalize their images before Wilde, but he was one of the first to realize the power of photography to *create* fame. Though it is a tribute to Napoleon Sarony's artistry that he took the most famous images of Wilde on one day in 1882 at his studio in New York, the credit for that achievement belongs equally to Wilde, who came to that studio with a clear idea of how he planned to present himself to America: as the Aesthetic Adonis, a man both of his time and removed from it. And it worked—so well that the images were used to sell not merely Wilde, but products ranging from cigarettes to women's "bosom enhancers."

AFTER RETURNING TO Europe, Wilde told Robert Sherard (eventually to become his first biographer) that the conclusion of his American lecture tour signified the demise of "the Oscar of the first period." His goal in that period had been to reverse the usual process of gaining stature as a literary man: to achieve fame first, and then to use that celebrity to build a career as a writer. The first period of Oscar had ended in resounding success. And though he didn't know it yet, so too would the second.

Until love interfered.

Don't Believe the Hype

Shortly after eleven p.m., on February 20, 1892, nine years after he returned to England, Oscar Wilde heard the words he had longed—and planned—to hear all his life. "AUTHOR! AUTHOR!" chanted the audience at St. James's Theatre, where the curtain had just fallen on the first of his comedies to be staged in London: *Lady Windermere's Fan*, his effervescent satire of morality and marriage. He would not disappoint them. Wearing a gray wool jacket with a black velvet collar, beige trousers, a white waistcoat edged in moiré ribbon, and a dyed green carnation in his buttonhole, Wilde emerged from the wings and bowed to his admirers. In his gloved left hand he held a gold-tipped cigarette, which he smoked with pleasure as the cheering continued, until he held up that hand and said: "Ladies and Gentlemen, I have enjoyed this evening *immensely*. The actors have given a *charming* rendering of a *delightful* play, and your appreciation has been *most* intelligent. I congratulate you on the *great* success of your performance, which persuades me that you think *almost* as highly of the play as I do myself." In one glorious night Wilde had achieved both goals he had set for himself at Oxford: he was famous as the writer of an adored new play; and he was notorious as the man who had delivered that cheeky speech.

Both demanded celebration. So after sending his beaming wife Constance home to their exquisitely decorated house in Chelsea—Wilde had married in 1884 and was now the father of two sons—he went for a late supper at Willis's, a spot favored by London's theater crowd. His dining companions, all of them young males, included the aspiring art critic Robbie Ross (who had lived for a time at the Wildes' home), Reggie Turner (a recent Oxford graduate who would become the gossip columnist for the *Telegraph*), Edward Shelley (a good-looking publishing clerk who, according to Neil McKenna, author of *The Secret Life of Oscar Wilde*, the playwright would take to bed that night at the Albemarle Hotel), and an even better-looking student from Magdalen College Wilde was just getting to know, the Marquess of Queensberry's third son—Lord Alfred Douglas, known to his friends as Bosie.

Wilde would have even more reasons to celebrate in the near future. *Fan* appeared before packed houses for six months at St. James's, then toured the provinces with equal success, after which it returned to London for another profitable run—especially for Wilde. He had rejected the actor-producer George Alexander's offer of £1,000 for all rights to his play, instead taking a percentage of the box-office receipts. (Alexander played Lord Windermere in the original cast of *Fan*.) By year's end Wilde had earned £7,000—the equivalent of £700,000 today—spending a good chunk of it on lavish meals and vintage champagne at London's best restaurants, almost always joined by a coterie of male acolytes, in lively soirees that often made the newspapers. Wilde wasn't just the conversational star of those dinners, he was the talk of all London, and, even more delightful from his point of view, he was often asked to speak about his play—which he took to mean himself—in public. When a left-leaning politician at one event praised him for "calling a spade a spade" in *Fan*, by lashing out against the hypocritical social mores of the ruling class, Wilde brought down the house by protesting that he had never called a spade a spade. The playwright who did so, he said, "should be condemned to *use* one."

His second hit, *A Woman of No Importance*, a biting take on the different rules of behavior set by society for men and women, especially in the realm of sex, opened on April 19, 1893, at the Theatre Royal, where it ran for 118 nights. When the Prince of Wales told him of his admiration for the play, Wilde confessed he worried his final act was too long. "Do not alter a single line," said the prince. "Sir, your wish is my command," said Wilde. After spending the next year showing off at parties for which the hostesses' invitations often included the message, "To Meet Mr. Oscar Wilde," he opened his next play, *An Ideal Husband*, on January 3, at the Haymarket Theatre. A hilariously astute look at the connections (and *dis*connects) between public and private behavior, *Husband* would run for 124 nights, earning Wilde even more fame and money, and this praise from the often cranky George Bernard Shaw: "Mr. Wilde is to me our only thorough playwright. He plays with everything: with wit, with philosophy, with drama, with actors and audiences, with the whole theatre." While *Husband* was still drawing crowds to the Haymarket, Wilde opened another play a few blocks away, his "trivial comedy for serious people," *The Importance of Being Earnest*. Just before it premiered on February 14, 1895, at St. James's, he was asked if he thought his new play— acclaimed today as his masterpiece—would be a success. "The play *is* a success," he said. "The only question is whether the first night's audience will be one." It was. Decades later, Allan Aynsworth, who played Algernon Moncrief that night, said: "In my fifty-three years of acting, I cannot remember a greater triumph than the first night of *The Importance of Being Earnest*. The audience rose in their seats and cheered again and again."*

---

* Wilde got one of his biggest laughs in *Earnest* when he doubled down on his "calling a spade a spade joke," in this exchange:

Wilde took a bow at St. James's but gave no speech. He had just given one at the Haymarket, he later explained; to give another one so soon after that, would make him feel like a German oompah band. For the first time in his life, Wilde knew he didn't have to blow his own horn. No playwright in the modern history of the British theater had experienced so much success so quickly.

But it would all end, even faster. This jarring turn began just four days later, when the Marquess of Queensberry, believing Wilde had lured his son Bosie, now Wilde's most visible companion, into a degenerate lifestyle, left a card for Wilde at the Albemarle Club that read: "For Oscar Wilde posing somdomite" (*sic*). Queensberry had been stalking Wilde for months, even showing up at Wilde's home on Tite Street. He had planned to humiliate Wilde from his seat in the audience for the opening of *Earnest* but was denied admission to the theater, after Wilde learned of his plan. (The marquess left a "bouquet" of rotting vegetables for the playwright.) Ignoring advice to ignore Queensberry's card, Wilde decided to sue the marquess for libel.

The resulting trial, covered on front pages across the English-speaking world, began on April 3, 1895, but Wilde withdrew his suit two days later when it became clear the marquess's barrister would call to the stand several male prostitutes whom Wilde (and Bosie) had consorted with at London hotels. ("Feasting with panthers" is how Wilde later described those encounters.) When, after the case was dropped, Queensberry sent the rent boys' affidavits to the police, Wilde—at the peak of his fame and notoriety—was arrested for, and after two additional trials convicted of, "gross indecency." He was sentenced to two years in prison at hard labor. (The first trial in which Wilde was the defendant had ended in a hung jury.) Even before that

---

CECILY: Do you suggest, Miss Fairfax, that I entrapped Earnest into an engagement? How dare you? This is no time for wearing the shallow mask of manners. When I see a spade I call it a spade.

GWENDOLEN: I am glad to say I have never seen a spade. It is obvious that our social spheres have been widely different.

verdict, Wilde's name was removed from the marquees, posters, and theater programs in London and New York that announced his plays. The man who had worked so hard to be seen was now invisible and soon to be incarcerated. In an equally harsh irony, the law that Wilde was to be punished for violating had been written in 1885 by the MP Henry Labouchère, a man Wilde had praised to the American press in 1882.

THE DETAILS OF Wilde's fall have been recounted often; they will not be retold at length here. But most of those studies have underestimated the role played—for better *and* worse—by Wilde's American lecture tour in the arc of his life. When Wilde said, just after that tour was over, that "the Oscar of the first period" was dead, he was speaking only sartorially: he cut his hair and put his breeches away. But the rest of that Oscar was very much alive. While vacationing in Paris in early 1883, using money he earned in America, he met the publisher Edmond de Goncourt, a towering figure in the French literary world. According to Goncourt's diary, Wilde spoke to him as if he were just another journalist sent to chronicle his recent triumph in the United States. "He told [me] of the theatre [he lectured in there] which . . . is used as a courtroom and where condemned men are hanged on the stage after the play is over," Goncourt wrote. "He said that he had seen one man being hanged . . . while the audience fired [bullets] at him from their seats."

Wilde told similarly self-glorifying whoppers about Leadville and other places in "Impressions of America," the lecture he gave at venues in and around London beginning in the summer of 1883, and then in the British provinces. One portion of this talk that always got a laugh was his tale of the American art patron who ordered a plaster cast of the Venus de Milo from Paris and, when it arrived "minus the arms," sued an American railroad line for damaging his property. Even more preposterously, Wilde said the patron won his case. A listener who tittered when this story was told in a Dublin lecture hall was Constance Lloyd, who became Mrs. Oscar Wilde on May 29, 1884. Many years later the poet W. H. Auden declared that marrying her the only immoral act Wilde ever committed.[*]

Wilde's success as a lecturer in Britain—he began to speak on "The House Beautiful," a staple of his speaking tour of the United States, as well as on his "Impressions of America"—increased his profile so much that he was offered the editorship of the English monthly *Lady's World*, which he accepted in 1887, upgrading the caliber of its contributors and making a small but significant alteration to the magazine's name. It is a sign of his growing celebrity—and the self-marketing savvy he exhibited in America—that his own name appeared on the cover of each issue: *WOMAN'S WORLD, edited by Oscar Wilde.* (just as Dickens name had appeared, he knew, on the covers of *Household Words* and *All the Year Round*). But Wilde wasn't cut out for office work; he quickly tired of the job and left the magazine in 1889.

He was far from idle, however. The man who, in America, had taught himself that promotion and provocation are synonymous, wrote "The Decay of Lying," as provocative a concept as had ever appeared in a serious journal in England, in the January 1889 issue of *Nineteenth Century*. He argued in his essay that too many nineteenth-century novelists—he cited Zola, Maupaussant, and Henry James as examples—rely too much on their powers of observation and too little on their powers of imagination, thus producing works of base realism rather than art. It was in "Decay" that Wilde wrote his famous lines "Life imitates Art far more than Art imitates life" and "As for the infinite variety of Nature, that is a pure myth. It is not to be found in Nature herself. It resides in the imagination."

"Decay" was followed five months later by "The Portrait of Mr.

---

[*] Auden believed Wilde used his wife as a prop to hide his homosexuality. But there is no conclusive evidence that Wilde had had any same-sex experiences by 1884 and there is much evidence, even today, that some people reach their late twenties unsure of his or her sexual identity. Apparently Auden wasn't one of them; perhaps Wilde was.

W.H." in *Blackwood's*, a short story that provoked an even more volca-
nic reaction with its suggestion that the dedicatee in several of Shakespeare's love sonnets may not have been a woman, but an adolescent
actor named Will Hughes. By coincidence—or maybe not—Wilde
had his first (documented) same-sex experience not long before this
article was written, with Robbie Ross, then a teenager. In July 1890,
Wilde published "The True Function and Value of Criticism," an
essay in *Nineteenth Century* in which he dared contradict the Great
Man of English Criticism, Matthew Arnold. As every Oxford man
knew, Arnold, who occupied that university's chair of poetry for a
decade, declared in 1864 that the aim of criticism is "to see the object
as in itself it really is." Wilde insisted the esteemed don got it back-
ward: the ultimate aim of criticism, he wrote, is to see the object as it
really is *not*. To use a term not then widely used in Britain, this was
chutzpah on a scale rarely seen in that nation. But Wilde wasn't merely
being brash; he was asserting the creative function of the critic, the
writer who uses the work of art he or she is studying as a starting place
for his or her own imagination. The higher that imagination soars,
Wilde said, the better the criticism. On some occasions the work of the
critic even surpassed the work of the artist.

An even more provocative work by Wilde, published simultaneously in America and Britain, appeared that same July in *Lippincott's
Monthly*. This was the novel *The Picture of Dorian Gray*, which owed its
very existence to Wilde's American tour. It was commissioned by the
American editor of *Lippincott's*, J. M. Stoddart, the man who had
accompanied Wilde on his first trip to meet Walt Whitman, in 1882.
Wilde was already a controversial figure; *Dorian*—the story of a beautiful, amoral young man whose appearance never changes as a painting of him does, becoming more and more grotesque as his behavior
worsens—made Wilde an icon of controversy. The title character's
embrace of hedonism as an aesthetic quest, encouraged by the cynical
epigrams of Lord Henry Wotton—epigrams many Londoners had
heard Wilde utter at parties—was said to be a coded text celebrating

the "indecent" behavior Wilde was so brazenly exhibiting with his clique of male admirers. A critic who believed he had cracked that code wrote in London's *Daily Chronicle*: "Mr. Oscar Wilde's story . . . is a poisonous [work], the atmosphere of which is heavy with the mephitic odours of moral and spiritual putrefaction. [It is] a gloating study of the mental and physical corruption of a fresh, fair and golden youth, which might be fascinating but for its effeminate frivolity, its studied insincerity, its theatrical cynicism, its tawdry mysticism [and] its flippant philosophizings." (*Dorian* was published in book form in 1891.)

A reader with a more positive take on the novel was a well-born undergraduate at Wilde's alma mater who claimed to have read it "fourteen times running." In June 1891, Lord Alfred (Bosie) Douglas arranged for an introduction to Wilde, who was immediately struck by the Magdalen man's pale beauty. It wasn't long before they were inseparable. (Douglas was twenty-one, Wilde thirty-seven.) Bosie was vain, arrogant, bigoted, and promiscuous, a free spender of other people's money, and a frequent thrower of tantrums, but Wilde had found love. With the triumphant launch of his playwriting career the following year, he would also find the glory he had sought for so long. Then Bosie's father left his card.

There has been much speculation in the intervening years about Wilde's decision to sue Queensberry. Wilde had to know he had committed acts deemed illegal by British law, so any suit he brought asserting that such an accusation was libelous could be defended by proving the truth of the accusation, which, if done successfully, would open the plaintiff—Wilde—to prosecution. This speculation typically has focused on Douglas, who despised his father and who saw Wilde's libel case, which he tirelessly urged his lover to file (even if it meant telling lies in court), as a chance to show the world why Queensberry deserved to be hated—not just by his son but by everyone. If Wilde had to play a supporting, and even suicidal, role in the Douglas family drama, that was fine with Bosie. It wouldn't be the first time he was selfish.

What's equally relevant is that Wilde had an accurate view of Queensberry's stamina. If Wilde ignored the card, the marquess wouldn't have dropped his campaign; he would have made more accusations in even more public places. If Wilde failed to respond, he knew his silence would be interpreted by Society as proof of the insults' truthfulness. As Auden later wrote: "Some artists are indifferent to their social reputations," but Wilde was not one of them. "The approval of Society was essential to his self-esteem."

There is another explanation for Wilde's decision, however, one that can be traced back to his yearlong stay in America. The man who, while touring that nation, had so presciently devised a winning—and lasting—formula for how to become a modern celebrity had failed to see a crucial pitfall of the new culture of self-promotion: the danger of believing the hype, especially your own. Wilde believed his hype. "I made art a philosophy, and philosophy an art," he wrote of himself. "I altered the minds of men and the colours of things: there was nothing I said or did that did not make people wonder. . . . I awoke the imagination of my century so that it created myth and legend around me." (Actually, Wilde was being modest on that final point: much of that myth and legend was created by him.)

Wilde thought he was too famous to fall—which is precisely why he *did*. Though it seems absurd in hindsight, Wilde sued Queensberry believing he would win. After his successful performance as an aesthete in America, and his ascension as a playwright in London, he approached his appearances in the witness box as one more "star turn"—another chance to lecture those less sophisticated than he, to show the world he really was the author of those witty plays, to take another curtain call. It was an error that only a man star-struck by his own stardom could make.

To be sure, he said many amusing things while testifying, such as when Edward Carson, Queensberry's barrister (and a former schoolmate of Wilde's at the Portora Royal School, in Ireland), asked him about a section of *The Picture of Dorian* Gray in which Basil Hallward, the painter of Dorian's portrait, tells his subject: "I ha[ve] never loved a woman. . . . [F]rom the moment I met you, your personality had the most extraordinary influence over me. I quite admit that I adored you madly, extravagantly, absurdly."

"Carson: Have you ever adored a young man madly? . . .

"Wilde: I have never given adoration to anybody except myself." (Loud laughter.)

But he would be serious when, at the first trial where he was the defendant, he was asked to define "the Love that dare not speak its name," a line taken from a poem written by Douglas. It is "such a great affection of an elder for a younger man as there was between David and Jonathan, such as Plato made the very basis of his philosophy, and such as you find in the sonnets of Michelangelo and Shakespeare," Wilde began.

It is that deep, spiritual affection that is as pure as it is perfect. . . .
It is beautiful, it is fine, it is the noblest form of affection. There is nothing unnatural about it. It is intellectual, and it repeatedly exists between an elder and a younger man, when the elder man has intellect, and the younger man has all the joy, hope and glamour of life before him. That it should be so the world does not understand. (Loud applause.)

What Wilde didn't understand was that he was the author of his own lines at his trials, but *only* those lines. He was in a drama, not a comedy, where the ending would be written by someone else—no matter how well he spoke. He thought his celebrity made him invincible. He was wrong.

WILDE SERVED HIS two-year sentence at three prisons: Pentonville, Wandsworth, and Reading. His petitions for early release, including one in which he asked for mercy on the grounds of insanity, were all denied. He was introduced to the "hard labor" part of his punishment immediately, finding himself forced to power a treadmill used to grind wheat. He stood in a cubicle alongside other prisoners he could hear but not see, with his left foot strapped onto the higher step of the treadmill, his right to the lower. For six hours a day—twenty minutes on, five off—Wilde pedaled that machine, the equivalent of climbing a staircase six thousand feet tall. When Robbie Ross visited Wilde at Reading, he found his friend and occasional lover emaciated and sobbing. His hearing had deteriorated as well, the result of a fall onto a cement floor. The food—thin soup, porridge, and suet (animal fat mixed with water)—was deplorable at each of the prisons where Wilde served time and, in his case, caused chronic diarrhea. This disorder made his sanitary "facilities," a bedpan that could be emptied only three times a day, especially humiliating. Perhaps even more dispiriting to Wilde—the greatest talker of his age—he was forbidden to talk.

When he was released on May 19, 1897, a piece in the *New York Times* larded with lies—Wilde "thrived under prison fare" and "not once [did he] enter the infirmary," to name but two—said that Wilde no longer desired notoriety but had no wish for oblivion either. In reality, the choice would not be up to him. His first visitors in London were the friends at whose house he had stayed while out on bond in 1895: Ernest and Ada Leverson. According to Mrs. Leverson, who had written a parody of *Dorian* that Wilde so adored he anointed her "the wittiest woman in the world," Wilde greeted them "with the dignity of a king returning from exile." If accurate, this was the greatest of all the poses ever struck by Wilde. For the truth was that the returning "king" had lost his career, his social standing, his money, his possessions (which had been sold at auction to pay Queensberry's legal costs), his mother (who died when he was incarcerated), and his children, who were being raised by his estranged wife with a new last name, Holland. He would never see them again.

Wilde began his second exile, this one of his own choosing, the next day, when he arrived by ferry in Dieppe, France. He was met there by Reggie Turner and Robbie Ross, who had dined with him five years earlier on the opening night of *Lady Windermere's Fan*. Before Wilde left prison, he had named Ross his literary executor. He now gave him the unmailed letter to Douglas he had written as an inmate, a letter filled with rage at Bosie for having created, for his own selfish ends, the situation that led to Wilde's imprisonment:

"Do you really think that at any period in our friendship you were worthy of the love I showed you?" Wilde wrote in that letter. "I had given you my life, and to gratify the lowest and most contemptible of all human passions, Hatred and Vanity and Greed, you had thrown it away. In less than three years you had entirely ruined me. . . .

"Blindly I staggered as an ox into the shambles. . . . What is loathsome to me is the memory of interminable visits to the solicitor in your company, when in the ghastly glare of a bleak room you and I would sit with serious faces telling serious lies to a bald man. . . .

"During the whole time we were together I never wrote one single line. . . . You were the absolute ruin of my Art. You couldn't know, you couldn't understand, you couldn't appreciate. . . . Your interests were merely in your meals and moods. . . . Your one idea of life, your one philosophy, if you are to be credited with a philosophy, was that whatever you did was to be paid for by someone else."

The author of these words checked into a hotel in Dieppe as "Sebastian Melmoth," a pseudonym based on his favorite religious martyr and the title character from a novel, *Melmoth the Wanderer*, written by Charles Maturin, a relative of Wilde's on his mother's side. A letter soon arrived from Bosie, who had neither written to Wilde nor visited him after he went to prison. Wilde probably knew it was a bad idea to respond, but as Emily Dickinson wrote: "The Heart wants what it wants." In August the inevitable happened. Bosie and he met for the first time in two years, in Rouen. Wilde wept at the train station. The two men walked arm in arm through the city and spent the night together at a hotel. After they parted, Douglas pledged his love in a telegram. Wilde responded as if he were not the man who had written those angry words about Bosie in the letter we now know as *De Profundis.* "I feel that my only hope of again doing beautiful work in art is being with you," he wrote.

The two met again weeks later, traveling to Naples, where they took a suite at the Hotel Royal and quickly ran up a bill of £60. This was no small matter, considering Bosie had no money, and Wilde was living on an allowance of £3 a week from his estranged wife who, after learning he was with Douglas, threatened to terminate that arrangement. "I forbid you to return to your filthy, insane life," she wrote. To subsidize that "insane" life, Wilde solicited a £100 advance from the composer Dalhousie Young to write a libretto for an opera Young was working on—an assignment Wilde never completed. This money allowed Wilde and Douglas to rent a villa in nearby Posilipo and to spend their days and nights flirting with local fishermen. "None of the English colony here have left cards [for] us," Wilde wrote to Ross. "Fortunately we have a few simple friends amongst the poorer classes." But after the money ran out in November, Bosie began to make ugly scenes, then vanished. "The facts of Naples are very bald and brief," Wilde told Ross.

> Bosie . . . offered me love, affection, and care, and promised that I should never want for anything. . . . I accepted his offer, but . . . on our way to Naples I found that he had no money, no plans, and had forgotten all his promises. His one idea was that I should raise money for us both. I did so. . . . On this Bosie lived, quite happily. When it came to his having to repay his own share, he became terrible, unkind, mean, and penurious, except where his own pleasures were concerned, and when my allowance ceased, he left.

There was more unhappiness to come. Wilde moved to Paris in February 1898, where he spent most of his nights chasing young men and drinking absinthe. (The word *alcoholic* was not then in wide usage; even so, it is a designation that merits serious consideration in Wilde's case—as well as that of his parents and his brother.) Before a month passed, Wilde's mounting bar tabs led him to write a letter to the Irish journalist Frank Harris, who lived in England, asking for a loan. The Australian opera diva Nellie Melba, who knew Wilde from London, was walking down a Parisian street when a large shabby man said to her: "Madame Melba—you don't know who I am? I'm Oscar Wilde and I'm going to do a terrible thing. I'm going to ask you for money." She gave him all the cash in her purse, after which he said thank you and turned on his heel, no doubt headed for the nearest bar. Wilde's finances improved somewhat in the spring of 1898 when his wife died, which resulted in his allowance being reinstated. A small sum also came his way after the publication of *The Ballad of Reading Gaol*, which had been released that winter with "C.3.3."—Wilde's former prison-cell number—on the title page as the author.

This good news was not enough to balm the snubs Wilde faced almost daily. The French writers Maurice Barrès (author of *Le Culte de moi*) and Catulle Mendès (*Le Roman d'une nuit*)—two "Parisians who licked my conqueror's boots only ten years ago," Wilde wrote—now ignored him when their paths crossed. James Whistler ran into Wilde at a restaurant in Paris but said nothing. Anna de Brémont, a friend of Wilde's wife and mother, covered her face with a fan when she saw him enter a Parisian café where she was seated. When Frank Harris took Wilde to the French Riviera, Wilde's walk along the sea was spoiled when George Alexander—who had starred in *The Importance of Being Earnest* and *Lady Windermere's Fan*—rode by on a bicycle and, after recognizing Wilde, failed to stop. Thirteen years earlier Wilde had been sold to the American public by the Carte agency as a freak—but the kind of freak you should see. Now he was the type of freak people wanted *not* to see: a celebrity who was no longer celebrated. The true cruelty of a prison sentence, Wilde told a friend, begins when you are released.

Paris would be the setting for Bosie's final act of cruelty. Just before his father died in early 1900, Douglas achieved a rapprochement. As a result, he inherited nearly £20,000, the equivalent of £2.2 million today (or 3.6 million, in dollars). When Wilde dined with Bosie in May at Café de la Paix, he asked Douglas if he could find it in his heart to give him some money. "When I spoke to him of this he went into paroxysms of rage, followed by satirical laughter, and said it was the most monstrous suggestion he had ever heard, that he was astounded at my suggesting such a thing, that he did not recognize I had any claim of any kind of him," Wilde wrote to Ross.

> When I remember his letters at Dieppe, his assurances of eternal devotion, his entreaties that I should always live with him, his incessant offers of all his life and belongings, his desire to atone in some way for the ruin he and his family brought upon me—well, it sickens me. . . ."I can't afford to spend anything except on myself," was one of his observations.

Wilde's spirit was broken by this encounter; his body, which had begun failing during his incarceration, accelerated its decline. The abscess that had developed in his ear after he took a fall in prison now caused excruciating pain. On October 10 a surgeon came to his room at the down-market Hotel D'Alsace, where Wilde had been living for months because its owner, Jean Dupoirier, rarely forced him to pay his bill. The surgeon's goal was to ease the pain and to stop the discharge from Wilde's ear; he succeeded at neither.

"I am dying beyond my means," Wilde told one visitor, after the procedure. To another he said: "My wallpaper and I are fighting a duel to the death. One or the other of us has to go." By November his illness led to bouts of semidelirium. His near-constant companions at his hotel were Reggie Turner and Robbie Ross; one day, after Turner had applied an ice pack to his head for nearly an hour, Wilde turned to him and said: "You dear little Jew, don't you think that's enough? Jews have no beautiful philosophy of life, but they are sympathetique."

Wilde knew his death was imminent. He told Turner he had "dreamt [he] was supping with the dead," to which Turner replied: "My dear Oscar, you were probably the life and soul of the party." Wilde hated to complain, but he told his friends: "My throat is like a limekiln, my brain a furnace and my nerves a coil of angry adders." He was no longer eating and had even stopped taking his medication of choice: champagne. His doctors concluded the abscess in Wilde's ear had penetrated his cranium; their diagnosis was cerebral meningitis, an infection of the lining of the brain. They placed leeches on either side of his forehead.

On November 29, Wilde's breathing became labored and he faded in and out of consciousness. Ross, a Roman Catholic, found an English-speaking priest and brought him to Wilde's bedside. Though raised a Protestant, Wilde had flirted often with the Roman Church. His great friend from Oxford, David Hunter Blair, had arranged an audience for the two of them with Pope Pius IX in 1877. Later Wilde said: "Catholicism is the only religion to die in." No one knew for sure if he really believed that. What's certain is that he couldn't make an intelligible sound when Father Cuthbert Dunne asked if he was ready to be received into the church. But he did raise his hand, so Dunne gave him the last rites. Just before sunrise on November 30, a loud death rattle began to emanate from Wilde's throat. So did blood. Oscar Wilde took his final breath just before two p.m. He was forty-six.

RICHARD ELLMANN CREATED a wave of controversy in his prize-winning biography of Wilde, published in 1988, by asserting that Wilde's meningitis had its origin in a case of syphilis he contracted at

Oxford from a female prostitute. Ellmann theorized that Wilde's habit of talking with a hand over his mouth—an idiosyncrasy noticed by many over the years—was caused by his anxiety that his listeners would notice his teeth had blackened, a well-known side effect of mercury treatments for syphilis. (Paul Ehrlich didn't discover salversan, his "magic bullet" cure for syphilis, until 1909.) Wilde "adopted mercury . . . as the [cure] for his dreadful disease," Ellmann wrote, and thus "the parable of Dorian Gray's secret decay began to form in his mind, as the spirochete began its journey up his spine towards the meninges." This link has been challenged by later biographers, who believe the true causes of Wilde's discolored teeth were more mundane: his lifelong smoking habit and his deficiencies in personal hygiene.

Of course, when the subject is Wilde—whether discussing his life *or* death—one must always consider his own words. "In this world there are only two tragedies. One is not getting what one wants, and the other is getting it," he wrote in *Lady Windermere's Fan*. To take those lines at face value is to believe that Wilde knew his life would end in disaster, and that he understood his enormous success would be the reason. But the case is much stronger that his fame as a wit, as an author, and as a "famous person" became dangerous to him in a way he *failed* to foresee. Wilde believed his own hype and reaped consequences he never anticipated. He learned too late that fame and notoriety are not identical and do not trigger the same response. The scholar from Oxford who won a double first in classics forgot the teachings of the ancient Greeks about hubris. He angered "the gods" by believing his celebrity made him all-powerful, just as he angered some of his fellow mortals by flaunting his earthly successes and his "aberrant" sexuality. He thought others were having as much pleasure watching him have pleasure, as he was having it. This was not true. "Morality is simply the attitude we adopt towards people we personally dislike," Wilde wrote in *An Ideal Husband*. He was looking for a laugh when he wrote that line. In the end, the joke was on him.

Fame makes you a star, but it also makes you a target. This is well understood today, in the age of Internet snark, but it was not widely appreciated in the late nineteenth century. One of the few who did see it then, the American psychologist William James (Henry's brother), attributed the "moral flabbiness" of the era he shared with Wilde to "the worship of the bitch-goddess SUCCESS," by which he meant not just money, but fame. What Wilde—who worshipped both—failed to understand was that the bitch-goddess he revered was capable of biting if not approached with humility. But it was not in Wilde's nature to be humble, so he was humbled. The rules of self-promotion he had pioneered in America did not make him invincible; they did the opposite. No matter what role syphilis did (or did not) play in his life, the best way to understand Wilde's death is not medically. It is metaphorically. The culture of celebrity he brought to life rose up to take *his*.

Acknowledgments

Much is owed to many. I'll start with Tom Mayer, an editor of uncommon ability whose insightful comments and unwavering commitment to this project made our collaboration a pleasure—and the book much better. Great thanks, also, to my agent David Black, who has always been a source of good advice and support.

Several friends read parts of the manuscript along the way. Ben Yagoda—the smartest person I know—provided invaluable help and was always available to give it. Every writer should have such a generous friend. Others who were equally lavish with their comments and/or encouragement were Erica Berger, John Capouya, Neal Hirschfeld, Stanley Mieses, Joel Rose, Lee Schreiber, and Michael Sorkin. The scholar Joseph Bristow, a professor of English at UCLA, who has written widely and well on Wilde, was a great help to me, as was Donald Mead, editor of *The Wildean*, and John Cooper, the host/writer of the wonderful *Oscar Wilde in America* website, and the leader of an enchanting walking tour of "Oscar Wilde's New York." Two geologists, Vince Matthews of the National Mining Hall of Fame, in

Leadville, Colorado, and Fred Mark (another Coloradan), taught me everything I know about nineteenth-century silver mining.

Librarians in several institutions were extraordinarily helpful to (and patient with) me. I owe special thanks to the staff at the William Andrews Clark Memorial Library, in Los Angeles, the home of an outstanding collection of Wildeana, and where every question I asked was answered with professionalism. Similar gratitude is owed to the staffs of the British Library in London, New York University's Bobst Library, and the Henry W. and Albert A. Berg Collection of English and American Literature at the New York Public Library, as well as the NYPL's Humanities and Social Science Library. This project also benefited from the excellent work of the photo researcher Donna Cohen and the copy editor Janet Biehl.

But, most of all, I'm grateful to my wife Marion Ettlinger, without whom this book never would have happened.

Notes

PROLOGUE: TAKE YOUR SHOW ON THE ROAD

000   "Have you anything": John Cooper, "Quotations by Oscar Wilde Made In or About America," at "Oscar Wilde in America" website, via Internet. The quotation is repeated in many books, including Arthur Ransome, *Oscar Wilde: A Critical Study* (London: M. Secker, 1912); Frank Harris, *Oscar Wilde: His Life and Confessions* (New York: Brentano's, 1916); Lloyd Lewis and Henry Justin Smith, *Oscar Wilde Discovers America [1882]* (New York: Harcourt, Brace, 1936); and Merlin Holland (Wilde's grandson), *The Wilde Album* (New York: Henry Holt and Company, 1998).

000   It is a belief system: Daniel J. Boorstin, *The Image: A Guide to Pseudo-Events in America* (1962; reprint New York: Vintage, 1992), p. 57. Boorstin was the first to define a "celebrity" as "a person known for being well-known." Two other excellent books on modern celebrity are Leo Braudy, *The Frenzy of Renown* (New York: Oxford University Press, 1986); and Neal Gabler, *Life: The Movie: How Entertainment Conquered Reality* (New York: Vintage, 2000).

CHAPTER ONE: BUILD YOUR BRAND

000   "Oscar, you have": David Hunter Blair, *In Victorian Days and Other Papers* (New York: Longmans, 1939), p. 121. (This book also gives an eyewitness

account of Wilde's parties at Oxford.) Hunter Blair's last name is occasionally cited as Hunter-Blair.

000 "Somehow or other": Ibid., p. 122.

000 Oscar's father: P. Froggatt, "Sir William Wilde, 1815–1876: A Centenary Appreciation of Wilde's Place in Medicine," *Proceedings of the Irish Royal Academy* 77 (1977): 261–78; Mark T. Watts, "Sir William Wilde, 1815-1876: Royal Ophthalmologist Extraordinary," *Journal of the Royal Society of Medicine* 83 (1990): 183–84; T. G. Wilson, *Victorian Doctor: Being the Life of Sir William Wilde* (London: Methuen, 1942); Terence de Vere White, *The Parents of Oscar Wilde* (London: Hodder and Stoughton, 1976).

000 "overdid the correction": George Bernard Shaw, *The Collected Works of George Bernard Shaw,* vol. 29, *Pen Portraits and Reviews* (New York: W. H. Wise, 1930), p. 298.

000 While unmarried: Barbara Belford, *Oscar Wilde: A Certain Genius* (New York: Random House, 2000), pp. 12–13.

000 "Why are Dr. Wilde's nails": Wilson, *Victorian Doctor,* p. 246.

000 though she claimed to be: Christine Kinealy, "The Stranger's Scoffing': Speranza, the Hope of the Irish Nation," *Scholars Library* (September 2008), www.oscholars.com/TO/Appendix/Library/Speranza1.htm. (Paper originally presented at Canadian Association for Irish Studies, Toronto, May 2008.)

000 "I, and I alone": C. J. Hamilton, *Notable Irishwomen* (Dublin: Sealy Bryers and Walker, 1909), p. 181.

000 This home was staffed: Richard Ellmann, *Oscar Wilde* (New York: Knopf, 1988), p. 18.

000 now Sir William and Lady Jane: On William Wilde's Knighthood, see P. Froggatt, "The Demographic Work of Sir William Wilde," *Irish Journal of Medical Science* 40, no. 5 (1965): 213–30.

000 The Wildes allowed: Ellmann, *Oscar Wilde,* p. 21.

000 "agglomerated together": Joy Melville, *Mother of Oscar: The Life of Jane Francesa Wilde* (London: John Murray, 1994), p. 115.

000 "thinking minds": Ibid.

000 She had long claimed: Ellmann, *Oscar Wilde,* p. 6.

000 After a patient: Wilson, *Victorian Doctor,* pp. 255–70.

000 "Those who did attend": Melville, *Mother of Oscar,* p. 115; Horace Wyndham, *Speranza: A Biography of Lady Wilde* (London: Boardman, 1951), pp. 69–70.

000 "there was a swaying": Melville, *Mother of Oscar,* p. 114.

000 "No. 1 Merrion Square": Ibid., p. 115.

000 Once when a friend: Wyndham, *Speranza,* p. 76.

000 "You must never": Davis Coakley, *Oscar Wilde: The Importance of Being Irish* (Dublin: Town House, 1995), p. 55.

000 "Epigrams are'": Davis Coakley, "The Neglected Years: Wilde in Dublin," in C. George Sandulescu, ed., *Rediscovering Oscar Wilde* (Gerrards Cross, UK: Colin Smythe, 1994), p. 56.

000 "I want to introduce": Hesketh Pearson, *The Life of Oscar Wilde* (Twickenham, UK: Senate, 1998), p. 34.

000 "Until you heard": Belford, *Wilde: A Certain Genius*, p. 42.

000 "For if a person": W. B. Stanford and R. B. McDowell, *Mahaffy: A Biography of an Anglo-Irishman* (London: Routledge & Kegan Paul, 1971), p. 78.

000 "Madam, I cannot": Clifton Fadiman and André Bernard, ed., *Bartlett's Book of Anecdotes* (Boston: Little, Brown, 2000), p. 367.

000 "Poets are born": Stanford and McDowell, *Mahaffy*, p. 80.

000 "a liar is a better": Ibid., p. 84

000 "is not to instruct": Ibid.

000 "I was only once caned": Ellmann, *Oscar Wilde*, p. 27.

000 "the telling of beautiful": Oscar Wilde, "The Decay of Lying," in *Complete Works of Oscar Wilde*, ed. Merlin Holland (London: Collins, 1998), p. 992.

000 "One should absorb": Oscar Wilde, *The Picture of Dorian Gray* (New York: Modern Library, 2004), p. 114.

000 "You're not quite clever": Richard Ellmann, "Oscar Wilde at Oxford," *New York Review of Books* 31 (March 29, 1984): 23–28.

000 (The youngest son: Heather Marcovitch, *The Art of the Pose: Oscar Wilde's Performance Theory* (Bern: Peter Lang, 2010), pp. 31–32.

000 "If I were alone": Ellmann, "Wilde at Oxford."

000 "Many men": John Pentland Mahaffy, *The Principles of the Art of Conversation* (New York: Macmillan, 1887), p. 3.

000 He was once seen: A.J.A. Symons, "Wilde at Oxford," in Symons, *Essays and Biographies* (London: Cassell, 1969), p. 151.

000 In opposition to: Doreen Bolger Burke et al., eds., *In Pursuit of Beauty* (New York: The Metropolitan Museum of Art, 1986), p. 15; Lionel Lambourne, *The Aesthetic Movement* (London: Phaidon Press, 1996), pp. 14, 214; George P. Landow, *The Aesthetic and Critical Theories of John Ruskin* (1971), www.victorianweb.org/authors/ruskin/atheories/contents.html; Karen Zukowski, *Creating the Artful Home: The Aesthetic Movement* (Layton, Utah: Gibbs Smith, 2006), p. 14.

000 "get rid at once": Lambourne, *Aesthetic Movement,* p. 15.

000 His usual venue: G. T. Atkinson, "Oscar Wilde at Oxford," *Cornhill Magazine* (May 1929): 559–64.

000 "Of all God's gifts": John Ruskin, *The Works of John Ruskin*, ed. E. T. Cook and Alexander Wedderburn (London: George Allen, 1904), p. 10:173.

000 "Mere colour": Oscar Wilde, *Intentions* (London: Heinemann and Balestier, 1891), p. 161.

000 "the most beautiful things": John Ruskin, *The Stones of Venice*, vol. 1, *The Foundations* (1851; reprint New York: Cosimo, 2013), p. 44.

000 "sureness of himself": Pearson, *Life of Oscar Wilde,* p. 35.

000 "I find it harder": Ellmann, *Oscar Wilde*, p. 45.

000 "a form of heathenism": Ibid., p. 45.

000 That Reverend Burgon: www.deanburgonsociety.org; Pearson, *Life of Oscar Wilde*, p. 33.

000 "scandal": Ellmann, *Oscar Wilde*, p. 45.

000 "like drapery": Horace G. Hutchinson, *Portraits of the Eighties* (London: Unwin, 1920), p. 273.

000 "It fell sideways": Ibid.

000 Most experts believe: Belford, *Wilde: A Certain Genius*, p. 139; Ellmann, *Oscar Wilde*, pp. 277; Jonathan Fryer, *Robbie Ross* (New York: Carroll & Graf, 2000), p. 18; Philip Hoare, *Oscar Wilde's Last Stand* (New York: Arcade, 1998), p. 16; Merlin Holland, *The Real Trial of Oscar Wilde* (New York: Fourth Estate, 2003), p. xx; H. Montgomery Hyde, *Oscar Wilde: A Biography* (New York: Farrar, Straus & Giroux, 1975), p. 209; Richard Pine, *Oscar Wilde* (Dublin: Gill & Macmillan, 1997), p. 51.

000 "one of those sophisticated": Rupert Croft-Cooke, *The Unrecorded Life of Oscar Wilde* (London: W.H. Allen, 1972), p. 40.

000 Lord Ronald Gower: On Gower as a model for Lord Henry Wotton, see Neil McKenna, *The Secret Life of Oscar Wilde* (New York: Basic Books, 2005), p. 11.

000 "Last night I strolled": Oscar Wilde to William Ward, August 6, 1876 in *The Complete Letters of Oscar Wilde*, ed. Merlin Holland and Rupert Hart-Davis (New York: Henry Holt, 2000), p. 28.

000 "The ordinary poseur": Hutchinson, *Portraits of the Eighties*, p. 276.

000 Sir Coutts Lindsay: Barrie Bullen, "The Palace of Art: Sir Coutts Lindsay and the Grosvenor Gallery," *Apollo* 102 (November 1975): 352–57;

000 "I was sent down": Ellmann, *Oscar Wilde*, p. 78; Patrick Sammon, "Oscar Wilde and Greece," *Oscholars Library*, www.oscholars.com/TO/Appendix/Library/sammon.htm. (Originally presented to the Third European Conference of Modern Greek Studies, Bucharest, Romania, June 2006.)

000 So in an exquisite: Ellmann, *Oscar Wilde*, p. 78.

000 an unforgettable act of peacockery: Belford, *Wilde: A Certain Genius*, p. 68.

000 He was thrilled: Rachel Teukolski, *The Literate Eye: Victorian Art Writing and Modernist Aesthetics* (New York: Oxford University Press, 2009), p. 117.

000 "The haunt of the very aesthetic": Lambourne, *Aesthetic Movement*, pp. 117–18.

000 "I always say I": Oscar Wilde to Keningdale Cook, ca. May–June 1877, in *Complete Letters of Wilde*, p. 39.

000 "I am little more": Oscar Wilde to William E. Gladstone, May 17, 1877, ibid., p. 46.

000   But he had read: William Butler Yeats, *The Collected Works of William Butler Yeats,* vol. 3, *Autobiographies,* ed. William H. O'Donnell and Douglas N. Archibald (New York: Scribner, 1999), p. 124.

000   "my golden book": Ellmann, *Oscar Wilde,* p. 47.

000   "Not the fruit": Walter Pater, *Studies in the History of the Renaissance* (London: Macmillan, 1873), p. 210.

000   "one of those timed": Pearson, *Life of Oscar Wilde,* p. 29.

000   "Why do you always": Ellmann, *Oscar Wilde,* p. 83.

000   On June 10 Wilde: "The Wilde Chronology," www.oscholars.com/TO/Appendix/The_Wilde_Chronology.htm.

000   Past honorees: Belford, *Wilde: A Certain Genius,* p. 61.

000   "Oh, Gloria, Gloria!": Ellmann, *Oscar Wilde,* p. 97.

000   "I understand that": Pearson, *Life of Oscar Wilde,* p. 40.

000   "The dons are 'astonied'": Oscar Wilde to William Ward, ca. July 24, 1878, in *Complete Letters of Wilde,* p. 70

000   "Worthless though": Oscar Wilde to Florence Balcombe, September 30, 1878, ibid., p. 71.

000   In January 1879: on London's population and street lighting. SeeWolf Von Eckardt, Sander L. Gilman and J. Edward Chamberlin, eds., *Oscar Wilde's London* (Garden City, N.Y.: Anchor Press, 1987), pp. ix–x.

000   "untidy": Oscar Wilde to Harold Boulton, December 23, 1879, ibid., p. 85.

000   The most romantic: Ellmann, *Oscar Wilde,* p. 111; Pearson, *Life of Oscar Wilde,* p. 47; Edward John Poynter, *Mrs.* Langtry, www.bbc.co.uk/arts/yourpaintings/paintings/mrs-langtry-18531929-137393.

000   "I want to introduce": Laura Beatty, *Lillie Langtry: Manners, Masks and Morals* (London: Chatto & Windus, 1999), p. 137.

000   "I with my pencil": Ronald Sutherand Gower, *My Reminscences* (London, Kegan Paul, Trench, & Co., 1883), 2:153.

000   "His face was large": Lillie Langtry, *The Days I Knew* (New York: George H. Doran Co., 1925), p. 83.

000   "always made a point": Ibid., p. 89.

000   It was said that Mr. Langtry: Belford, *Wilde: A Certain Genius,* p. 72; Heather Marcovitch, "Oscar Wilde, Lillie Langtry, and the Fashioning of Persona," in *Oscar Wilde: The Man, His Writings, and His World,* ed. Robert N. Keane (New York: AMS Press, 2003), pp. 25–33; Sheridan Morley, *Oscar Wilde* (New York: Holt, Rinehart & Winston, 1976), p. 35.

000   "There is only one thing": Oscar Wilde, *The Picture of Dorian Gray* (New York: Modern Library, 2004), pp. 2–3.

000   When Sir Charles Newton: Ellmann, *Oscar Wilde,* pp. 113–14.

000   "O Helen!": Langtry, *Days I Knew,* pp. 86–88. The poem was originally published in 1881.

000 "There goes that": Ellmann, *Oscar Wilde*, p. 109.

000 "Oscar Wilde, though he": "Oscar Wilde," *Biograph and Review* 4 (1880): 130–35.

000 "The Bard of Beauty": Frederick S. Roden, "The Scarlet Woman: Wilde and Religion," *Reading Wilde: Querying Spaces* (New York: Fales Library, New York University, 1995), p. 24.

000 "Nincompoopiana": Langtry, *Days I Knew*, p. 85; Morley, *Oscar Wilde*, p. 38; Jerold Savory and Patricia Marks, *The Smiling Muse: Victoriana in the Comic Press* (Philadelphia: Art Alliance Press, 1985), pp. 150–73; Gary Smidgall, *The Stranger Wilde* (New York: Dutton, 1994), pp. 43–63.

000 "Which of you two created": Leonee Ormond, *George du Maurier* (London: Routledge, 1969), p. 468.

000 "the sign [one] has become": Roland Barthes, *Mythologies* (New York: Macmillan, 1972), p. 69.

000 He was mingling: Ellmann, *Oscar Wilde*, p. 108.

000 "she is a celebrity": Henry James, "The Comedie Francais in London" (1879), reprinted in *The Scenic Art: Notes on Acting and the Drama, 1872-1901*, ed. Allan Wade (New Brunswick, N.J.: Rutgers University Press, 1948), p. 128.

000 One night he appeared: Ibid.

000 His typical uniform: Langtry, *Days I Knew*, p. 84; Pearson, *Life of Oscar Wilde*, p. 49.

000 *A Private Viewing*: Alison Hennegan, "Personalities and Principles: Aspects of Literature ad Life in *Fin-de-siècle* England," in *Fin de Siècle and Its Legacy*, ed. Mikulas Teichy and Roy Porter (Cambridge: Cambridge University Press, 1990), pp. 170–214; Linda M. Shires, "The Author as Spectacle and Commodity," in *Victorian Literature and the Victorian Imagination*, ed. Carol T. Christ and John O. Jordan (Berkeley: University of California Press, 1995), pp. 198–212.

000 "Beauty had existed": Sir Max Beerbohm, *The Works of Max Beerbohm* (New York: Charles Scribner's Sons, 1896), p. 47.

000 "I can resist": There are several excellent compilations of Wilde's epigrams. Two of the best are Karl Beckson, *I Can Resist Everything Except Temptation* (New York: Columbia University Press, 1996), and Ralph Keyes, *The Wit and Wisdom of Oscar Wilde* (New York: Gramercy, 1999).

000 "You are so evidently": Coulson Kernahan, *In Good Company* (London: Ayer, 1917), pp. 216–17.

000 "I wish I could": Ellmann, *Oscar Wilde*, p. 136.

000 "What has he done": G. T. Atkinson, "Oscar Wilde at Oxford," *Cornhill Magazine* 66 (May 1929): 559–64.

000 "I do know know Mr. Wilde": Ellmann, *Oscar Wilde*, p. 128.

000 "Mr. W. Irving Bishop": Anonymous, *The Ladies' Treasury*, July 1, 1881.

000 "succeed in literature": George Gissing, *New Grub Street* (Teddington, Middlesex: Echo Library, 2007), p. 18.

000 "I am anxious": Oscar Wilde to David Bogue, May 1881, in *Complete Letters of Wilde*, p. 110.

000 The contract made: Hyde, *Wilde: A Biography*, p. 53.

000 "If you wish": Frank Harris, *Oscar Wilde: His Life and Confessions* (New York: Brentano's, 1916), pp. 1:103–104. (It must be noted here that Harris, despite knowing Wilde well, is not considered a wholly reliable source.)

000 "To Helen": Ellmann, *Oscar Wilde*, p. 143.

000 *"Poems by Oscar Wilde"*: Anonymous, "Swinburne and Water," *Punch*, July 23, 1881.

000 "Aesthete of Aesthetes!": "O.W.", *Punch*, June 25, 1881.

000 "It is not that": Pearson, *Life of Oscar Wilde*, p. 52.

000 After Frank Miles's father: Molly Whittington-Egan, *Frank Miles and Oscar Wilde: Such White Lilies* (High Wycombe, UK: Rivendale, 2008), pp. 71–72.

000 "My son must not": E. H. Mikhail, ed., *Oscar Wilde: Interviews and Recollections* (London: Macmillan, 1979), p. 1:30.

000 "I am working at": Oscar Wilde to E.F.S. Pigott, September 1880, in *Complete Letters of Wilde*, p. 98.

000 In the fall of 1881: Ellmann, *Oscar Wilde*, p. 124.

000 "Mr. Oscar Wilde has": "A Wilde Enterprise," *Moonshine*, December 17, 1881.

000 His first idea: Jane W. Stedman, "The Genesis of *Patience*," *Modern Philology* 66, no. 1 (August 1968): 48–58.

000 *"Though the Philistines"*: Ian Bradley, ed., *The Complete Annotated Gilbert & Sullivan* (Oxford: Oxford University Press, 1996), p. 293.

000 "I should like to go": Oscar Wilde to George Grossmith, April 1881, in *Complete Letters of Wilde*, p. 109.

000 "a fierce clamour of screams": Morley, *Oscar Wilde*, 40.

000 But Carte was nervous: Lambourne, *Aesthetic Movement*, p. 123.

000 passed on an idea: Hyde, *Wilde: A Biography*, pp. 55–56.

000 "Responsible agent asks": Ellmann, *Oscar Wilde*, p. 152.

000 "Yes, if offer good": Ibid.

000 "I want a natural": Ibid., p. 118.

000 "The gentleman who": Edward Burne-Jones to Charles Eliot Norton, December 23, 1881, in *Complete Letters of Wilde*, p. 132n.

000 His optimism: Regina B. Oost, *Gilbert and Sullivan: Class and the Savoy Tradition, 1875–1896* (Farnharm, UK: Ashgate, 2009), p. 57.

000 "In ancient mythology": "Narcissus," *New York Herald*, December 22, 1881.

000   "Wilde is slightly": Lambourne, *Aesthetic Movement*, p. 136.

000   "two great gods": Oscar Wilde to William Ward, March 1877, in *Complete Letters of Wilde*, p. 39.

CHAPTER TWO: WORK THE ROOM

000   When launched from Liverpool: Stephen Fox, *Transatlantic* (New York: HarperCollins, 2003), pp. 284–85; C. R. Vernon Gibbs, *Passenger Liners of the Western Ocean* (London: Staples, 1952), pp. 165–67; Arnold Kludas, *Record Breakers of the North Atlantic* (Washington: Brassey's, 2002), pp. 59–60; "S/S Arizona, Guion Line," www.norwayheritage.com.p–ship.asp?sh-arizo.

000   "My God, men": Fox, *Transatlantic*, p. 287.

000   *Arizona* had a hole: "Great Disasters: The Guion Line Steamer Arizona Colliding with an Iceberg," http://bit.ly/MmJjVH.

000   "Oscar Wilde, Gentleman": "Immigrant Ships Transcribers Guild, SS Arizona," http://bit.ly/1hXz23D.

000   "I have lately had": Richard Ellmann, *Oscar Wilde* (New York: Knopf, 1988), pp. 152–153.

000   Now he began: Nick Frigo, "Oscar Wilde: A Celebrity in the Making," *Traffic* (January 2007), http://bit.ly/LwERdW.

000   "with a soul steeped": "Oscar Wilde and His Literary Circle: Wildeiana," Box 10: "Oscar Wilde in America," William Andrews Clark Memorial Library, University of California Los Angeles.

000   (These very words": Lionel Lambourne, *The Aesthetic Movement* (London: Phaidon Press, 1996), p. 123.

000   P.T. Barnum's Aerican Museum: "The Lost Museum," American Social History Project / Center for Media and Learning, the City University of New York, www.lostmuseum,cuny,edu/home.html.

000   "Aestheticism is a search": "Oscar Wilde's Arrival," *New York World*, January 3, 1882.

000   "Missing Link": "What is It? Archive," "The Lost Museum," www.lostmuseum.cuny.edu/home.html.

000   "He was found": "Ten Minutes with a Poet," *New York Times*, January 3, 1882.

000   "His manner of talking": "Oscar Wilde's Arrival," *New York World*, January 3, 1882.

000   "I am not exactly pleased": Richard Ellmann, "Wilde in New York: Beauty Packed Them In," *New York Times*, November 1, 1987; Lloyd Lewis and Henry Justin Smith, *Oscar Wilde Discovers America [1882]* (New York: Harcourt, Brace, 1936), p. 32.

000 "the grandest sight": Ellmann, "Wilde in New York."

000 "I am disappointed": Ellmann, *Oscar Wilde*, p. 158.

000 "I am here to diffuse": "Oscar Wilde," *New York Evening Post*, January 4, 1882.

000 "(It was definitely": "About Delmonico's Firsts," www.delmonicosrestaurant group.com/restaurant/about-firsts.html.

000 Built for Chickering & Sons: "Chickering Hall," www.nycago.org/Organs/ NYC/html/ChickeringHall.html.

000 (Bell made the first": Ibid.

000 "Everybody seems in a hurry" Oscar Wilde, *Impressions of America* (Sunderland: Keystone Press, 1906), pp. 22–23.

000 "I now understand": Oscar Wilde to Mrs. George Lewis, ca. January 7, 1882, in *The Complete Letters of Oscar Wilde*, ed. Merlin Holland and Rupert Hart-Davis (New York: Henry Holt, 2000), p. 124.

000 Among those attending: "Events in the Metropolis: In Honor of Oscar Wilde," *New York Times*, January 6, 1883.

000 "A line of private": Ibid.

000 "His face is": "Oscar Wilde: The Aesthetic Apostle's First Appearance in New York Society," *New York World*, January 6, 1882.

000 "a heathen idol": "Oscar Wilde: The Aesthetic Apostle's First Appearance in New York Society, *New York World*, January 6, 1882.

000 "I stand at the top": Oscar Wilde to Mrs. George Lewis, ca. January 15, 1882, *Complete Letters of Wilde,* p. 124.

000 "America reminds me": Lewis Broad, *The Friendships and Follies of Oscar Wilde* (New York: Thomas Y. Crowell, 1955), p. 63; Martin Fido, *Oscar Wilde* (New York: Viking, 1973), p. 51.

000 "Why arrange them": Stephen Fry, "Oscar Wilde: Aesthete in America," *Civilization* (August–September 1998): 53–55.

000 After the party ended: Ellmann, *Oscar Wilde*, p. 160.

000 *"Am I alone"*: *Patience*, Gilbert and Sullivan Archive, diamond.boisestate.edu/ gas/patience/webop/operhome.html.

000 "[As] the whole audience": "Oscar Wilde Sees 'Patience'—the Poet at the Standard—His Comments on the Part of Bunthorne," *New York Tribune*, January 6, 1882.

000 "doctrine of corporate personhood": Jesse Matz, "Wilde Americana," in *Functions of Victorian Culture at the Present Time*, ed. Christine L. Krueger (Athens: Ohio University Press, 2002): 65–78.

000 three parties: "Among the Aesthetes: Oscar Wilde Feted in New York," *Toronto Daily Star*, January 14, 1882.

000 "immediately drew off part": "A Reception in Miss Alcott's Honor," *New York Tribune*, January 9, 1882.

000 "I am torn": Oscar Wilde to Norman Forbes-Robertson, January 15, 1882, in *Complete Letters of Wilde*, p. 127.

000 "This Philistine town": Edmund Clarence Stedman, *The Life and Letters of Edmund Clarence Stedman,* ed. Laura Stedman and George M. Gould (New York: Moffett, Yard, 1910), ed., p. 2:31.

000 "I have not seen": Bette Roth Young, ed., *Emma Lazarus in Her World* (Philadelphia: Jewish Publication Society, 1995), p. 189.

000 "If I am not a success": Oscar Wilde to Mrs. George Lewis, ca. January 7, 1882, in *Complete Letters of Wilde*, p. 124.

000 every ticket had been sold: Ellmann, *Oscar Wilde*, p. 164.

000 "Wilde's topic": Ibid., p. 152.

000 "The Beautiful as Seen": Frances Winwar, *Oscar Wilde and the Yellow Nineties* (New York: Harper & Brothers, 1940), p. 80.

000 Its 1,250 members were staring: Ellmann, *Oscar Wilde*, p. 164; Winwar, *Wilde and Yellow Nineties*, p. 81.

000 "I have the great": "Oscar Wilde's Lecture," *New York Times*, January 10, 1882.

000 "Among the many debts": Oscar Wilde, "The English Renaissance of Art," in Wilde, *Essays and Lectures* (London: Methuen, 1908).

000 "It is to no avail": Ibid.

000 "I am asking": Whitney Helms, *Symbolic Capital and the Performativity of Authorship,* Ph.D. thesis, University of Nebraska, 2013, p. 181.

000 "Well, let me tell you": Wilde, "English Renaissance of Art."

000 "And so with you": Ibid.

000 "blushed like a school-girl": "Oscar Wilde's Lecture," *New York Times*, January 10, 1882.

000 "to [whom] the gods gave": Oscar Wilde to John Ruskin, June 1888, in *"Complete Letters of Wilde,"* p. 349.

000 Once inside Mrs. Mack's: Ellmann, *Oscar Wilde*, p. 166

000 "Scores upon scores": "Living Up to Beauty," *New York Herald*, January 10, 1881.

000 "Loving virtuous obscurity": Oscar Wilde to Mrs. George Lewis, ca. January 15, 1882, in *Complete Letters of Wilde*, p. 86.

000 "long, melodious sentences": Winwar, *Wilde and Yellow Nineties*, p. 86.

000 "The craze over Oscar": "The Fooler and the Fools," *Daily Graphic*, January 10, 1882.

000 Ward had received: Maude Howe Elliott, *Uncle Sam Ward and His Circle* (New York: Macmillan, 1938), p. 602.

000 "In two days I got": Ibid., p. 605.

000 "Oscar Wilde was entertained": "The Aesthetic Poet: He Dines With Sam Ward," *New York Times*, January 12, 1882.

000 *"Take, O gardener"*: Stephen Mallett and Samuel Ward, "The Valley Lily," in Music for the Nation: American Sheet Music, Library of Congress, memory. loc.gov/music/sm/sm1881/14700/14797/001.jpg.

000 "He is no slouch": Lloyd Lewis and Henry Justin Smith, *Oscar Wilde Discovers America [1882]* (New York: Harcourt Brace, 1936), p. 50.

000 General George McClellan: Ibid., p. 47.

000 "At the Century": Henry Irving Brock et al., *The Century, 1847–1946* (New York: Century Association, 1947), p. 49.

000 "Where is she?" Ellmann, *Oscar Wilde*, p. 176.

000 Mr. and Mrs. Samuel L. M. Barlow: On Barlow's $25,000 fee, see BarlowGenealogy.com, "Samuel Latham Mitchell Barlow."

000 "filled with pictures": Ibid.

000 "Nothing like it": Oscar Wilde to Norman Forbes-Robertson, January 15, 1882, in *Complete Letters of Wilde*, p. 127.

000 When Dickens arrived: Ada Nisbet, "Dickens in America: The Boz Ball," *American Heritage* 9, no. 1 (December 1957).

000 According to clippings: Richard Butler Glaenzer, "Collection of Working Papers, Folder 1: Diary of Wilde's Trip in America," William Andrews Clark Memorial Library, University of California Los Angeles.

000 "A conscious youth": "The Aesthetic Boom: The New Narcissus," *New York World*, January 11, 1882.

000 "[He's] a clever young man": Lewis and Smith, *Wilde Discovers America*, p. 61.

CHAPTER THREE: STRIKE A POSE

000 Born in Canada: Ben L. Bassham, *The Theatrical Photographs of Napoleon Sarony* (Kent, Ohio: Kent State University Press, 1978), p. 6; "A Biographical Chronology for Napoleon Sarony," www.classyarts.com/saron/Sarony_Chronology.htm

000 "FACES OF NOTED PEOPLE": Barbara McCandless, "The Portrait Studio and the Celebrity," in *Photography in Nineteenth-Century America*, ed. Martha A. Sandweiss (New York: Abrams, 1991), p. 68.

000 One New York dealer: "Faces of Noted People," *New York Times*, February 25, 1883.

000 Sarony's reputation: Graham Murdock, "Celebrity Culture and the Public Sphere," in *Media, Markets and Public Spheres*, ed. Jostein Gripsrud and Lennart Weibul (Bristol, UK: Intellect Books, 2010), p. 275.

000 "She has in a supreme": Henry James, *The Scenic Art: Notes on Acting and the Drama, 1872–1901*, ed. Allan Wade (New York: Hill & Wang, 1957, p. 129.

000 These portraits created: Joseph A. Harriss, "The First Superstar," *American*

Spectator (December 2010-January 2011), spectator.org/articles/38468/first-superstar.

000 In exchange for Sarony's: Mary Watson, "Oscar Wilde at Home," *San Francisco Examiner*, April 9, 1882. Watson claimed that Wilde expressed regret that he had signed an exclusive contract with Sarony because "he admires the pictures produced by some of our local photographers, and, in an art sense, apparently believes in the superiority of San Francisco workmanship to that of New York." However, there is no evidence that this assertion is anything but local boosterism on the part of Ms. Watson.

000 In truth, Wilde had: Daniel A. Novak, "Sexuality in the Age of Technological Reproducibility," in *Oscar Wilde and Modern Culture*, ed. Joseph Bristow (Athens: Ohio University Press, 2008), p. 92n33.

000 "Oscar,—How dare you!": Richard Ellmann, *Oscar Wilde* (New York: Knopf, 1988), p. 154.

000 "a genuine Egyptian mummy": Richard Edwards, *New York's Great Industries* (New York: Ayer, 1884), p. 213.

000 "the smell of a chemical": Richard Grant White, "A Morning at Sarony's," *Galaxy* 9 (1877): 408–11.

000 "look our beloved science": Bassham, *Theatrical Photographs of Sarony*, p. 4.

000 A recent technological: Brian Coe, "The Techniques of Victorian Studio Photography," in *Victorian Studio Photographs*, ed. Bevis Hillier (Boston: David R. Godine, 1976), p. 26.

000 This was Sarony's posing machine: Bassham, *Theatrical Photographs of Sarony,* p. 11; McCandless, "Portrait Studio and Celebrity," p. 64.

000 "iron instrument of torture": White, "Morning at Sarony's."

000 "A picturesque subject": Lloyd Lewis and Henry Justin Smith, *Oscar Wilde Discovers America [1882]* (New York: Harcourt, Brace & Company, 1936), p. 39.

000 When photographing the British: Bassham, *Theatrical Photographs of Sarony,* p. 15.

000 On the day Wilde and Sarony: Merlin Holland, *The Wilde Album* (New York: Henry Holt & Co., 1998), p. 64.

000 In the late nineteenth: Jane M. Gaines, *Contested Culture* (Chapel Hill: University of North Carolina Press, 1991), p. 43.

000 "far exceeds any possible": "What Mr. Wilde Says About Himself," *Manchester* (England) *Examiner and Times*, May 23, 1882.

000 "His face is well known": "Aesthetic: An Interesting Interview with Oscar Wilde," *Dayton Daily Democrat*, May 3, 1882.

000 "some large lithographs": Oscar Wilde to Richard D'Oyly Carte, March 1882, in *The Complete Letters of Oscar Wilde*, ed. Merlin Holland and Rupert Hart-Davis (New York: Henry Holt, 2000), p.152.

000   Such visual materials: Robert Jay, *The Trade Card in Nineteenth-Century America* (Columbia: University of Missouri Press, 1987), p. 61.

000   And, as Wilde surely: Waleska Schwandt, "Oscar Wilde and the Stereotype of the Aesthete," in *The Importance of Reinventing Oscar*, ed. Uwe Boker, Richard Corballis and Julie Hibbard (Amsterdam: Rodopi, 2002), p. 97.

000   "staged celebrity": Chris Rojek, *Celebrity* (London: Reaktion Books, 2001), p. 125.

000   the work of the biologist Francis Galton: Novak, "Sexuality in the Age," p. 69; Kathleen R. Slaugh-Sanford, *Declaring Genius: Literary and Scientific Claims of Artistic Genius in Late-Victorian Britain*, Ph.D thesis, University of Delaware, 2011.

000   "O wad some Power": Robert Burns, "To a Louse," www.robertburns.org/works/97.shtml.

000   "fake it till you": Julia Hanna, "Power Posing: Fake It Until You Make It," *Working Knowledge,* an online publication of the Harvard Business School; Dana R. Carney, Amy J.C. Cuddy, Andy J. Yapp, "Power Posing: Brief Nonverbal Displays Affect Neuroendocrine Levels and Risk Tolerance," *Psychological Science* 21, no. 10 (October 2010): 1363–68.

000   "The Work of Art": Walter Benjamin, "The Work of Art in the Age of Mechanical Reproduction" (1936), www.marxists.org/reference/subject/philosophy/works/ge/benjamin.htm.

000   "undoubled genius": Slaugh-Sanford, *Declaring Genius.*

000   Trade cards: Kit Barry, "Interpreting Popular Culture Through Advertising Trade Cards: The Oscar Wilde Event," *Ephemera News* 27, no. 1 (Fall 2008): 9–16.

000   "Mme Marie Fontaine's Bosom Beautifier": "Antique 1880s Oscar Wilde Card," Dave's Great Cards Galore, Ebay.com.

000   "the first modern marketed celebrity": Barry, "Interpreting Popular Culture."

000   Burrow-Giles Lithographic Company: Michael North, "The Picture of Oscar Wilde," *Publications of the Modern Language Association of America* 125, no. 1 (January 2010): 185–91; Kerry Powell, *Acting Wilde: Victorian Sexuality, Theatre, and Oscar Wilde* (New York: Cambridge University Press, 2009), p. 23.

000   "DID SARONY INVENT": "DID SARONY INVENT OSCAR WILDE?", *New York Times*, December 14, 1883.

000   the Supreme Court: Novak, "Sexuality in the Age," p. 80; Lee Schulman, "Thank Napoleon Sarony," *ASMP Bulletin* (April 2002): 5; Mitch Tuchman, "Supremely Wilde," *Smithsonian* (May 2004).

000   "I will take the furniture": Oscar Wilde, "The Canterville Ghost," in *The Complete Works of Oscar Wilde* (London: Collins, 1998), p. 193.

000   A man named: Ibid., p. 204.

CHAPTER FOUR: CELEBRITY IS CONTAGIOUS

000   "Oscar Wilde sent me": Walt Whitman to Harry Stafford, January 31, 1882, in *Collected Writings of Walt Whitman: The Correspondence*, ed. Edwin Haviland (New York: New York University Press, 1961–77), p. 266.

000   "Have you read": Walt Whitman to Harry Stafford, January 25, 1882, ibid., p. 264.

000   "I am very tired": "A Talk with Wilde," *Philadelphia Press*, January 17, 1882.

000   "I was up": Ibid.

000   "Look, there he is": Ibid.

000   "How dreadful": Ibid.

000   "Velvet is such a": Ibid.

000   "I think Walt Whitman": Ibid.

000   "I admire him intensely": Ibid.

000   "Massa Wilde": Lloyd Lewis and Henry Justin Smith, *Oscar Wilde Discovers America [1882]* (New York: Harcourt, Brace, 1936), p.71; Hesketh Pearson, *The Life of Oscar Wilde* (Twickenham, UK: Senate, 1998), p. 62.

000   Davis had mailed: Lewis and Smith, *Wilde Discovers America*, p. 71.

000   "surrendered his devotion": "A Reception for the Aesthete," *Philadelphia Press*, January 17, 1882, in "Oscar Wilde and His Literary Circle: Wildeiana," Box 10: "Oscar Wilde in America," William Andrews Clark Memorial Library, University of California Los Angeles.

000   "I am an invalid": Walt Whitman to Mrs. George W. Childs, January 17, 1882, in Haviland, ed., *Collected Writings* of Whitman, p. 263.

000   "Walt Whitman will": Walt Whitman to Oscar Wilde and Joseph M. Stoddart, January 18, 1882, ibid., p. 263.

000   There was some giggling: Lewis and Smith, *Wilde Discovers America*, p. 72.

000   "my hearers [at the lecture]": Ibid, p. 73.

000   "a weak, vain, pretentious crank": "The Shoddy and Aesthetic Climaxes," *Philadelphia Times*, January 20, 1882, in Richard Butler Glaenzer, "Collection of Working Papers, Folder 1: Diary of Wilde's Trip in America," William Andrews Clark Memorial Library, University of California Los Angeles; Lewis and Smith, *Wilde Discovers America*, p. 73.

000   "I come as a poet": Ellmann, *Oscar Wilde*, p. 168.

000   The first book by Whitman: Sherwood Smith, "William Michael Rossetti," *Walt Whitman Archive*, www.whitmanarchive.com/criticism/current/encyclopedia/entry_48.html.

000   "the old teacups treasur'd by": Gary Schmidgall, *Walt Whitman: A Gay Life* (New York: Dutton, 1997), p. 291.

000   "talk[ed] readily with": *The Poetry and Prose of Walt Whitman*, ed. Louis Untermeyer (New York: Simon & Schuster, 1949), p. 539.

000 "I will call you": "Wilde and Whitman, The Aesthetic Singer Visits the Good Gray Poet," *Philadelphia Press*, January 20, 1882.

000 "I am not blind": Ralph Waldo Emerson to Walt Whitman, July 21, 1855, *Walt Whitman Archive*, www.whitmanarchive.org/criticism/current/pdf/anc .02044.pdf.

000 "almost always perfumed": "Wilde and Whitman," *Philadelphia Press*, January 20, 1882.

000 "Tennyson's rank is too well": Ibid.

000 "Who may this be": "Narcissus in Camden," *Century* (November 1882).

000 "the most influential portrait": Ed Folsom and Kenneth M. Price, "The First Edition of *Leaves of Grass*," *Walt Whitman Archive*, www.whitmanarchive. com/biography/walt.whitman/index.html#firstedition.

000 "Its author is Walt": "*Leaves of Grass—An Extraordinary Book,*" *Brooklyn Eagle*, September 15, 1855.

000 "was very much hatcheted": "Image 003: Gallery of Images," *Walt Whitman Archive*.

000 "2/3rd length with hat": "Image 086: Gallery of Images," ibid.

000 "have used me for a show-horse": Ed Folsom, "This Heart's Geography Map: The Photographs of Walt Whitman," *Walt Whitman Archive*, www. whitmanarchive.org/multimedia/gallery/introduction.html.

000 "The public is a thick-skinned": Justin Kaplan, *Walt Whitman: A Life* (New York: HarperCollins, 2003), p. 22.

000 "I've always had the knack": William Roscoe Thayer, "Personal Recollections of Walt Whitman," *Scribner's* 65 (June 1919): 674–94.

000 "'How it happened": Ibid.

000 "butterfly": David Haven Blake, *Walt Whitman and the Culture of American Celebrity* (New Haven: Yale University Press, 2006), p. 2.

000 "God bless you, Oscar": "Wilde and Whitman," *Philadelphia Press*, January 20, 1882.

000 "If it had been vinegar": Ibid.

000 "He is the grandest man": "Oscar Wilde," *Boston Herald*, January 29, 1882.

000 Philadelphia was the second-largest city: "Table 11: Population of the 100 Largest Urban Places, 1880," www.census.gov/population/www/document ation/tops0027/tab11.txt.

000 It is a sign: "The War Correspondent," *Hartford Courant*, November 18, 1881.

000 "Oscar Wilde is here": Ellmann, *Oscar Wilde*, p. 174.

000 Forbes claimed that P.T. Barnum: Ibid.

000 "It is reported that Barnum": Robert Herron, "Have Lily, Will Travel: Oscar Wilde in Cincinnati," *Bulletin of the Historical and Philosophical Society of Ohio* 25 (1957): 215–33.

000 "Now I wish it understood": Lewis and Smith, *Wilde Discovers America*, p. 80.

000 "Our views are": Ellmann, *Oscar Wilde*, p. 175.

000 "How far is it": "How Far is It from This to This?" *Washington Post*, January 22, 1882.

000 "mushy face, his long and plastered": A.J.A. Symons, *Essays and Biographies* (London: Cassell, 1969), p. 179.

000 "back-door": Michele Mendelssohn, *Henry James, Oscar Wilde and Aesthetic Culture* (Edinburgh: Edinburgh University Press, 2007), p. 27.

000 "I believe that Washington": Henry James to Sir John Clark, January 8. 1882, in *Henry James: Selected Letters,* ed. Leon Edel (Cambridge, Mass.: Belknap Press of Harvard University, 1987), p. 178.

000 "I have asked Henry James": Clover Adams to Dr. Robert William Hooper, January 18, 1882, in *First of Hearts: Selected Letters of Mrs. Henry Adams*, ed. Ward Thorton (AuthorHouse Books, 2011), p. 105.

000 "the sexes of my nouns": Mendelssohn, *James, Wilde and Aesthetic Culture*, p. 29.

000 "I went last night": Henry James to Isabella Stewart Gardner, January 23, 1882, in *James: Selected Letters*, p. 179.

000 "One prominent feature": George Monteiro, "A Contemporary View of Henry James and Oscar Wilde, 1882," *American Literature* 35, no. 4 (January 1964): 528–30.

000 Arlington Hotel: On Wilde requesting candles, see "Wilde Oscar, the Lover of the Big Sunflower, Has Arrived in the Capital," *National Republican*, January 20, 1882.

000 "no living Englishman can": Ellmann, *Oscar Wilde*, p. 178.

000 "I am very nostalgic": Ibid.

000 "Oh, Mr. Wilde": Lewis and Smith, *Wilde Discovers America*, p. 114.

000 "a fatuous fool": Richard A. Kaye, *The Flirt's Tragedy* (Charlottesville: University Press of Virginia, 2002), p. 177.

000 "A clever and accomplished man": James Russell Lowell to Oliver Wendell Holmes, December 21, 1881, *The Complete Letters of Oscar Wilde*, ed. Merlin Holland and Rupert Hart-Davis (New York: Henry Holt, 2000), p. 131.

000 "They say that when good Americans": Oscar Wilde, *The Picture of Dorian Gray* (New York: Modern Library, 2004), p. 43.

000 "And where do bad Americans": Ibid., p. 44

000 "Suddenly a hush": Alice Cary Williams, *Thru the Turnstile* (Boston: Houghton Mifflin, 1976), pp. 19–20.

000 Longfellow and Ward's shared love: Charles C. Calhoun, *Longfellow: A Rediscovered Life* (Boston: Beacon Press, 2004), p. 242.

000 "Mr. Wilde has written": Ellmann, *Oscar Wilde*, pp. 180–81.

000 "Oh, I assure you": Calhoun, *Longfellow*, p. 3.

000 "There were blond wigs": Mary Warner Blanchard, *Oscar Wilde's America* (New Haven: Yale University Press, 1998), p. 18.

000   "As a college man": Douglass Shand-Tucci, *The Crimson Letter* (New York: St. Martin's, 2003), p. 67.

000   "Mr. Wilde achieved": Boris Brasol, *Oscar Wilde: The Man, the Artist, the Martyr* (New York: Charles Scribner's Sons, 1938), p. 106.

000   "Oh, I could sympathize:" "Oscar Wilde in Brooklyn," *New York Sun*, February 4, 1882.

000   "WILDE AND SULLIVAN": "WILDE AND SULLIVAN / The Great Fight," *Puck* 10, no. 258 (February 15, 1882), p. 375.

000   "A man who wishes": "Editor's Easy Chair," *Harper's New Monthly Magazine* 64, no. 383 (April 1882): 786–90. Pieces published under the "Easy Chair" rubric were unsigned, but as was widely known in 1882, the author was George William Curtis.

000   "What a tempest": Ellmann, *Oscar Wilde*, p. 184.

000   "I am indestructible": Ibid., p. 185.

CHAPTER FIVE: THE SUBJECT IS ALWAYS YOU

000   "Interviewers are a product": "The Aesthetic Apostle," *Boston Globe*, January 29, 1882.

000   "We have no interviewing": "Oscar as He Is," *St. Louis Republican*, February 26, 1882.

000   The journalist credited: Lucy Brown, *Victorian News and Newspapers* (Oxford: Clarendon Press, 1985), p. 163; Michael Schudson, *The Power of News* (Cambridge, Mass.: Harvard University Press, 1995), p. 79; W.T. Stead Resource Site, www.attackingthedevil.co.uk.

000   "During the three years": W.T. Stead, "Chinese Gordon for the Soudan," January 9, 1884, www.attackingthedevil.co.uk/pmg/soudan.php.

000   "The interview is": Schudson, *Power of News*, p. 76.

000   "James Gordon Bennett": Ibid., p. 73

000   Brigham Young: George Turnbull, "Some Notes on the History of the Interview," *Journalism Quarterly* 13 (1936): 272–79.

000   "An Encounter with an Interviewer": R. Kent Rasmussen, *Critical Companion to Mark Twain* (New York: Facts on File, 2007), p. 1:114; Mark Twain, "An Encounter with an Interviewer," http://twain.lib.virginia.edu/wilson/encounter.html.

000   "I love acting": Oscar Wilde, *The Picture of Dorian Gray* (New York: Modern Library, 2004), p. 90.

000   "an idea is of no value till": Oscar Wilde to Lord Alfred Douglas, January–March 1897, in *The Complete Letters of Oscar Wilde*, ed. Merlin Holland and Rupert Hart Davis (New York: Henry Holt, 2000), p. 746.

000 "The aesthetic young man": "The Apostle of Art," *Chicago Inter-Ocean*, February 11, 1882.

000 "coat and natty rest": "With Mr. Oscar Wilde," *Cincinnati Gazette*, February 21, 1882.

000 "tete-d'tete covered with": "Wilde," *Cleveland Leader*, February 20, 1882.

000 "Will you kindly": Oscar Wilde to Col. W. F. Morse, February 26, 1882, in *Complete Letters of Wilde*, p. 141.

000 "[It] is based on a principle": "Oscar Wilde," *Salt Lake Herald*, April 12, 1882.

000 "I hope that the masses": "Oscar Arrives," *Sacramento Record-Union*, March 27, 1882.

000 "My dear Jimmy": Oscar Wilde to James McNeill Whistler, February 1882, in *Complete Letters of Wilde*, p. 139.

000 "My philosophy": "Our New York Letter," *Philadelphia Inquirer*, January 4, 1882.

000 "animated": Mary Watson, "Oscar Wilde at Home," *San Francisco Examiner*, April 9, 1882.

000 "A boy could": "The Theories of a Poet," *New York Tribune*, January 8, 1882.

000 "In 1873 [I] entered": "The Science of the Beautiful," *New York World*, January 8, 1882.

000 "I came back": Ibid.

000 "Facts . . . are usurping:" Oscar Wilde, "The Decay of Lying," in *The Complete Works of Oscar Wilde* (London: Collins, 1988), p. 980.

000 "To have done it": Joseph Pearce, *The Unmasking of Oscar Wilde* (New York: HarperCollins, 2000), p. 86.

000 no evidence that Wilde ever declared: John Cooper, "Quotations by Oscar Wilde Made In or About America," *Oscar Wilde in America*, www.oscarwildeinamerica.org/quotations/index.html.

000 "and so this is Oscar Wilde": "A Man of Culture Rare," *Rochester Democrat and Chronicle*, February 8, 1882.

000 "Never complain": John Morley, *The Life of William Ewart Gladstone* (1903; reprint New York: Kessinger, 2005), p. 1:123.

000 "Wilde thought so highly of Disraeli": Nicholas Mirzoeff, "Disorientalism: Minority and Visuality in Imperial London," *TDR: The Drama Review* 50, no. 2 (Summer 2006): 52–69.

000 (He also brought novels: Oscar Wilde to Julia Ward Howe, July 6, 1882, in *Complete Letters of Wilde*, p. 175.

000 "I regard all caricature": Oscar Wilde to Col. W. F. Morse, June 1882, ibid., p. 141.

000 "An artist should not": "Oscar Wilde," *Boston Herald*, January 29, 1882.

000 "in New York they wrote": "Oscar as He Is," *St. Louis Republican*, February 26, 1882.

000   "Do *not* call it": "Aesthetic: An Interesting Interview with Oscar Wilde," *Dayton Daily Democrat*, May 3, 1882.

000   "The best service of god": "Oscar Arrives," *Sacramento Record-Union*, March 27, 1882.

000   "treated me outrageously": "A Man of Culture Rare," *Rochester Democrat and Chronicle*, February 8, 1882.

000   "When I read the papers": "Oscar Wilde," *Rocky Mountain News*, April 13, 1882.

000   "If you expect English": "Wilde and Forbes," *New York Herald*, January 21, 1882.

000   "I am extremely impressed": "Truly Aesthetic," *Chicago Inter-Ocean*, February 13, 1882.

000   "I am quite conscious": "Oscar Wilde," *Salt Lake Herald*, April 12, 1882.

000   "Narcissuses of imbecility": Oscar Wilde to Joaquin Miller, February 28, 1882, in *Complete Letters of Wilde*, p. 143.

000   "Byron of the Rockies": Kathi Morrison-Taylor, "The Poet's Cabin: Joaquin Miller in Washington," *Beltway Poetry Quarterly* 9, no. 3 (Summer 2008).

000   "A wonderful appetizer!": Carey McWilliams, *Ambrose Bierce: A Biography* (New York: A. & C. Boni, 1929), p. 100.

000   "Yours (from Boeotia)": Oscar Wilde to the Hon. George Curzon, February 15, 1882, in *Complete Letters of Wilde*, p. 139.

000   "In old days men had": Alvin Redman, ed., *The Wit and Humor of Oscar Wilde* (Mineola, N.Y.: Dover, 1959), p. 129.

000   "I was dressing": "Utterly Utter," *St. Louis Post-Dispatch*, February 25, 1882.

000   "some of the brightest hours": "Oscar Wilde," *Cincinnati Enquirer*, February 21, 1882.

000   "I have met [reporters who]": "Speranza's Gifted Son," *St. Louis Globe-Democrat*, February 26, 1882.

000   "upon the whole I'd rather": "Oscar Dear, Oscar Dear!" *Charleston News and Courier*, July 8, 1882.

000   "no one sees a country": "Oscar Wilde," *Boston Herald*, January 29, 1882.

000   "The greatest fault": Ibid.

000   "The best cities": "The Apostle of Art," *Chicago Inter-Ocean*, February 11, 1882.

000   "Do I contradict": "Song of Myself," in *Walt Whitman's Leaves of Grass*, ed. David S. Reynolds (New York: Oxford University Press, 2005), p. 43.

000   "[Wilde] is scholarly": "Oscar Arrives," *Sacramento Record-Union*, March 27, 1882.

000   "The fact is [Wilde] has been": Lilian Whiting, "They Will Show Him," *Chicago Inter-Ocean*, February 10, 1882.

000 "I think nothing of [them]": "Oscar Arrives," *Sacramento Record-Union,* March 27, 1882.

000 "What possible difference": "A Man of Culture Rare," *Rochester Democrat and Chronicle,* February 8, 1882.

000 "Oh, yes, I read": "Utterly Utter," *St. Louis Post-Dispatch,* February 25, 1882.

000 By mid-June: Richard Ellmann, *Oscar Wilde* (New York: Knopf, 1988), p. 192.

000 $5,605, a sum equal: "The Inflation Calculator," westegg.com/inflation/.

000 "I'm a very ambitious": "Oscar Wilde in Omaha," *Omaha Weekly Herald,* March 24, 1882.

000 "The supreme object": Ellmann, *Oscar Wilde,* p. 191.

CHAPTER SIX: *PROMOTE* IS JUST ANOTHER WORD FOR *PROVOKE*

000 "hundreds of starry-eyed": "Wilde Dazzled Niagara's Fair Sex in 1882," *Niagara Falls Gazette,* June 21, 1958.

000 "Santa Claus, Alaska": Mike Belasco, "'Santa Claus' 1882 Visitor to Falls," *Niagara Falls Gazette,* December 24, 1961.

000 "I was in a manner": Charles Dickens, *American Notes* (1842), www.gutenberg,com/ebooks/675

000 "Of all the sights": Anthony Trollope, "Niagara," in *North America* (1862), http://ebooks.adelaide.edu.au/t/trollope/anthony/north/chapter7.html.

000 "I was disappointed": "Wilde Sees the Falls," *Buffalo Express,* February 10, 1882.

000 "They told me that": "Wanted—A New Universe," *New York Tribune,* October 31, 1882.

000 "Every American bride": Oscar Wilde, *Impressions of America* (Sunderland: Keystone Press, 1906), p. 25.

000 "UNIVERSE, you are": "Disappointed Again," *Fun* (March 8, 1882): 103.

000 "We like to look": "Wilde," *Chicago Daily News,* February 10, 1882.

000 "in a neat-fitting black": "Oscar Wilde, The Esthetic Apostle Greeted by an Immense Audience," *Chicago Tribune,* February 14, 1882.

000 "wicked and imaginative editor": Philip Kinsley, *The Chicago Tribune: Its First Hundred Years,* vol. 3, 1880–1890 (New York: Knopf, 1943).

000 "might paint sunsets": "Oscar Wilde, The Esthetic Apostle," *Chicago Tribune,* February 14, 1882.

000 "I was shocked:" Ibid.

000 "I didn't expect to learn": Ibid.

000 "Mr. Wilde, are you aware": "Oscar Wilde, He Has Seen Quite Enough of Chicago," *Chicago Tribune,* February 15, 1882.

000 "failed to note the degree": Lloyd Lewis and Henry Justin Smith, *Oscar Wilde Discovers America [1882]* (New York: Harcourt, Brace, 1936), p. 179.

000 "Oscar's knee-breeches": John T. Flanagan, "Oscar Wilde's Twin Cities Appearances," *Minnesota History* 17, no. 1 (March 1936): 38–48.

000 "My audiences are": Oscar Wilde to Hon. George Curzon, February 15, 1882, in *The Complete Letters of Oscar Wilde*, ed. Merlin Holland and Rupert Hart-Davis (New York: Henry Holt, 2000), p. 139.

000 "Go, Mr. Wilde": "Oscar Wilde," *Chicago Daily News*, February 14, 1882.

000 "Commercially [Chicago] is": "Oscar Wilde," *Fort Wayne Gazette*, February 15, 1882.

000 "Oscar Wilde tomorrow": "City News," *Fort Wayne Gazette*, February 15, 1882.

000 "His lecture is": "Oscar, Which His Last Name is Wilde, His Appearance Last Night," *Fort Wayne Gazette*, February 17, 1882.

000 "those people who go": "Oscar Wilde's Visit," *Detroit Free Press*, February 14, 1882.

000 "the sickly atmosphere": "The Aesthetic Youth Discourses Upon Decorative Art at Music Hall," *Detroit Free Press*, February 18, 1882.

000 "advertise their inferiority": Francis X. Roellinger, Jr., "Oscar Wilde in Cleveland," *Ohio History* 59, no. 2 (April 1950): 129–38.

000 "great heaven, they speak": "With Mr. Oscar Wilde," *Cincinnati Gazette*, February 21, 1882.

000 "You have no architecture": Robert Herron, "Have Lily, Will Travel: Oscar Wilde in Cincinnati," *Bulletin of the Historical and Philosophical Society of Ohio* 25 (1957): 215–33; Kerry Powell, "The Importance of Being Audacious," *Cincinnati* (May 1983): 34–38.

000 "The aesthetic young man": "Patti," *Cincinnati Enquirer*, February 21, 1882.

000 "the best first book": John Spalding Gatton, "The Sunflower Saint: Oscar Wilde in Louisville," *Filson Club History Quarterly* (January 1978): 5–25.

000 "[Wilde] has . . . an effeminacy": "The Aesthetic Craze: Oscar Wilde, the Long-haired Apostle of Aestheticism, at the National Capital," *Louisville Courier-Journal*, January 22, 1882.

000 On the same night: Gatton, "Sunflower Saint."

000 "perfectly natural, with the": "Hoaxes of Joseph Mulhattan," at www.museumofhoaxes.com/hoax/archive/permalink/josephmulhattan.

000 "delicate sense of colour harmonies": Oscar Wilde, "Keats's Sonnet on Blue," in Wilde, *Miscellanies,* ed. Robert Ross (1904).

000 "reading the letters of [John]": Ibid.

000 "not a charlatan": Gatton, "Sunflower Saint."

000 "What you have given": Oscar Wilde to Mrs. Emma Speed, March 21, 1882, in *Complete Letters of Wilde,* p. 157.

000 "tumultuous silence": Lewis and Smith, *Wilde Discovers America*, pp. 196–98.

000 Once opened: Ibid.

000 "cunningly arranged into a lily": Robert Herron, "Have Lily, Will Travel: Oscar Wilde in Cincinnati," *Bulletin of the Historical and Philosophical Society of Ohio* 25 (1957): 215–33.

000 "They were dreadfully": Oscar Wilde to Colonel Morse, February 26, 1882, in *Complete Letters of Oscar Wilde*, p. 141.

000 "I send you a line": Oscar Wilde to Mrs. George Lewis, February 28, 1882, ibid., p. 143.

000 "seen Indians": Oscar Wilde to Mrs. Bernard Beere, March 20, 1882, ibid., p. 152.

000 "I don't know where": Oscar Wilde to Mrs. George Lewis, March 20, 1882, ibid., p. 154.

000 "Beautiful women are": "Philosophical Oscar," *Chicago Times*, March 1, 1882.

000 "He is one of": Ibid.

000 "All ornaments": Oscar Wilde, "The House Beautiful," in *The Complete Works of Oscar Wilde* (London: HarperCollins, 2003), pp. 913–25.

000 "appreciative": "Oscar Wilde, The Second Lecture of the Apostle of Aestheticism," *Chicago Tribune*, March 12, 1882.

000 "ASS-THETE": John T. Flanagan, "Oscar Wilde's Twin City Appearances," *Minnesota History* 17, no. 1 (March 1936): 38–48; Ben Welter, "Thursday, March 16, 1882: Oscar Wilde, 'Ass-thete,'" *StarTribune*, March 17, 2008, http://blogs2.startribune.com/blogs/oldnews/archives/216.

000 "Ladies and gentlemen," "St. Patrick—St. Paul Observes the Day in Appropriate Style," *St. Paul Daily Globe*, March 18, 1882.

000 the San Francisco impresario: Lois Foster Rodecape, "Gilding the Sunflower: A Study of Oscar Wilde's Visit to San Francisco," *California Historical Society Quarterly* 19, no. 2 (June 1940): 97–112.

000 "Six lectures a week": Oscar Wilde to Col. W. F. Morse, March 21, 1882, in *Complete Letters of Wilde*, p. 155.

000 "The biggest sunflower": Carl Uhlarik, "Oscar Wilde in Omaha," *Prairie Schooner* 14, no. 1 (Spring 1940): 45–53.

000 "went with the sincere desire": Ibid.

000 "You will see flocks": Ibid.

000 "Big Nose George": Chuck Woodbury, "The Crook Who Grew Up to be a Shoe," www.outwestnewspaper.com/bignose.html; "Wyoming Legends: Outlaw Big Nose George Becomes a Pair of Shoes in Rawlins," www.legendsofamerica.com/wy-bignose.html.

000 "Corrine, Utah": Rodecape, "Gilding the Sunflower."

000 "At first grey": Oscar Wilde to Norman Forbes-Robertson, March 27, 1882, in *Complete Letters of Wilde*, p. 158.

000 "civilians": Rodecape, "Gilding the Sunflower."

000 "poised on one leg": "Lo! The Aesthete," *San Francisco Chronicle*, March 27, 1882.

000 Los Angeles didn't: "Population of the 100 Largest Urban Places: 1880," www.census.gov/population/www/documentation/twps0027/tab11.txt, Internet.

000 "churned into aggressive life": "Lo! The Aesthete," *San Francisco Chronicle*, March 27, 1882.

000 "psychology of perfumes": Oscar Wilde, *The Picture of Dorian Gray* (New York: Modern Library, 2004), pp. 150–51.

CHAPTER SEVEN: KEEP YOURSELF AMUSED

000 "A really beautiful city": Oscar Wilde, *Impressions of America* (Sunderland: Keystone Press, 1906), p. 28.

000 "It is an odd thing": Oscar Wilde, *The Picture of Dorian Gray* (New York: Modern Library, 2004), p. 241.

000 "four thousand people": Oscar Wilde to Norman Forbes-Robertson, March 27, 1882, in *The Complete Letters of Oscar Wilde*, ed. Merlin Holland and Rupert Hart-Davis (New York: Henry Holt, 2000), p. 158.

000 "The Modern Messiah": Lucy Shelton Caswell, "The San Francisco Wasp: An Illustrated History (Review)," *American Periodicals* 15, no. 2 (2005): 225–26; Lois Foster Rodecape, "Gilding the Sunflower: A Study of Oscar Wilde's Visit to San Francisco," *California Historical Society Quarterly* 19, no. 2 (June 1940): 97–112; "Oscar Wilde: The Modern Messiah," *Virtual Museum of the City of San Francisco*, www.sfmuseum.org/hist5/wilde1.html.

000 "Hail! Brother, hail!": Rodecape, "Gilding the Sunflower."

000 "Oscar Wilde is at hand": "Amusements," *San Francisco Chronicle*, March 25, 1882.

000 "Wilde in San Francisco": Papers Past, National Library of New Zealand, http://paperspast.natlib.govt.nz/cgi-bin/paperspast?a-d&d-AS188205b.2.34.1b.

000 "An Irishman whose": "Footlight Flashes," *San Francisco Chronicle*, March 26, 1882.

000 "the Palace Hotel": Charles A. Fracchia, "Palace Hotel," *Encyclopedia of San Francisco*, www.sfhistoryencyclopedia.com/articles/p/palacehotel.html.

000 "There is much here": "Oscar Wilde: An Interview with the Apostle of Aestheticism," *San Francisco Examiner*, March 27, 1882.

000 "I never saw so many": Rodecape, "Gilding the Sunflower."

000 "gentlemen connected professionally": Peter Martin Phillips, *A Relative Advantage: Sociology of the San Francisco Bohemian Club*," Ph.D diss., University of California–Davis, 1994.

000 One thing the membership: Richard Reinhardt, "The Bohemian Club," *American Heritage* 31, no. 4 (June–July 1980).

000 "Oscar Wilde's lecture": "The Renaissance," *San Francisco Chronicle*, March 28, 1882.

000 "as soon as the first feeling": Rodecape, "Gilding the Sunflower."

000 "teel-a-phone": "The Renaissance," *San Francisco Chronicle*, March 28, 1882.

000 "That sovereign of insufferables": Ambrose Bierce, "Prattle," *Wasp*, March 31, 1882.

000 "the poem in breeches": Rodecape, "Gilding the Sunflower."

000 "Mobbing the Esthete'": "American Barbarism: The Apostle of Estheticism Exposes Our Sins," *San Francisco Chronicle*, March 30, 1882.

000 "Last night, after the close": Rodecape, "Gilding the Sunflower."

000 There were more than two hundred: "Chinatown's Opium Dens," FoundSF. org/index.php?title-Chinatown%27s_Opium_Dens.

000 "At the end of the hall": Wilde, *Picture of Dorian Gray*, pp. 212–13.

000 "Under the guidance": "Oscar Wilde," at *Gay Bears: The Hidden History of the Berkeley Campus*, bancroft.berkley.edu/collection/gaybears/wilde.

000 "Oscar Wilde, the apostle": "Local Brieflets,", *Livermore Herald*, April 6, 1882.

000 "Mr. Wilde's lecture was one": "Oscar Wilde, His Last Lecture Night— What He Had to Say," *Sacramento Daily Union*, April 1, 1882.

000 "High Jinks": Lloyd Lewis and Henry Justin Smith, *Oscar Wilde Discovers America [1882]* (New York: Harcourt, Brace, 1936), pp. 255–56; Rodecape, "Gilding the Sunflower."

000 "Why not go further back": Robert D. Pepper, "San Jose Greets Oscar Wilde: April Third, 1882," *San Jose Studies* 8, no. 2 (Spring 1982): 6–32.

000 "The poetry and music of Ireland": "Celtic Song: Oscar Wilde's Farwell Lecture in the City," *San Francisco Chronicle*, April 6, 1882.

000 "This is where I belong!": Isobel Field, *This Life I've Loved* (New York: Longmans Green, 1937), pp. 139-40.

000 "I think he was little": Ibid.

000 "the jollity was kept up": Rodecape, "Gilding the Sunflower."

000 He left San Francisco: "Oscar Wilde's Last Lecture: How We Should Adorn Our Homes, Furniture and Dress," *Sacramento Daily Union*, April 10, 1882.

000 "palpable hit:" Rodecape, "Gilding the Sunflower."

000 "so-called aesthete": Helen L. Warner, "Oscar Wilde's Visit to Salt Lake City," *Utah Historical Quarterly* 55, no. 4 (Fall 1987): 322–34.

000 "Is it possible my poems": "Oscar Wilde Paralyzed by Youngster," *Salt Lake Tribune*, April 15, 1882.

000 "a personal tour of Salt Lake City": Warner, "Wilde's Visit to Salt Lake City."

000 "God's vice-regent": On Taylor's titles), see Walter Gore Marshall, *Through*

America: Or, Nine Months in the United States (London: S. Low, Marston, Searle & Rivington, 1882), p. 178.

000 "The Upper California": Ibid., p. 181.

000 "soup kettle": Wilde, *Impressions of America,* p. 29; "Art and Aesthetics," *Denver Tribune,* April 13, 1882.

000 "The building next": Wilde, *Impressions of America,* p. 30.

000 The Salt Lake Theatre: "Salt Lake Theatre," utahtheaters.info/theatermain. asp?10-249; Ronald W. Walker, "Salt Lake Theatre," historytogo.utah.gov/ utah_chapters/utah_today/saltlaketheatre.html.

000 "How is it that": Warner, "Wilde's Visit to Salt Lake City"; "Oscar Wilde," *Salt Lake Herald,* April 12, 1882.

000 "because it was the first city": "Art and Aesthetics," *Denver Tribune,* April 13, 1882.

000 "pathetically homely": Mark Twain, *The Innocents Abroad / Roughing It* (New York: Modern Library, 1984), p. 610.

000 The Tabor Grand: "Tabor Grand Opera House," cinematreasures.org/ theaters/19055; "Denver's Tabor Grand Opera House," theautry.org/ collections/opera-5.

000 Most of those seats: Lewis and Smith, *Wilde Discovers America,* p. 303; "Art and Aesthetics," *Denver Tribune,* April 13, 1882.

000 "an ingenious manner": Lewis and Smith, *Wilde Discovers America,* p. 305.

000 The hotel's best suite: Ibid., pp. 300–301.

000 "Of all things that which": Ibid., p. 306; "Art and Aesthetics," *Denver Tribune,* April 13, 1882.

000 "I want to see Leadville": "Truly Aesthetic," *Chicago Inter-Ocean,* February 13, 1882.

000 By 1879 the total value: Lewis and Smith, *Wilde Discovers America,* p. 31.

000 "The ominous command": Richard Patterson, *Historical Atlas of the Outlaw West* (Boulder: Johnson Books, 1985), p. 42.

000 "eighty-two saloons": Caroline Bancroft, *Tabor's Matchless Mine and Lusty Leadville* (Boulder, Colo.: Johnson, 1990), p. 17.

000 "I was told that, if": Wilde, *Impressions of America,* pp. 80–81.

000 "practice[d] with [his] new": "Mr. Wilde's Presentation," *Denver Times,* April 12, 1882.

000 Born in Vermont, Tabor: Duane A. Smith, *Horace Tabor: His Life and Legend* (Niwot: University Press of Colorado, 1989), p. 59.

000 "grubstaking": Evelyn E. Livingston Furman, *The Tabor Opera House* (Aurora, Colo.: National Writers Press, 1984), p. 15.

000 "sole owner of the Matchless": Smith, *Horace Tabor,* pp. 122–23.

000 "Prescription $1": Lewis and Smith, *Wilde Discovers America,* p. 312.

000 "a whole house of curiosity": "Oscar Dear: Wilde Wrestles Wildly with the

Art Decorative in this Mountain Wilderness," *Leadville Daily Herald*, April 14, 1882.

000 "Notice to all thieves": Patterson, *Historical Atlas of the Outlaw West*, pp. 42–43.

000 *Serious Family!*: Furman, *Tabor Opera House*, p. 68.

000 "stumbled onto the stage": "Oscar Dear: Wilde Wrestles Wildly," *Leadville Daily Herald*, April 14, 1882.

000 "We live in adobes": Ibid.

000 "read them passages from": Wilde, *Impressions of America*, p. 31.

000 "My audience [in Leadville]": Oscar Wilde to Mrs. Bernard Beere, April 17, 1882, in *Complete Letters of Wilde*, pp. 161–62.

000 The wooden sidewalks: Elliott West, *The Saloon on the Rocky Mountain Mining Frontier* (Lincoln: University of Nebraska Press, 1979), p. 66.

000 "French section": Lewis and Smith, *Wilde Discovers America*, pp. 315–16.

000 "In Leadville at night": Ernest Ingersoll, "Ups and Downs in Leadville," *Scribner's Monthly* 18, no. 6 (October 1879): 801–21.

000 PLEASE DO NOT SWEAR: West, *Saloon on the Mining Frontier*, p. 68.

000 PLEASE DO NOT SHOOT: Wilde, *Impressions of America*, p. 31.

000 "the only rational method": Ibid.

000 "I was struck by this": Robert Harborough Sherard, *The Life of Oscar Wilde* (New York: Mitchell Kennerley, 1906), p. 226.

000 "carried his coins": Lewis and Smith, *Wilde Discovers America*, p. 316; West, *Saloon on the Mining Frontier*, p. 68.

000 "complete dress of India rubber": Lewis and Smith, *Wilde Discovers America*, p. 316.

000 "the finest sight in the": Ibid., p. 317.

000 "The first course [was] whisky": Wilde, *Impressions of America*, p. 32.

000 "art and appetite could": Oscar Wilde to Mrs. Bernard Beere, April 17, 1882, in *Complete Letters of Wilde*, p. 162.

000 "I brilliantly performed": Ibid.

000 "chatted incessantly": Lewis and Smith, *Wilde Discovers America*, p. 317.

CHAPTER EIGHT: GO WHERE YOU'VE
WANTED (AND EVEN WHERE YOU'RE NOT)

000 "In all of my journeys": Oscar Wilde, "The House Beautiful," in *The Complete Works of Oscar Wilde* (London: Collins, 2010), p. 1,862.

000 "an advertising dodge": Lloyd Lewis and Henry Justin Smith, *Oscar Wilde Discovers America [1882]* (New York: Harcourt, Brace, 1936), p. 320.

000 "Oscar Wilde, whose name is now": "Oscar Wilde Hung," *Leadville Herald*, April 19, 1882.

000 "an exaggeration": "Death," www.twainquotes.com/Death/html.

000 "Oscar Wilde, the long-haired": Lewis and Smith, *Wilde Discovers America*, pp. 330–31.

000 "Oscar Wilde and a circus": Felicia Hardison Londre, *The Enchanted Years of the Stage* (Columbia: University of Missouri Press, 2007), p. 84.

000 Both buildings: "Last Night at the Opera House," Kansas City Public Library, www.KCLibrary.org/blog/week-kansas-city-history/last-night-opera-house.

000 the lure of seeing Zazel: Lewis and Smith, *Wilde Discovers America*, p. 332.

000 Charles and Robert Ford: "Jesse James's Murderers," *New York Times*, April 18, 1882; Ted P. Yeatman, "Jesse James's Assassination and the Ford Boys," *Wild West* (December 2006), www.historynet.com/jesse-james.

000 "Jesse ain't no Oscar": "Doubting Jesse James' Death," *Sacramento Daily Union*, April 12, 1882 (reprinted from the *Chicago Times*).

000 "a big crowd at the opera": Lewis and Smith, *Wilde Discovers America*, p. 334.

000 "Outside my [hotel] window": Oscar Wilde to Hattie (last name unknown), April 19, 1882, in *The Complete Letters of Oscar Wilde*, ed. Merlin Holland and Rupert Hart-Davis (New York: Henry Holt, 2000), pp. 164–65.

000 "dreaming of a long, dry": Charles Harmon Cagle, "Oscar Wilde in Kansas," *Kansas History* 4, no. 4 (Winter 1981–82): 227–45.

000 "He is a very pleasant": Ibid.

000 "I lecture at Corinthian": Ibid.

000 "Oscar Wilde Disgusted": "Oscar Wilde Disgusted," *Louisville Courier-Journal*, April 26, 1882.

000 "The summer is just": Oscar Wilde to Norman Forbes-Robertson, April 21, 1882, *Complete Letters of Wilde*, p. 165.

000 "In the eastern cities": "What Mr. Wilde Says About Himself," *Manchester Examiner and Times*, May 6, 1881.

000 "the talk of London": Richard Ellmann, *Oscar Wilde* (New York: Knopf, 1988), p. 191.

000 "I have come here": "Argus and the Ass," *Omaha Daily Bee*, April 26, 1882.

000 "guile taken with the pretty": Lowry Charles Wimberley, "Oscar Wilde Meets Woodberry," *Prairie Schooner* 21, no. 1 (Spring 1947): 109–16.

000 "Poor sad types": Oscar Wilde to Helena Sickert, April 25, 1882 in *Complete Letters of Wilde*, p. 166.

000 "[Wilde] is the first artistic": Wimberley, "Wilde Meets Woodberry."

000 "vain imagining of a morbid": "Oscar Wilde," *Columbus Daily Times*, May 4, 1882.

000 "The kiss of Walt Whitman": Ellmann, *Oscar Wilde*, p. 171.

000 "You made a great sensation": Charles Godfrey Leland to Oscar Wilde, May 11, 1882, William Andrews Clark Memorial Library, *University of California, Los Angeles.*

000 "P.T. Barnum": Lewis and Smith, *Wilde Discovers America*, p. 344.

000 "not an empty seat": Oscar Wilde to Norman Forbes-Robertson, May 12, 1882 in *Complete Letters of Wilde,* p. 169.

000 "I have already civilized": Oscar Wilde to James McNeill Whistler, May 16, 1882, ibid., p. 172.

000 "I am making": "The New Costume: How the Aesthetic Young Men of New York Are Expected to Dress," *New York World*, May 4, 1882.

000 "$50 for a jacket": Oscar Wilde to Col. W. F. Morse, May 15, 1882, in *Complete Letters of Wilde,* p. 169.

000 "Peter Tracy": William W. Rogers, Robert David Ward, and Dorothy McLeod MacInerney, "Aesthetic Messenger: Oscar Wilde Lectures in Memphis, 1882," *Tennessee Historical Quarterly* 63, no. 4 (Winter 2004): 250–65.

000 Maria Teresa McCarthy: Ibid.

000 "aflaming while canvas": Lewis and Smith, *Wilde Discovers America*, p. 358.

000 "largea nd recherché audience": Eileen Knott, William Warren Rogers, and Robert David Ward, "Oscar Wilde in Vicksburg, at Beauvoir, and Other Southern Stops," *Journal of Mississippi History* 59, no. 3 (Fall 1997): 183–210.

000 "He is a fine scholar": "Oscar Wilde," *Vicksburg Daily Herald*, June 16, 1882.

000 Bonfouca, Louisiana: Mary Louise Ellis, "Improbable Visitor: Oscar Wilde in Alabama, 1882," *Alabama Review* 39 (October 1886): 243–60; William W. Rogers, Robert David Ward, and Dorothy McLeod MacInerney, "Oscar Wilde Lectures in New Orleans and Across the South in 1882," *Southern Studies* 11, nos. 3 & 4 (Fall–Winter 2004): 31–65.

000 "Oscar Wilde ran across a lynching": "News Notes," *Sedalia* (Missouri) *Weekly Bazoo,* June 27, 1882.

000 "encountered more that was": Rogers, Ward, and MacInerney, "Wilde Lectures in New Orleans."

000 "A mule race!": Ibid.

000 "Nothing in the way": "Oscar Wilde Talks of Texas," *New Orleans Picayune,* June 25, 1882.

000 I saw them everywhere": Ibid.

000 "We Americans are": Norman W. Alford, "Oscar Wilde in Texas," *Texas Quarterly* 10, no. 2 (Summer 1967): 193–203; Dorothy McLeod MacInerney, William Warren Rogers, and Robert David Ward, "Oscar Wilde Lectures in Texas, 1882," *Southwestern Historical Review* 106, no. 4 (April 2003): 550–73.

000 The electric power: MacInerney, Rogers, and Ward, "Wilde Lectures in Texas."

000   "arrested": Ibid.

000   (When telling the same: Oscar Wilde, *Impressions of America* (Sunderland: Keystone Press, 1906), p. 27.

000   Henry Ryder-Taylor: MacInerney, Rogers, and Ward, "Wilde Lectures in Texas."

000   "Those old Spanish churches": "Oscar Wilde Talks of Texas," *New Orleans Picayune*, June 25, 1882.

000   "monstrous": MacInerney, Rogers, and Ward, "Wilde Lectures in Texas."

000   "too long between drinks": Ibid.

000   "The original and only": Norman W. Alford, "Oscar Wilde in Texas," *Texas Quarterly* 10, no. 2 (Summer 1967): 193–203.

000   "He may insist too roundly": MacInerney, Rogers, and Ward, "Wilde Lectures in Texas."

000   George W. Cable: Eileen Knott, William Warren Rogers, and Robert David Ward, "Oscar Wilde in Vicksburg, at Beauvoir, and Other Southern Stops," *Journal of Mississippi History* 59, no. 3 (Fall 1997): 183–210.

000   "It seems incredible that": "Oscar Wilde and One Enchanted Evening in 1882," *Montgomery Daily Advertiser*, June 23, 1882, montgomeryhistorical. org/oscarwilde.html.

000   the visit was the result: Hudson Strode, *Jefferson Davis, Tragic Hero: The Last Twenty-Five Years, 1864–1889* (New York: Harcourt, Brace & World, 1964), p. 459.

000   "in disorder, with magazines": Ibid.

000   "Jefferson Davis is the one": Ibid.

000   "That's a long way": Ibid.

000   "[Davis's] fall, after such": "Oscar Wilde Talks of Texas," *New Orleans Picayune*, June 25, 1882.

000   "It is feared": Knott, Rogers, and Ward, "Wilde in Vicksburg, at Beauvoir."

000   "It's like a butterfly": Ibid.

000   "I did not like the man": Strode, *Jefferson Davis, Tragic Hero*, p. 461.

000   "How beautiful the moon": Wilde, *Impressions of America*, pp. 32–33.

000   "The modern androgynous": Ellen Crowell, "The Picture of Charles Bon: Oscar Wilde's Trip Through Faulkner's Yoknapatawpha," *MFL Modern Fiction Studies* 50, no. 3 (Fall 2004): 595–631.

000   The photo left by Wilde: Merlin Holland, *The Wilde Album* (New York: Henry Holt, 1997), photo insert following p. 63; Knott, Rogers, and Ward, "Wilde in Vicksburg, at Beauvoir"; and James L. Swanson, *Bloody Crimes: The Chase for Jefferson Davis and the Death Pageant for Lincoln's Corpse* (New York: William Morrow, 2010), p. 364–65.

000   "THE EIGHTH WONDER": On the attractions at Frascati Park, see advertisement in the *Mobile Register,* July 5, 1876.

000 "extra horse-car facilities": Mary Louise Ellis, "Improbable Visitor: Oscar Wilde in Alabama, 1882," *Alabama Review* 39 (October 1886): 243–60.

000 "OSCAR WILDE—": "Oscar Wilde," *Montgomery Daily Advertiser*, June 29, 1882.

000 "something in the shape": Ellis, "Improbable Visitor."

000 "select": William Warren Rogers, Dorothy McLeod MacInerney, and Robert David Ward, "The Wilde Alabama Lecture Circuit," *Alabama Heritage* (Fall 2005): 6–13.

000 "utter absence of that": Doris Lanier, "Oscar Wilde Tours Georgia," *Georgia Historical Quarterly* 65, no. 4 (Winter 1981): 329–40.

000 "Oh, the patriots": "Oscar Wilde: Arrival of the Great Aesthete," *Atlanta Constitution*, July 5, 1882.

000 "against the rules of the company": "Oscar Wilde and His Negro Valet," *New York Times*, July 9, 1882, (reprinted from *Atlanta Constitution*, July 6, 1882).

000 "I write to you from": Oscar Wilde to Julia Ward Howe, July 6, 1882, *Complete Letters of Wilde*, p. 175.

000 "thrown into a flutter": Lewis and Smith, *Wilde Discovers America*, p. 382.

000 "I have just returned": Oscar Wilde to Charles Eliot Norton, July 15, 1882, in *Complete Letters of Wilde*.

000 Newport Casino Theatre: Lewis and Smith, *Wilde Discovers America*, p. 382; "The Newport Casino," International Tennis Hall of Fame & Museum, www.tennisfame.com/museum-and-grounds/the-newport-casino.

000 "two of the greatest talkers": Ellmann, *Oscar Wilde*, p. 203.

000 "I put it back": Lewis and Smith, *Wilde Discovers America*, p. 383.

000 other vacation spots: Richard Butler Glaenzer, "Collection of Working Papers, Folder 1: Diary of Wilde's Trip in America," William Andrews Clark Memorial Library, University of California Los Angeles.

000 New Jersey Shore: Ibid.

000 Long Beach, New York: John Cooper, "A Scene at Long Beach," oscar wildeinamerica.org/lecture-tour/a-scene-at-long-beach.html; "New York—A Scene at Long Beach, the New and Popular Seaside Resort," *Frank Leslie's Illustrated Newspaper*, August 12, 1882.

000 the unnamed friend of Helen Lenoir: Lewis and Smith, *Wilde Discovers America*, pp. 23–24.

000 "lover of the beautiful": Ibid, pp. 387–88.

000 "in the wake of the professional": Ibid, p. 391.

000 "It was about 2 o'clock": "Oscar Wilde in Wall Street," *Washington Post*, September 21, 1882.

000 "I would rather have discovered": Ellmann, *Oscar Wilde*, p. 206.

000 "dressed as probably no man": "Mrs. Langtry's Reception," *New York Times*, October 24, 1882.

000   "She has a fine": Lewis and Smith, *Wilde Discovers America*, p. 419.

000   "You have made": Ibid.

000   "I thought that I": "Mr. Wyndham at the Lotos Club, He and Mr. Wallack Exchange Oratorical Compliments which Mr. Oscar Wilde Supplements," *New York World*, October 29, 1882.

000   "It is only in": Oscar Wilde, "Mrs. Langtry as Hester Grazebrook," *New York World*, November 7, 1882.

000   Mary Anderson: Ellmann, *Oscar Wilde*, pp. 208–209; Oscar Wilde to Mary Anderson, several dates in late 1882, in *Complete Letters of Wilde*, pp. 178–79, 180–81, 185, 187.

000   "Have you made": "Oscar Wilde Thoroughly Exhausted," *New York Tribune*, November 27, 1882.

000   "'Excuse me, Mr. Wilde": "Oscar Fleeced at Banco," *New York Times*, December 29, 1882; "The Poet and the 'Banco' Man," *New York Tribune*, December 29, 1882.

000   "the most famous sucker game": Luc Sante, *Low Life* (New York: Macmillan, 2003), pp. 166–68.

000   "'Captain Williams, in your": "The Poet and the 'Banco Man,'" *New York Tribune*, December 28, 1882.

000   "fallen into a den": Oscar Wilde to John Boyle O'Reilly, December 15, 1882, in *Complete Letters of Wilde*, p. 192.

000   "Mr. Wilde, is it true": "Mr. Wilde Undisturbed by Rumors," *New York Tribune*, December 25, 1882.

000   Helena Modjeska: Ellmann, *Oscar Wilde*, p. 210; "Modjeska as Camille," *New York Times*, December 22, 1882.

000   "What has he done": G.T. Atkinson, "Oscar Wilde at Oxford," *Cornhill Magazine* 66 (May 1929): 559–64.

000   "Oscar Wilde took a sorrowful": "Farewell to Oscar Wilde," *New York Tribune*, December 28, 1882.

000   "the most determined and sustained": Ellmann, *Oscar Wilde*, p. 205.

000   "the Oscar of the first period": Ibid., p. 220.

EPILOGUE: DON'T BELIEVE THE HYPE

000   "AUTHOR! AUTHOR!": Richard Ellmann, *Oscar Wilde* (New York: Knopf, 1988), p. 366; Hesketh Pearson, *The Life of Oscar Wilde* (Twickenham, UK: Senate, 1998), p. 224.

000   "Ladies and Gentlemen": A.E.W. Mason, *Sir George Alexander and the St. James's Theatre* (London: Macmillan, 1935), p. 224.

000   So after sending his beaming wife: H. Montgomery Hyde, *Oscar Wilde* (New

York: Farrar, Straus & Giroux, 1975), pp. 153–54; Neil McKenna, *The Secret Life of Oscar Wilde* (New York: Basic Books, 2005), p. 174.

000 Wilde had earned £7,000: Hyde, *Oscar Wilde*, p. 156; "Historical UK Inflation and Price Conversion Chart," http://safalra.com/other/historical-uk-inflation -price-conversion/

000 "calling a spade a spade": Ellmann, *Oscar Wilde*, p. 368.

000 "Do not alter": Ibid., p. 382.

000 "Mr. Wilde is to me": Christopher Innes, ed., *The Cambridge Companion to George Bernard Shaw* (New York: Cambridge University Press, 1998), pp. 67–68.

000 "The play *is* a success": Mason, *Sir George Alexander and the St. James's Theatre,* p. 78.

000 "In my fifty-three years": Pearson, *Life of Oscar Wilde*, p. 257.

000 "a German oompah band": Ibid.

000 "For Oscar Wilde posing": Linda Stratmann, *The Marquess of Queensberry* (New Haven: Yale University Press, 2013), p. 211.

000 "Feasting with panthers": Oscar Wilde to Lord Alfred Douglas, January– March 1897, in *The Complete Letters of Oscar Wilde*, ed. Merlin Holland and Rupert Hart-Davis (New York: Henry Holt, 2000), p. 758; the letter was later published as *De Profundis.*

000 In an equally harsh irony: F. B. Smith, "Loubouchère's Amendment to the Criminal Law Amendment Bill," *Historical Studies* 17, no. 67 (October 1976): 165–73.

000 "He told [me] of the theater": Edmond and Jules de Goncourt, *Pages from the Goncourt Journals* (New York: New York Review of Books, 2007), p. 285.

000 "minus the arms": Oscar Wilde, *Impressions of America* (Sunderland: Keystone Press, 1906), p. 33.

000 the only immoral act: W. H. Auden, "An Improbable Life," *New Yorker* (March 9, 1963): 155–77.

000 "to see the object as": Matthew Arnold, "The Function of Criticism at the Present Time," *National Review* (November 1864): 230–51.

000 J. M. Stoddart: Ellmann, *Oscar Wilde*, p. 313.

000 "Mr. Oscar Wilde's story": Stratmann, *Marquess of Queensberry*, p. 147.

000 "fourteen times running": Ellmann, *Oscar Wilde*, p 324.

000 "Some artists are indifferent": Auden, "Improbable Life."

000 "I made art": Oscar Wilde to Lord Alfred Douglas, January–March, 1897, in *Complete Letters of Wilde*, p. 729.

000 "I ha[ve] never loved a woman": Oscar Wilde, *The Uncensored Picture of Dorian Gray*, ed. Nicholas Frankel (Cambridge, Mass.: Harvard University Press, 2011), p. 144. This passage is from the original version of *Dorian*, published in *Lippincott's Monthly* in July 1890. It was deleted from the book version published in April 1891.

000 "Carson: Have you": Ellmann, *Oscar Wilde*, p. 449; Merlin Holland, *The Real Trial of Oscar Wilde* (New York: Fourth Estate, 2003), pp. 90–91.

000 "such a great affection": Ellmann, *Oscar Wilde*, p. 463.

000 "thrived under prison fare": "Oscar Wilde Released," *New York Times*, May 20, 1896.

000 "the wittiest woman": Ada Leverson, *Letters to the Sphinx from Oscar Wilde, with Reminiscences of the Author* (London: Duckworth, 1930), p. 45.

000 "Reggie Turner and Robbie Ross": Barbara Belford, *Oscar Wilde: A Certain Genius* (New York: Random House, 2000), p. 278.

000 "Do you really think": Oscar Wilde to Lord Alfred Douglas, January–March 1897, in *Complete Letters of Wilde*, pp. 714–15.

000 "Blindly I staggered": Ibid., p. 690.

000 "What is loathsome": Ibid., p. 759.

000 "[D]uring the whole": Ibid., p. 685, 687, 764.

000 "The Heart wants what": Emily Dickinson, *The Letters of Emily Dickinson* (Cambridge, Mass.: Harvard University Press, 1958), p. 1:405.

000 "I feel that my only": Oscar Wilde to Lord Alfred Douglas, August 31, 1897, in *Complete Letters of Wilde*, p. 932–33.

000 "I forbid you to return": Oscar Wilde to More Adey, November 28, 1897, ibid., p. 994.

000 Dalhousie Young: Ellmann, *Oscar Wilde*, p. 550.

000 "None of the English colony": Oscar Wilde to Robert Ross, October 3, 1897, in *Complete Letters of Wilde*, p. 955.

000 "The facts of Naples": Oscar Wilde to Robert Ross, March 2, 1898, ibid., p. 1029.

000 the Irish journalist Frank Harris: Oscar Wilde to Frank Harris, March 3, 1898, ibid., p. 1029.

000 "Madame Melba": Nellie Melba, *Melodies and Memories* (Cambridge: Cambridge University Press, 2011), p. 75.

000 "Parisians who licked": Ellmann, *Oscar Wilde*, p. 575.

000 Anna de Bremont: Ibid., p. 578.

000 George Alexander: Ibid., 571.

000 The true cruelty of a prison: Ibid., p. 565.

000 inherited nearly £20,000: Ibid., p. 577; "Historical UK Inflation and Price Conversion Chart," http://safalra.com/other/historical-uk-inflation-price-conversion/

000 "When I spoke": Oscar Wilde to Robert Ross, May–June 1900, in *Complete Letters of Wilde*, p. 1188.

000 a surgeon came to his room: Belford, *Wilde: A Certain Genius*, p. 304; Oscar Wilde to Robert Ross, October 11, 1900, in *Complete Letters of Wilde*, p. 1199.

000 "I am dying beyond": Ellmann, *Oscar Wilde*, p. 580.

000 "My wallpaper and I": Ibid., p. 581.

000   "You dear little Jew": Reginald Turner to Robert Ross, November 28, 1900, in *Complete Letters of Wilde,* p. 1218; Reginald Turner to Robert Ross, November 27, 1900, ibid., p. 1216.

000   "dreamt [he] was supping": Robert Ross to More Adey, December 14, 1900, in *Complete Letters of Wilde,* p. 1213.

000   "My throat is like": Sean McCann, ed., *The Wit of Oscar Wilde* (New York: Barnes & Noble, 1969), p. 11.

000   "Catholicism is the only": Joseph Pearce, *Literary Converts* (London: HarperCollins, 1999), p. 6.

000   "adopted mercury": Ellmann, *Oscar Wilde*, p. 95.

000   "moral flabbiness": William James to H. G. Wells, September 11, 1906, in *The Letters of William James,* ed. Henry James (New York: Cosimo, 2008), p. 260.

Index